Hungry Tigers

A Candid Account of Addiction and Recovery

Gary Swoboda

PublishAmerica
Baltimore

First printing

ISBN: 1-60672-870-9 (softcover)
ISBN: 978-1-61582-454-0 (hardcover)
PUBLISHED BY PUBLISHAMERICA, LLLP
www.publishamerica.com
Baltimore

Printed in the United States of America

The young boy said to the teacher: "Pretend you were surrounded by a thousand hungry tigers. What would you do?"

The teacher thought for a while, and unable to come up with a solution, finally answered, "Well, I don't know. What would *you* do?"

The young boy replied, "I'd stop pretending."

—Catherine Ingram

For Casey, Michael and "Luke"

I have little understanding of certain events as they unfold. Lesser still, it sometimes seems, upon their passing. But what I have come to believe is that everything happens for a reason, whether we understand the implications or not.

A LIFE ONCE LIVED

I got clean when Luke died.

It seems a lifetime ago that I witnessed Luke propped up against the old, beige wall of the now-deserted second-grade building at St. Peter's School in Southeast Portland, his artificial leg lying several feet away. I remember watching with empathy as he fought back the tears, a heart-wrenching picture of aloneness etched upon his eight-year-old face. None of the other kids at school had to put up with their limbs coming off during play at recess. In retrospect, I think about the terrible injustice Luke must have felt in that regard, yet in all the years I knew him, he never once voiced it. Never once.

I would do well to remember that, as I toss around my own feelings of injustice—such petty little kernels of discontent, paling in comparison to anything actually "bitch-worthy." Luke often reminded me of my gratitude list, since I appeared to be incapable of compiling one on my own. For a long time, it seemed, Luke had a tremendous gift for looking at the bright side of life. However, as his physical pain grew through the years, along with his psychological and spiritual suffering, his view became restricted to the bright side of other people's lives. Nonetheless, he seemed genuinely pleased at the fortune of others and was able to stave off the natural temptation of envy throughout most of his life.

It never ceased to amaze me when I would visit Luke in that dilapidated, immobile bus he lived in for seventeen years, or at other, even more depressing residences he inhabited over time, how he could *ever* be in a good mood, yet his moods seemed positive far more often than my own.

And so it is that the memory of that stoic eight-year-old face, trying so valiantly not to cry, can still conjure up feelings of great sadness and empathy. I am reminded of Luke's death occasionally, a barrage of emotions suddenly invading my being: grief, guilt, regret—as well as gratitude for the good times and relief that his pain on this planet has finally come to a close.

A lady named Meg Crawford had been with Luke on the day he died, and she met with me a few weeks after his death to tell me of his final hours. She had known Luke for more than two decades, and at various times during those years she had been his landlord, his "mother," his spiritual compatriot, and his guardian angel. On the day Meg imparted this dire news to me she was a tired-looking woman in her late sixties. Short in stature with a roundish face, her eyes, though at times troubled, somehow always communicated kindness. It had been difficult for us both. I was quite a mess, only twenty-one days clean and sober at the time. After thirty years of active addiction to one substance or another, I had entered recovery for the first time in my life. With hands clenched tight in my coat pockets, I sat shivering in the front seat of Meg's ailing Chevy Caprice, waiting with trepidation as this world-weary woman began to tell me of Luke's last day on earth.

Meg had been looking the other way, as always, she told me, because she hated to watch Luke do this to himself. When she turned back he was just pulling the needle from his arm. He cried out immediately, almost reverently, Meg said.

"Oh, my God!" were Luke's last words on Earth, this planet Earth that had both enticed and delighted him, both seduced and tortured him mercilessly all the days of his life. And then, as though to make sure the irony and relevance of the statement were heard and understood, he cried out once more, "Oh, my God!" and then fell back onto that small, shoddy bed in that desolate, flea-bag motel room he had been living in the last few months of his life.

He died within minutes as Meg tried desperately to resuscitate him, shouting out woefully, "Please don't do this to me, Luke! Please don't do this!"

Thirty-seven years after that forsaken eight-year-old child had tried so gallantly to stifle his tears on that cruel playground a million memories ago, that little boy, older now but every bit as alone, lay lifeless in the distant town of Kalama, Washington.

That had been his biggest complaint during his stay there—the isolation. Luke was a people person. He loved people of all ages and backgrounds, yet he had been forced into relative isolation in the remote town of Kalama the last year of his life, due to financial hardships and life circumstances. Now Luke's tortured existence on this sphere had ended, dead from an overdose, from a syringe full of too much heroin, heroin that I had purchased the night before.

Though it had been relatively mild outside on that 18th day of April in the year

1999, I shivered uncontrollably beneath my winter coat as I sat listening to Meg. I just couldn't keep warm those days, it seemed. They had discovered on my second day in detox that I'd contracted what they termed opiate-induced pneumonia sometime during my addiction. I was subsequently transferred down to the medical ward on the third floor of the hospital, the only addict ill enough in the twelve days I was there to meet this fate. They fed me through an IV for five days, so sick from drug abuse that I was unable to ingest sustenance on my own. Five days in the medical ward, six more back up in the chemical-dependency unit, and then out into the world, ready or not. And I was definitely not. But being subject to the limitations of insurance coverage, I was compelled to leave after twelve days, many weeks (or months) shy of being ready to face the world.

I empathized with what Meg had undergone on that fateful evening, having to watch someone she had seen suffer for so many years finally succumb to his addiction, leaving this world more quietly than when he had entered, but sadly, just as lost. I thanked Meg for sharing her painful story with me. She assured me that I was doing great and that she was proud of me. But as I exited that faded blue Chevy, I felt anything but great. At the time, I did feel somewhat proud that I'd managed to go twenty-one days without a drink or a drug. Not bad, considering that for most of the last twenty-five years of abuse, if I had gone more than a day or two without a drink or a drug, it had definitely been a very conscious, white-knuckle effort.

It wasn't Luke's untimely death that had spurred me into detox. Though he had died the evening before I checked into rehab, I hadn't learned of his overdose until my eighth day in the hospital, a full nine days after his death. (My family had learned the news early on, but hadn't wanted to risk telling me while I was still in withdrawal, out of fear that the grief might jettison me back into using.) And because my mind was still in such a huge fog at that point, it wasn't until a full twenty-four hours later that I recalled with horror that I was the one who had bought my friend his fatal dose.

More than several years have passed now, but I remember my last conversation with Luke as if it were yesterday. I had known that I was going into rehab when I talked to him at noon, just hours before his death. A few days prior, my wife Judy had found a small amount of heroin on a piece of foil that I had evidently dropped in one of my stupors. She had called me on my cell phone as I was weaving my way home from work, absolutely loaded to the gills, yet unable to feel anything at all. That's the way it was toward the end—no feelings of any kind. No euphoria, no joy, but then again, no pain—or so I kept trying to convince myself, since I knew of no way out of my addiction. Of course there was the psychic pain that the deepest part of my being was experiencing, the very pain I had tried to escape through drugs in the first place. And there was the horrible shame and guilt of knowing what I was doing to myself and to those who loved me. That and the underlying desperation of wanting out but not knowing how to escape my bondage.

It was odd how life had turned to this. A seemingly carefree youth with "endless potential" and "his father's sense of humor" had become this depressed, unfeeling, suicidal heroin addict. I remember my beautiful niece, Jennifer, writing to me once from California, "How can the funniest man I know also be the saddest man I know?" Indeed—like tears of the clown. How *had* it turned to this? I'm sure my wife had wondered that a thousand times as she watched me slowly sink deeper and deeper into my addiction, viewing first-hand my desperate, unsuccessful attempts at alleviating my psychic pain. Self-medication only served to mask, not to cure, and the cloth the mask was woven of was becoming more transparent each passing day.

I had responded robotically to the ringing of my cell phone. "Hello," I mumbled.

"I know you're doing heroin," my wife had blurted out bravely and abruptly, her voice even, yet something in it reflecting what must have been excruciating anxiety. My wife is a so-called "normy" (a recovery term denoting a "non-addict") and although she had been aware of my abuse of alcohol and pain-killers, the heroin had come as quite a shock to her.

"No, I'm not!" came my immediate, well-trained addict denial, my heart racing with the dread of having been found out.

"I'm holding some in my hands," she replied firmly, "and I've had it verified."

Those words somehow gave me a sense of relief I hadn't felt in years. Although being discovered frightened me, it also instilled in me a shred of hope, for I felt then that somehow, just possibly, help was on the way.

"I've only been snorting it!" I quickly responded, knowing how shocked she must have been, and trying to alleviate some of her concern. It was a bit of a half-truth in that I had "only" been snorting it the last couple of months. In the beginning I had used it both intravenously and intramuscularly. Somewhere along the line I had made the conscious decision to stop injecting the heroin, my diseased and irrational mind telling me that I would somehow become less addicted, or would at least be able to put off the severity of an addiction awhile longer. (I remember using this same line of misplaced logic on the admitting nurse in the chemical dependency ward a few days later, thinking she would tell me my withdrawal would somehow be made easier with this bit of information. "Heroin is heroin, honey," had been her matter-of-fact response.)

There were a few seconds of silence while my mind raced (as much as it could race, loaded as I was), searching for an answer. "I'm going into detox!" I remember exclaiming, trying to assuage whatever fears my wife was experiencing, and mine as well. It was all I could think of to say.

And so it was that I called my mother that evening, who had a friend in the mental-health field by the name of John Parker. John was an ex-priest who had been a friend of the family for years. He gave her the name of someone in the recovery field for me to call. Gathering up every ounce of nerve I could muster, I called this man, a compassionate man by the name of John Emerson. John strongly suggested that I check into a hospital so that I could be medically supervised while I detoxed. Frightened to death, but more desperate than frightened, I called around and found a hospital that would take me in on Saturday morning. It was the middle of the week when I called, "forcing" me to stay loaded for a few more days.

I scored my last hundred dollars' worth of heroin on a Thursday night from my Mexican dealer, Alejandro. As usual, I could barely understand what street he wanted me to meet him on, his English was so broken, his accent so thick. On occasion, one of his compadres would answer the phone, but none of them spoke with any greater clarity. The connection point was always somewhere different and I always had to have them repeat several times the name and number of the street intersection where they wanted me to meet them. (They made sure that their customers never knew where they lived.) Of course, I was always ultimately able to decipher their words.

In any event, I had my gram and a quarter of heroin, plus a half gram remaining from my prior purchase the day before, enough to get me through until Saturday morning with some left over to trade Luke for a few Lorcet 10s (double-strength Vicodin). I called Luke on Friday just before noon on the day of his death. He was already loaded on his muscle relaxers and pain pills by this time, having gotten his latest batch that morning. He was barely able to speak he was so out of it. I had told him the day before that I was going into rehab, but I wanted to make sure he remembered, to make sure he knew that it meant the end of our thirty-seven-year relationship. I knew intuitively that I couldn't afford to have Luke in my life anymore if I was to have any chance of staying clean. He had never expressed a desire to get clean—and I can't judge another man's desires or suffering. He had endured legitimate back pain over the years, partly due to ill-fitting prostheses, having grown up with half a leg (a leg that had been taken from him at the tender age of three, due to a tragic car accident). His journey was his journey. But I knew I had never been able to resist buying pills from him in the past, and I was still at least sane enough to sense that I didn't stand a snowball's chance in hell of resisting such a direct opportunity for narcotics in the future, especially from someone I knew so well.

Aside from reminding Luke about my plans to get clean, I wanted to get some pills from him that day so I could augment my last few highs. This was a laughable notion, considering that my tolerance had skyrocketed so horrendously I was no longer able to *feel* high. Toward the end of my active addiction, I had taken up to eight Lorcet 10s at once—the equivalent of sixteen regular-strength Vicodin—along *with* my next dose of heroin, and had still felt no high, no sense of euphoria whatsoever. But I was an addict, and that meant "repeating the same mistakes over and over again, expecting different results" (Einstein's definition of insanity). I had also wanted to sneak some pills into rehab in case the pain of withdrawal from all the opiates became more than I could bear.

We agreed upon the exchange—actually I was the one who decided how much heroin for how many pills, since Luke had been far too out of it to indulge in our usual bartering (arguing) process. I would give him forty dollars' worth of heroin for twenty Lorcet 10s. I was taking advantage of his stupor, since he normally charged much more than that (heroin was far easier to get than Lorcet 10s). But addicts do what they can for themselves, first and foremost, and I was no different from anyone else in this regard.

Things were working out better than I had hoped. Meg was with Luke—she was going to help him move later that day. He had been evicted from the motel in Kalama for failure to pay rent. I knew after I talked to Luke that I could talk with Meg and arrange to meet her during my lunch hour for the exchange. That way I wouldn't have to deal with Luke in person—dealings that had become more frequently combative over the previous couple of years.

(Although odds were Luke would be unconscious by that time anyway—his patterns were highly predictable. He would eat so many pills he would pass out, usually within a half an hour, and he wouldn't begin regaining consciousness until a couple of hours or so later.)

In talking with Luke that day I emphasized that I was going into rehab and that we couldn't communicate at all in the future. I wanted to make sure he understood that I was very serious about attempting to turn my life around.

"I'm going into detox tomorrow, Luke."

"I know—I know," came his slow, slurry reply.

"I can't afford to talk to you anymore after that," I reminded him.

"I know—I know," he repeated.

And then I uttered the words (words that haunt me to this day), "This is our last conversation, my friend."

"I know—I know," he slurred again.

And five hours later, after injecting approximately thirty dollars' worth of heroin into his arm, my life-long friend, Luke, was gone.

On that same fateful day I had used three times the amount of heroin that had ended up killing Luke. However, my use had been spread out over the full day, as opposed to the one dose he had taken. More telling, though, was that I had built up a heavy tolerance, whereas Luke had next to none, having used only sporadically over the preceding months, unable to afford more. Was that a curse or salvation? It depends upon one's perspective, I suppose. Salvation, I imagine. The suffering was over, at least.

My high tolerance had been built up from using heroin many times a day, every day, for more than three straight months—all except for a forty-two hour kick attempt, that is. A grueling, nightmarish forty-two hours somewhere near the middle of a ninety-four-day run. After several weeks of daily use, I had shut myself in my bedroom (*our* bedroom had become *my* bedroom since my wife had become so fed up with my addiction she had stopped sleeping with me several months prior) to try to kick the dope. I had stashed a small amount of heroin in my car in case I couldn't make it through the pain of withdrawal. I had experienced many opiate kicks over the years, and knew how intense the suffering could be.

It's not until about twenty-four hours into it that you begin to feel the pain of withdrawal. Then, as the hours mount, the pain, both physical and psychological, gradually takes over your entire being. Each moment begins to seem like hours, each hour like days—relentlessly cruel, tortuous, merciless days. Absolutely freezing cold one minute, trembling like a soaked puppy, only to be drenched in sweat the next, only to be freezing again seconds later. Constant nausea. Heavy dry-heaving for me. Indescribable weakness. A horrific taste in my mouth, irremovable, inescapable. An overall body ache that seemed inhuman, as if some alien disease had been transported into my body from another world. But far worse than any of the physical pain or discomfort is the tormenting, ever-present knowledge that all of these symptoms and more are going to be with you unceasingly for the better part of four or five days, without so much as a split second of conscious relief. Sadly, that dreadful awareness becomes your closest companion. And forty-two hours had been the limit of my endurance. I don't know which particular thought it was that had put me over the edge, but once the decision was made, I leapt off the bed and headed for the dope in my car like there was no tomorrow. After doing the ten dollars' worth that I had stashed for just such an "emergency," I hastily called my Mexican connection and immediately left the house to get more. That single dose had merely served to lessen the suffering—it had not deadened it nearly enough. My "amigos" were uncharacteristically slow that day. I had never waited more than ten minutes for them before, and except for that particular day, when I had to wait an agonizing forty-five minutes, I never waited more than ten minutes again.

Between that day and the day I checked into detox many weeks later, I stayed loaded twenty-four seven, never going more than two hours during my waking hours without a fix, never going much more than that during the night. I was so afraid of feeling anything that I kept a syringe full of heroin in the top drawer of my night stand, ready to do my next dose at the slightest sign of awakening from my stupor. And so my tolerance had skyrocketed, whereas Luke had basically built up none.

That day in her Chevy Caprice, Meg and I discussed whether or not we thought Luke had ended his life on purpose. It's something we will never know for sure, of course, at least not while we're members of this realm. He had to have known that he didn't have any tolerance built up. Though he was more often than not loaded on some form of opiate, it was usually painkillers and not heroin, and there were often many days between his using sprees. Although Luke was consistently getting over six hundred pills a month (a combination of pain pills and muscle relaxers) from three different doctors, and had been for several years, his supplies would never last long. He usually sold me at least half of the pain medication (I had no desire for the muscle relaxers, but Luke often called his Soma his "wife") and neither of us could make them last very long. We would supplement his regular prescription medications with "ER hits" (emergency room visits to scam for painkillers), but we never had enough to satisfy us, and the more the years passed, the truer this became.

As far as Meg and I had known, Luke hadn't used heroin for at least a couple of weeks prior to his death. Knowing this, he surely would have been aware of his lack of tolerance. Luke had not been ignorant about many things in life and certainly not about narcotics. He had been very well-versed in drug lore.

A few weeks before his death, Luke had mentioned to me that if he ever wanted to kill himself, all I had to do was bring him forty dollars' worth of heroin. It was strange how he had worded that—if *he* ever wanted to kill himself, all *I* had to do was bring him forty dollars' worth of heroin. I remember sounding surprised, not surprised so much that he had uttered the thought, but at the amount he had chosen as lethal. I recall asking him with some measure of doubt, "Forty dollars' worth would be enough to kill you?"

He had responded in a very assured manner, "Oh, absolutely—if I hadn't used in a couple of weeks or more."

It wasn't until many days after I'd learned of Luke's death that I remembered that particular conversation—and even then my mind was still so clouded I didn't immediately grasp its significance. *Forty dollars' worth*— exactly the amount *I* had decided to trade to Luke in exchange for twenty of his pills.

Luke sat on his bed that last day as he talked with Meg. The bed, a small chair, and table were the only pieces of furniture to grace his motel cell. Meg said Luke was unusually nostalgic that afternoon as he spoke with her. The initially debilitating effects of his muscle relaxer and pain pill intake had passed a couple hours after I talked with him that day. Shortly after I had spoken with him, I had talked to Meg and agreed to meet her at a freeway rest area halfway between Luke's motel and my place of work during lunch hour. Meg had since returned to the motel and given the heroin to Luke, but he didn't touch it until much later in the afternoon, she told me. That in itself was odd. Luke had no such willpower that I had ever been aware of. Was he consciously spending a last few relatively lucid hours with the only woman who had loved him in many years? Luke's own mother had died a number of years prior. (He had never known his father.) He had no living relatives in the state, save for a half-sister he was estranged from. He had had a girlfriend in his late teens, but hadn't had one since. My own mother and father loved Luke, but he rarely saw them over the years, and my dad had passed away quite some time before. He had been close to my brother, Tim, and his ex-wife Lisa, and their four children. (The kids called Luke "Uncle Goofy," aptly enough), but Tim had told Luke several years before that he couldn't come around anymore—Luke's drug abuse was far too negative for the kids. Meg and I were the only people left in his life that he saw with any regularity. So had this been Luke's way of saying good-bye, reminiscing with the person who probably understood him best?

Meg sat listening to Luke for several hours that afternoon. Luke would have rolled his own cigarettes as he talked, one after the other, his ever-jaundiced eyes meeting with his tobacco far more often than with hers. His full and scraggly beard, no hint of color aside from gray, roughly framed a haggard face. Just a trace of his lips would have been revealed through the whiskers as he spoke. His lightly tinted John Lennon specs, which it seems he had worn since before Lennon had made them popular, would have only slightly obscured the sadness in his blue eyes, eyes that had once sparkled with humor and with life, and on occasion still visited there. Luke stood about six feet tall, I would guess. (It seems odd to me that I never knew exactly how tall he was—I'm not sure why I never knew nor why it seems odd.) I'm guessing one side of him stood taller than the other, surmising that his artificial leg never matched up perfectly with his own. In earlier days, before Luke's addiction had turned the corner and become the master, he would have weighed around one hundred and eighty pounds. In later years, his once-healthy frame would support a meager one sixty or so. At forty-five years of age he still had a full head of hair, though the rust red had all but vanished long ago, swapped for a gray that matched his beard. Combined with the harsh miles of his life's journey, he looked as though he had seen at least a decade more. "Rode hard and put away wet" would have been a fitting bumper sticker for Luke.

Although I was a year and a half older than Luke and had abused my body nearly as much as he had, I often felt like he was the older one. Somehow, genetics had allowed me to retain most of my hair as well, though there was no gray in mine as yet, a living example that worry absolutely does not prematurely gray one's hair, or mine would have attained that hue ages ago.

As such, my hair still lined up with my brown eyes. At five foot nine, I stood beneath Luke three inches or so (unsure as to whether one of my legs might be shorter than the other, having never thought to measure them). I, too, sported spectacles, mine being oval as opposed to the perfectly round ones that rested on the bridge of Luke's nose. At the time I weighed one hundred and sixty pounds, about the same as Luke, which was actually ten pounds over my normal weight. (I remember the nurses in rehab finding it unusual that I had actually gained weight at the height of my addiction, but the tolerance of my sweet tooth had escalated in stride with my capacity for opiates. I maintained a voracious appetite for unhealthy foods throughout my heroin use, my pockets forever jammed with lemon drops, candy corn, M & M's, or some other sugar-laden substance.)

I sensed that Meg had been ever-patient with Luke on what was to be his last day on Earth, something in his demeanor commanding her attention more so than usual. She said he was strangely subdued but at the same time strangely serene that afternoon. It was quite some time, Meg told me, before he eventually looked toward the balloon of heroin that lay innocently enough on the table. He would have taken his sweet time with the ritual, a ritual we had all been warned somewhere along the path not to fall in love with. Yet fall in love with it (in a twisted sense of the phrase) we all somehow did. For Luke, it would be a particularly time-consuming affair. He liked to savor it, as if sampling a fine wine at a private gala. From the peeling off of the balloon wrap to the opening of the foil, from the heating of the heroin and water in the spoon to the drawing up of the drug into the awaiting needle, from the vein "making" to the final act of injection into the vein, Luke was meticulous and mindful of each and every move.

From Meg's description that day in her Chevy of how much heroin Luke had left in the foil, I conjectured that he had shot up about thirty dollars' worth of the forty-dollar bag I had traded to him. Had he been saving a few dollars' worth just in case his suicide attempt failed? Or was he simply trying to reach a deeper state of oblivion than usual, knowing he was leaving his motel room with nowhere to go? I had seen in the past what a mere ten dollars' worth of heroin did to Luke if he hadn't used in a while—it would completely wipe him out—and he knew that. Surely he would have known that thirty dollars' worth was more than flirting with danger.

Yet Meg and I also knew how steadfastly opposed to suicide Luke had been. Meg reiterated this to me when we spoke of his death. Luke believed that if you took your own life you would have to come back in another life and go through the suffering all over again, until you got it right.

Of course, we will never know for sure. Luke left no note, and had made no mention of suicidal thoughts to anyone. Occasionally I am bothered by this not knowing. What bothers me much more, however, is the fact that I had brought Meg exactly the amount of heroin that Luke had told me, just a few weeks before, would be enough to end his life. A conscious decision? Most definitely not. But disturbing nonetheless. I sometimes wonder if Luke and I had some sort of *subconscious* connection that day, his distressed mind somehow communicating to mine his desire to leave this planet, and my distressed mind somehow agreeing that this would be the best thing for him— and for me?

Thirty dollars' worth of the heroin I had sent to Luke had killed him. I am not particularly biblically minded, but I am aware of your more notable biblical facts. Thirty dollars' worth. *Thirty pieces of silver*. The correlation has often visited my mind.

"What was it they used to call it?" Zephram Cochrane asked, as he returned his gaze to Captain Kirk. "A *Judas* goat?" He then walked out the door to summon his loyal alien caretaker, "The Companion," to her demise.

Luke would be pleased, at least, with the *Star Trek* reference.

It is now more than several years past, and I remain clean and sober. I still reflect from time to time upon Luke's premature death, as well as his life. His life wasn't always so lonely and so sad.

As for me, I wasn't always a depressed, unfeeling, suicidal heroin addict.

EARLIER YEARS

YOUTHFUL INNOCENCE

My parents threw a birthday party for me when I was five years old. To this day it is the only surprise party I've ever had (which, incidentally, is not something I regret). I remember this particular event with startling clarity, if only for the emotional response it conjured up within me. As I walked into the living room of our small, three-bedroom home in Southeast Portland on the afternoon of my fifth birthday, I was greeted with a rousing rendition of "Happy Birthday to You" by what seemed like an overwhelming number of adults (in truth it was probably no more than six or seven, but "overwhelming" is a relative term, especially at the fragile age of five). I recall immediately bursting into tears, running frantically down the short hallway, and lunging head-first onto my bed. My confused and worried mother came into the room seconds later to find me lying face down on my bed literally sobbing so hard I could barely breathe, my small face buried in my still smaller hands.

"What's the matter, honey?" she asked, perplexed by my reaction. "Did we scare you?"

It was everything I could do to talk, my sobbing was so pronounced that my chest was heaving violently. The words came in little spurts.

"No," I managed through the gasps. "I'm crying—because—because they love me," I sobbed, "and it makes—it makes me happy."

And so begins the memory of my childhood. The event in itself is of little interest to an outside observer, I would suppose. However, upon reflection these many years past, I have come to recognize its profound significance to me. It is the first powerful emotional event in my memory. These many years later it remains as one of the most powerful experiences of my life. And it has reminded me in retrospect to recognize that there *is* overwhelming power in love. I'm not speaking of romantic love, or of a mother's instinctual love for her child—I'm talking of a love that comes from a different place, a place we can't explain, but that is always available to us. A love emanating from connectedness, from oneness. It is my belief today that this oneness is the ground of all being.

BAD TRIP, BROKEN HEART

The memories of my youth are scattered, as I'm sure it is with most of us. Certain moments stand out above others, many moments remain lost in time. The events and memories of my grade school years are like that, Luke and his separated leg among them.

I can tell you that the innocence of my youth left me gradually, only not so gradually in retrospect. I can also tell you that the loss of that innocence, and my impending journey into the darker nature of things, had little to do with my upbringing—at least not to my way of thinking. I have listened to the stories of a great many recovering addicts over the years, many of whom had truly bona fide excuses for their downfalls in life. It would be an insult to those people to blame the problems in my adult life on my childhood. The levels of abuse some of these poor souls endured in their earlier years would both sicken and enrage the hardest of hearts. I can tell you I have no such excuses. My deviation from the norm may have had genetic factors (addiction is a disease, I am told), but I won't blame my later behavior on the treatment I received growing up. My parents were of the most loving and nurturing natures possible. Neither of them abused drugs or alcohol. (My dad never drank, and my mom rarely did.) I went to Catholic schools for twelve years, and though I love to kid about being a "recovering Catholic," I hold much of what I learned and derived from that influence sacred to my heart. The truth is, the underlying reasons for everything that happened in my life aren't overly significant to me. It's my belief they could not have occurred any other way. But I digress. (You might want to get used to that.)

Although it would make sense to do this thing chronologically, making sense has never seemed to have been an established pattern or priority of mine. And so, with my own permission, I would like to jump ahead to my nineteenth year on this planet. It was in this year that I first discovered just how little sense I did make, how little sense life seemed to make and, most apparent at the time, how it seemed appropriate to label me (euphemistically) a tad touched.

26

Yes, I was definitely certifiable. Now, some may consider this a judgment call, but one of the parameters for this type of certification, it seems to me, is fairly cut and dried. It's my opinion that when they go to the trouble of hooking you up to one of those "shocker machines," it's a pretty safe bet that you've fallen off the deep end—dropped your other oar—system overload—crash-city.

Getting plugged into the shocker machine is a pretty fair indication that you've jumped the meridian, so to speak. They just don't go connecting all those electrodes to the scalps of normal, well-adjusted, *sane* people. Gotta have your marbles pretty well scrambled in the first place for them to want to zap your God-given brain with electricity. EST—Electric Shock Therapy is what they called it. Therapy—that's a laugh. Barbarism seems a more accurate term, at least from my perspective, and I feel I'm pretty well entitled to a perspective, considering I was a first-hand recipient of this "therapeutic" procedure. But they claimed to know what they were doing, or at least they believed they knew what they were doing. And I guess I believed them— believed that they actually believed they knew what they were doing. Or is that part of the process, getting you to buy their story? Here I was, messed up beyond all rational belief at the impressionable age of nineteen, and they're telling me about this EST stuff, and I'm thinking, *It must be effective; why else would they have it?* Of course, the key here being I was all messed up. Obviously, anything being told to me by someone who wasn't messed up immediately possessed more credibility than anything I could come up with on my own. Especially if it was coming from the "professional medical community."

What bothers me is how, in retrospect, it's so easy for me to deduce that cooking a person's brain with electricity just can't be all that good for them. Kind of like the smoking thing. It took the medical community how many years to deduce that cigarettes weren't good for you? Gosh, it takes a logical thinking person, what? About thirty seconds to figure that one out if he or she thinks about it. It shouldn't have taken a legion of medical personnel thirty years of research to ascertain that sucking smoke from a flaming object into your body probably isn't good for you. (Although a smoker friend of mine always contended it was safer to suck our polluted air in through a filter. You have to almost admire this desperate level of deductive reasoning—if only for the fact that he didn't spend thirty years researching the subject to reach his conclusion.) It's the same with this EST stuff. I'm thinking that little six-year-old Tommy down the street might take thirty, forty seconds tops to deduce that plugging your brain into an electric outlet probably isn't one of the healthier options in life.

The truth was, though, I wanted them to do it. I begged them, actually, since neither my parents nor the psychiatrist I was seeing wanted me to go that route initially. But neither therapy nor medication had done anything to alleviate the depression and anxiety that had consumed me. I was all torn up inside and grasping at anything I thought might heal me. I just couldn't figure out how to fix myself. No one else seemed to be able to either.

Several months before I had those shock treatments I had gone to my parents, pleading for help. It had taken every ounce of courage I could assemble to tell them I had taken a lot of drugs in high school and that I thought the drugs had messed up my mind. My reticence in sharing these thoughts with my parents wasn't because they were unapproachable. On the contrary, they were quite approachable. I was simply ashamed to admit to them the level of my drug use. I was afraid they would be disappointed in me, the kid with all the good grades and "so much to offer." But I was at the point of complete and utter despair, and I simply couldn't live any longer with the crazy thoughts that were bouncing around inside my skull. So I had gone to my parents and told them that I thought I was losing my mind, beginning to sob as I opened my heart to them. I wasn't being melodramatic. I truly thought I was going insane.

They took me to a place called *Outside In* at first. One of the services this non-profit organization provided at the time was assisting young people with drug problems. After a couple of visits there, it was obvious I needed help of a more professional nature. They recommended that I see a psychiatrist. My parents, although they didn't have much in the way of money, took me to one of the top psychiatrists in the state, Dr. Dickel (president of the Oregon Psychiatric Association at the time).

I spent a few months in weekly psychotherapy sessions before it was agreed they would see if the shock treatments could bring me some relief (since therapy and medication hadn't). A deep state of depression coupled with massive anxiety were the clinical terms for my condition. My depression became so severe that at one point (I learned many years later) the doctor had told my mother there was a chance I might never come out of it. Prior to each of these psychotherapy sessions I had also been taken into a room to learn relaxation techniques, where some female person (I don't recall what her name or her title was) would start at one end of my body or another and tell me to tighten, then release, all the individual muscles groups in my body. I didn't see how something this insanely simple could help cure something as insanely complicated as the madness in my mind, but I was willing to do whatever they asked of me, since I was clueless as to how to help myself. They put me on anti-depressants during this time as well. But none of these therapies proved effective, which is why, when I first heard about shock treatments, they began to pique my interest, and I began probing the doctor about them.

As I think about it now, I wonder how any progress *could* have been made during those therapy sessions. I barely even talked to Dr. Dickel, from what I remember (there are large gaps in my memory from that time). I only recall attempting to explain to the doctor the feelings I was experiencing, and having a terribly difficult time doing so. How does one describe feeling so sad that they don't want to live anymore, other than to say, "I feel so sad that I don't want to live anymore"? How does one describe feeling like they're going insane, other than to say, "I feel like I'm going insane"? How does one describe fear other than to say, "I'm afraid"?

Well, what are you sad about? Why do you feel like you're going insane? What are you afraid of? The good doctor would have attempted to dig deeper, I'm sure, trying to draw something out of me that would have helped him treat my illness.

However I tried to describe my pain to Dr. Dickel, the fact was that my own thoughts were terrifying me—they were screaming to me that I was losing it, that I was going insane. I had told the doctor the same thing I had told my parents—that I thought a bad trip on mescaline had triggered this madness in my mind (I had no other explanation for it). And after this venture into psychedelic psychosis, I had eventually become so inundated with these frightening thoughts that I was unable to see old friends anymore. I was embarrassed to tell anyone how disturbed my mind had gotten. It had been hard enough to tell my own parents. So I became a virtual recluse, which only compounded my feelings of abnormality, which in turn exacerbated my thoughts of madness.

There is only one bit of conversation with Dr. Dickel that I remember verbatim. He had been interrogating me as to why I was afraid of seeing old friends. I didn't know exactly how to explain it, but I recall telling the doctor that I was afraid I wouldn't be myself.

He had quickly responded with, "Who else can you be?"

I remember liking that line, but I also remember not believing that it could benefit me in any lasting way.

My recollection of Dr. Dickel is of a very soft-spoken, gentle, and sincere man somewhere in his sixties. He was accomplished in his field and seemed to genuinely want to help me, but I was locked so deep within my own mind that I'm sure it would have been impossible for anyone with less credentials than God to have helped me at that point. And I guess God was too busy in 1972 to bother with me—or else He was saving that for later. Much later, as it turned out.

My parents, of course, were very involved in all of this. I sure as hell hadn't picked up the phone and started dialing for shrinks. I was busy reclusing in my bedroom at their house, spending my days in an almost catatonic state and my tortured nights riddled with anxiety. Mom and Dad had multiple conversations with the doctor in the ensuing months, doing their best to rescue me from my hell. My parents were not the type of people who gave up trying, no matter what the situation. They would have turned over every stone in the state of Oregon if they thought there was a chance it would uncover a solution to my tormented state of mind. I know that my various forms of treatment must have cost them a small fortune, a fact they never once mentioned to me. (I harbor guilt to this day, figuring that all those psychiatric expenses my parents took on were at least partially responsible for their having to sell their home and move into an apartment less than a year after my medical care had ended.)

Whatever theories might have been bantered about regarding my psychoanalysis, the professionals seemed to reach a consensus among them that my plunge into the darker side of consciousness had indeed been a direct result of my drug abuse in high school. Mescaline, LSD, psilocybin, MDA, hashish, speed, pot—whatever my friends and I could get our hands on at the time. Kids experimenting with getting high. Fairly common back in the late sixties and early seventies. We were in the minority, I must say, but it's not like we were the only ones messing with the stuff. Curiosity, boredom, whatever. It was fun for the most part until I had the bad trip. It wasn't worth all of the fun put together then—not even close. I took two hits of brown organic mescaline and smoked way too much hashish at a party during my senior year in high school. And I flipped out. Thought I was going insane, wouldn't you know? (Maybe I was having a premonition.)

The terror of that night can't justly be put into words. The closest way I can come to describing it would be to have a person imagine being scared out of their wits by something—suddenly startled by an unexpected noise in a dark forest, for example. Then take that initial instant of fear, that very first heart-grabbing, mind-bending, spine-tingling jolt of fear, intensify it a hundredfold and then freeze-frame that nanosecond of peak terror. Then replay this feeling every second of every minute of every hour for the next six or seven hours. Then imagine that the imagined reason behind the fear was a completely convincing sense of going insane, or of actually *being* insane. A hideously nightmarish scenario—not something I would wish upon my (or anyone else's) worst enemy.

My friends took care of me on that night, while I proceeded to think I was losing my mind. I owe them a debt of gratitude that I can never adequately repay. The party that night had been at my friend Terry Milton's house. His parents were out of town for the weekend.

I remember I had begun to feel extremely paranoid at one point and had gone outside to sit on the porch steps. Suddenly it was as if I could see myself "from above," only from my new vantage point it appeared as if I had literally shrunk to about twelve inches in height. The paranoia blossomed rapidly from there. A few minutes later I was heading to my car to get the hell out of there. I instinctively knew I shouldn't drive and was terrified, actually, of the prospect, but the fear of facing people in my current mental state was even greater.

Fortunately my best friend, Duane Keaton, saw me heading to my car and stopped me to ask what I was doing. I told him I was freaking out and that I was leaving. He told me I wasn't going anywhere. He gathered our gang of close friends and we all left the party together—including Terry, who was throwing the party. Duane and I, along with Sam Bauer and Matt Larson, piled into Terry's panel truck. All night long I would tell them, "I need to get out of the truck," or "I need to get back in the truck"—a constant, intense terror guiding my thoughts, words, and actions. They babysat me until dawn, when the effects of the drugs began to slowly wear off. It was an extremely ugly and debilitating, life-changing experience. It was, without a doubt, the most hellish six or seven hours of my life (and I've had a few hellish hours since).

Over the next few months I began suffering from severe bouts of anxiety, frightening thoughts, and social paranoia. The only explanation I could come up with for these new maladies was that I might be having flashbacks from my bad trip. And it scared the hell out of me.

But as intense and mind-altering as my drug experience proved to be, I still can't say for sure what the definitive cause was for my eventual institutionalization and shock treatments. Right around the same time as my bad trip I had my heart broken pretty well. Really well, actually. I loved her from the moment I saw her freshman year in high school. I knew when I heard her laugh that she was the one for me. Fourteen years old and already had a wife picked out. I waited a year for her to break up with her boyfriend, then dated her until we were out of high school. We were madly in love with each other.

The problem was, I had felt the need to test the waters a bit before we actually got married (as we had fully planned). All I wanted was to make sure that down the road I didn't regret not experiencing a wider variety of other women—in the physical sense (I was eighteen, damn it!). I had only kissed one other girl before Sarah. It wasn't that I wanted to go have sex with a bunch of different women. Hell, my girlfriend and I were still virgins, for God's sake. It wasn't uncommon back then. I had tried, of course, but she had wanted to "save herself" for when we got married. That Catholic thing. Frustrating for me, but it actually made me respect and love her all the more. (A lot of guys might not believe that, but it's the truth. And if there's one thing I am, it's honest. Insane, but honest. Of course, I'm not saying that I still didn't want to "do it" with Sarah, because if I said that, I wouldn't be being honest anymore. I'm simply saying that I wasn't that persistent on the subject out of respect for her. That and probably a little of that ol' Catholic thing weighing in on my own damn head.)

I sincerely wanted my first time to be with Sarah. Before we got married and did that, though, I simply wanted to have some decent physical contact with a couple of different girls in order to sate that wild-oats thing—to at least give the physical aspect of playing the field some sort of effort. It was an attempt to preempt any future misgivings in that area. Quite a thoughtful, selfless, and mature act if you stop to analyze it—I wanted to grope other women for the sake of our long-term relationship. You've got to respect that, I'm thinking.

The emotional side of a new relationship wasn't a factor to me. I already had my emotional partner. I wanted some "strange stuff," is what it boiled down to. And, of course, I couldn't just fool around on the side. That guilt thing again. So I had confronted Sarah with my plan. We would separate for thirty days—so we could be absolutely sure about each other, I explained to her.

Caught her totally by surprise. Broke her heart. Devastated her, her mother had told my mother (I found out years later). She spent three days in her room crying her eyes out.

Well, those three days must've been awfully damn therapeutic—it turns out after the month was up she wasn't sure she wanted to come back to *me*. (Poetic justice?) She actually thought she might be in love with some guy she had dated in the last couple of weeks—what in the hell was that all about? Who said anything about falling in love with someone else? Gloves off, young fella. Back at ya, pal. Hard to get happy after that one. Fall in love with someone else in a couple of weeks? We were going to be married, for God's sake! A couple of make-out sessions and some strange bare tit (as we used to say) had cost me a wife, a heart, and quite possibly my mind. Who knew?

I spent the next few lunar periods in varying degrees of heartache—vacillating from merely agonizing to downright unbearable. I must have played Rod Stewart's "Maggie May" and The Beatles' "Oh, Darling," eight or nine trillion times each over the next few months. (My poor parents—I had no headphones, and I would blast these songs on the record player in my room, over and over and over again. Certainly, no obsessive/compulsive mentality here.)

The bottom line was, this woman was everything I had ever dreamed of in my young life, and I had blown it, plain and simple. And I just couldn't bear the thought of living my life without her.

UPON FURTHER ANALYSIS

I could delve deeper into my childhood to try to further sort out some of what ailed me in later years, although as I've already disclosed, any deviation from the norm in my upbringing pales in comparison to countless other stories I have heard. Nor do I think the "why" of it matters much, as I've also pointed out. It is my firm belief that most of us do the best we can in this life, parents and children alike, and playing the blame game serves no purpose. That said, there *are* environmental factors in our childhoods that obviously have lasting effects on us, some positive, some not so positive. How much effect they have on us, and how lasting they are, is a pretty ambiguous call, it seems to me. There are so many variables in life, it's impossible to say for sure what combination of conditions or circumstances may have led to a person's specific traits or trends.

But I suppose at least a partial understanding of some of these traits and trends can be gleaned from an examination of one's earlier surroundings. How much such an examination can aid in reducing further suffering in one's life is debatable. At some point a person has to take responsibility for his or her own life. I have been led to believe in more recent years that only a shift in our current perspective can improve our lives in the present moment. Yesterday is gone. Accepting things as they are, regardless of what happened in the past, is the path to serenity.

But if I were to play along with Freud and his cohorts for a moment, I might begin such an analysis by noting that my mother was a worrier (a syndrome that surfaced partly from her own upbringing, I'm sure), and remarking that some of that rubbed off on me. (Not to pick on Mom, but they always appear to start these things with the mother.) I could add that she was a bit of a screamer at times, too, vocal emissions that were more often than not brought on by my older brother and me fighting like cats and dogs several times a day, seemingly every day, for as much of my youth as I can remember. At other times my mother's yelling would be the result of our refusal to do our chores, chores that she would line up for my two brothers and me (an older brother, Joe, and a younger brother, Tim) and that we evidently had very little interest in performing. There were three chores that she alternated weekly among us—vacuuming, drying the dishes (we grew up long before the existence of dishwashers—long before they existed in our neighborhood, anyway), and taking out the garbage. The "taking out the garbage" brother would automatically elicit scorn and hatred from the other two, having, through no fault of his own, drawn the easy job of the week. There were days we cooperatively did our chores and days we needed prodding. It was on the prodding days that the screaming would begin.

I could bring up the time that my mother went ballistic, shouting at my brothers and me for one damn thing or another, and ended up tossing a pan of spaghetti sauce all over the beautiful new wallpaper (beautiful to my mother, at least) in the dinette, as well as on the ceiling and the floor. Now *that* seemed whacked to me. After all, even at the relatively naive age of twelve it seemed pretty obvious to me that the person she was hurting most was herself. I guess it was the pointlessness of what she had done that had started my brothers and me laughing. And I have to hand it to Mom—even she started laughing at this point, recognizing the absurdity of the mess she had created. (Mom could always readily laugh at herself, an endearing trait for anyone.) I remember Dad had come home right about then and had joined us all in the laughter when he saw the dining room carnage. Moments like that seemed in some bizarre way to make us more of a family than any church, school or sporting event ever did.

If I was talking to a shrink today, I would probably make it clear somewhere in here that my mother loved her children (and later, her grandchildren) as much or more than any mother I've ever known. If I was to use one word to describe my mother it would be "selfless." I know of no mother who was there for her offspring (and later, for her offspring's offspring) more. I know of no mother who was more involved in her children's lives, whether it be schoolwork or sports or anything that should rightfully call for a parent's attention. And there is no doubt in my mind (nor was there ever) that she would have done (and would do) anything within her power to end whatever level of suffering any of her children or grandchildren might be going through. This would include, of course, the insanity that preceded my shock treatments.

At this point an analyst might want to know why my older brother and I fought so much, I imagine. And I would tell them that I haven't the foggiest, other than while growing up it always seemed to me that disliking one's older brother was a very normal and proper thing to do. My best friend, Jeff Carson, didn't care for his older brother, Cliff, either—so why do you ask such a thing? Only eleven months of life separated Joe and me, about the same span of time that separated Jeff from his brother. I'm sure the closeness of our ages brought with it some Freudian sense of competition, vying for attention early in life and then gaining momentum as the years went by. Jeff and I were the "Blackjacks" and Joe and Cliff were the "Renegades," clever little names we had come up with to further distinguish our alienation from each other. Of course, more often than not, Jeff and I would lose whatever battles we partook in, being the younger, smaller, and therefore, weaker ones.

Being physically weaker than my older brother put me on a quest to locate equalizers in my youth. As a fight would escalate and I would start getting the hell beat out of me, I would be compelled to balance the scales in any manner that seemed convenient at the time. Various weapons availed themselves to me over the years and I took full advantage of their appearances in my life. Sticks, stones, vacuum cleaner parts, baseball bats, ashtrays, whatever. Sometimes these things would be wielded merely as threats, but at other times it would become necessary to actually use them in self-defense. (Tell it to the judge.)

I'm not sure exactly how many holes appeared in the walls of our home on S.E. 86th and Woodstock (where we lived from the time I was six until I was fifteen) as a result of these engagements. (The fights seemed to lessen in frequency after we moved to S.E. 129th and Harold halfway through my high-school years, probably because they were just too damn intense, and as we got bigger we became more fearful of inflicting serious damage, either upon our surroundings or upon ourselves.) One such hole surfaced above the couch in the living room because my brother's elbow had missed my head (these fights did improve my reflexes over the years). A hole near the bottom of the bathroom door came into being because I had slung my foot into it. (If it was more toward the beginning of a confrontation I would be brave enough—or pissed enough—to be the aggressor, and on this occasion Joe had locked himself in the bathroom to escape my wrath.) An unsightly gouge in the hardwood floor in the hallway loomed into existence one day because of a metal object (the specific identification of which escapes me) I had tossed at my brother. I suppose the most insane thing I ever did in these regards was to throw a butcher knife at my brother's head from about fifteen feet away. It was actually a bit of a compliment to him on my part, if one dissects the scene appropriately. I knew without a doubt that my brother had some of the better reflexes in the city (he was a talented athlete), and that he would relatively easily duck the incoming missile. And he did. To this day, my only regret is that the knife didn't stick in the wall (that same abused wallpapered wall that had taken the spaghetti hit) behind where his head had been seconds before. That would have gotten my point across much more effectively, I think. Plus it would have looked cool.

The fights usually ended with my running as fast as I could in any direction where my brother wasn't. Unfortunately, he was not only stronger, but faster as well, and I would find myself tackled and underneath him at some point, begging him to let me go. If I yelled loud and long enough, this usually worked. I would promise to stop hitting him if he would stop pummeling me. I might tell him that the whole thing was my fault and that I was sorry and that he was the greatest brother in the whole, wide world or whatever I felt might appease him, and then as soon as he let me go and I could get far enough away from him I would bombard him with one disgustingly vile name or another. And that would start another series of chase, tackle, pummel, etc. It wasn't that I was just plain stupid—I simply couldn't control the anger that would well up inside me.

I know a shrink would ask me at this point what it was that I was so angry about (and Dr. Dickel may have asked this of me, but I doubt that I had gotten that in depth with him) and I would have to say, "I don't know. I just didn't like my brother back then." Of course, that would have been misleading, because the truth of the matter is we did love each other in some way, I know. Hell, there is no doubt in my mind that my older brother would have stuck up for me in a Portland minute if some stranger had been hassling me. And, as adults, Joe and I learned to love and appreciate one another a great deal. But growing up there was just this sense of rivalry, and it stirred some hidden rage within each of us, I guess. Where that rage came from beats the hell out of me. I do know that in my heart of hearts I never believed I was the instigator in a single one of these altercations. (I'm confident NBA sports analysts would have loved saying about me, "In his mind, he's never committed a foul in his life.") Of course, the notion is ludicrous—I'm sure out of the thousands of fights we engaged in, I must have started one or two of them.

37

My younger (by two and a half years) brother, Tim, was kind of like that poor wallpaper, an observer throughout most of his childhood. It's surprising that he grew up to be probably the sanest of the bunch of us, with what he had to witness. But it would probably come as no surprise to anyone to learn that as a young adult he became very interested in karate and over the ensuing decades became a fifth-degree black-belt master and teacher of Tae-kwon-do. Perhaps watching me lose most of my battles instilled in him a sense of wanting to know how to protect himself (and a desire to share this knowledge with as many "little brothers" as he could).

I would confess to a shrink today that my dad seemed relatively flawless to me, and I only throw in the "relatively" because I assume he could not have been. I do remember him spanking me on maybe a handful of occasions in my youth. Not that I deem the act of spanking as being flawed, but it's all I can come up with that seems negative in any sense. (And that *is* the point of psychoanalysis, isn't it? To focus on the negative aspects of one's past? I would assume we're not looking to alter the positive influences in our lives.) I don't recall what prompted any of these corporal incidents. I do know that my brother and I rarely fought when Dad was around. We reserved those lovely occasions for my mother—or outside the house where there was no parent around. My dad worked full time, of course, mostly as a loan officer for the Small Business Administration when we were growing up. We always had at least a couple of hours after school to stir up whatever problems for Mom that we could. She worked as the school secretary during our grade-school years, so she was home, for the most part, after school. The culturally common entreaty, "Wait until your dad gets home," was oft heard in our home, too. When she couldn't stop us with this threat (which was most of the time, since we didn't fret too much about the future in those days), she would sometimes resort to trying to spank us as well. I say "trying" because we weren't nearly as cooperative with her as we were with Dad.

So, what deductions could be derived from any of this delving? Had my drug use sparked my high anxiety, as I had initially thought? Did this anxiety then lead to my depression? Did my broken heart serve to exacerbate this condition, or was it fuel enough for its own form of illness? Was my inability to cope with these things a result of youthful immaturity, a drug-fractured psyche, or the fault of inherent biological chemistry? And how did my upbringing influence any of this, if at all?

I don't know if there are, or ever will be, definitive answers to these questions. I only know that the pain I experienced during the period surrounding those shock treatments was all too real and that it affected me in profound ways for many years to come.

A SHOCKING EXPERIENCE

Analysis aside, I was pretty damn insecure after the break up and the flip out. I couldn't tell you which damaged my psyche more. And it wouldn't change anything if I could. Things are as they are. As I've said, it never did make sense to me how finding out what causes you to go bonkers is somehow going to be the basis for a cure: "Well, it turns out, Bob, that your grandpa's neighbor molested you when you were four, your mother was an alcoholic who turned tricks on the side, you were adopted, and your Aunt Stephanie used to be your Uncle Steve. There, feeling better now? That'll be two hundred dollars, thank you very much."

All I *can* tell you is that those shocker machines do exactly what any normal thinking person would expect them to do—they give you one excruciatingly intense headache. Make your next migraine seem like an orgasm. Shock your poor, already screwed-up brain with a thousand-or-how-ever-many volts of electricity—makes a lot of sense, doesn't it? (I guess they've turned the voltage down quite a bit since the sixties and seventies—less hard core "bad-trippers" to contend with, I imagine. I've been told that this milder form can be beneficial for some people. Still, intentionally inducing seizures seems a bit mad to me—at least now it does—but this is coming from someone whose brain has been fried, scrambled, *and* seized.)

They wait awhile after they've zapped you. Then a pair of trustees helps you shuffle down the hall à la Jack Nicholson in *One Flew Over The Cuckoo's Nest*, each labored step a mighty struggle to survive, your brain unable to communicate properly with your now-rubbery legs and your head about to explode from the internal pounding of a thousand jackhammers that have taken root inside. They take you immediately to the main living section of the ward, they do—the day room. Right there where all your other wigged-out brothers and sisters, your fellow "inmates," can view your misery first-hand. I suppose the real reason they did that was so that we could get some support from our peers, because truly no one is more empathetic than a fellow sufferer. They relate better to your pain, not to mention that those who suffer from psychic pain often have a "higher sensitivity level" to begin with (in my sometimes-not-so-humble, often-uneducated, but usually derived-from-experience, opinion).

I blame myself mostly, though. I was the one who had asked them to do it. Begged them, for sure. (This part of my story never ceases to amuse a recovering addict friend of mine—he finds it somehow delightfully entertaining that I actually begged people to electrocute my head.) I was (by the normally accepted measuring standards) an intelligent human being. I heard about this EST stuff, asked the doctor to explain the theory behind it, evaluated it, and decided I wanted to try it. It seemed the quick and easy way out—right up my alley. The theory, as my agitated mind understood it at the time, was that there's something in your past causing you to be all screwed up, and the electricity will somehow shock those portions of your brain that are disturbed and cause you to forget those disturbances. Sounded good to me. Quick and simple. Never mind how those bolts of electricity magically seek out and destroy only the bad stuff up there in your head. They must have access to intelligent electricity in those places (I must have assumed in my desperation). But I had heard what I wanted to hear, disregarded any logical skepticism, and began begging both the doctor and my parents to let me try these shock treatments. I think they were each experiencing their own levels of desperation when they finally acquiesced to my pleadings, having made zero progress with my mental state using other therapies and medication.

It turns out I probably should have paid more attention to my logical self. To this day, there are large segments of my life prior to and several years after that so-called shock "therapy" that I remember little or nothing about. This isn't old age sneaking up on me, either. I never could remember those periods, all through my twenties and beyond. People would say things like, "Remember that time we kidnapped the pope?" (or some actual event that should've been almost as memorable as kidnapping the pope), and because I was embarrassed that I couldn't remember (hardly anyone outside my immediate family knew I had been to the funny farm) I would say, "Yeah, that was a blast! That pope was a pretty funny dude, you know," or whatever I felt the appropriate response should have been. I had been deathly afraid of anyone learning that I had seen a psychiatrist, let alone been in a psych ward. I know now that the people in my life would have felt only compassion for me. But because of the stigma mental illness carried, my pride wanted those secrets guarded. My parents had to explain my absence in some manner, however, and I didn't mind them telling people that I had had some problems with drugs, or that I was depressed about my breakup with Sarah, but the shrink and the psych ward were taboo.

I spent three weeks in that psych ward, located at Holladay Park Hospital in Northeast Portland. (The hospital shut down years ago, but the atmospheric disturbance from our torched thalami must surely still linger there.) Well—I was *supposed* to spend three weeks. I left after two and a half. I had some sort of panic attack, only back then they didn't have a name for them—they just figured you were loony. All I knew was I had to get the hell out of there.

I loved my fellow inmates, though. I got rather close to a few of them, although I couldn't even tell you one of their names. Seven visits to the shocker machine made sure of that. I sure as hell don't remember what they looked like, either. I just remember loving them. Vague recollections. A tall, long-haired blond kid, my age, in there for the same thing as me—bad trip. At least, that's what they told him, and that's what he believed. (That was an oft-heard cry of the late sixties and early seventies: "Bad trip fried his brain, man. Fucked him way up.") This blond kid, whom I'll name Randy, and I—we hit it off right from the start. Same age, same likes and dislikes, same affliction, same treatment. If we weren't both so messed up I'm sure we could have been lifelong friends.

Then there was the girl, twenty or so. She was in there because she couldn't cope with the guilt she was experiencing after having slept with her husband's brother once. Some people might not understand how that would put you in a psych ward, but then they're not dealing with that "heightened sensitivity" thing I mentioned earlier. She was probably Catholic, too—had the added guilt thing going. (See, it's okay to make fun of something if you've ever been a member. That's the rule. Well, my rule, anyway. And I was a long-standing member of the Catholic Church, at least from a baptismal perspective, if not a practicing one.) Anyway, nicest girl in the world, but all bollixed up and nowhere to go but the psych ward.

There was the attractive lady in her early thirties, in there on account of she got hooked on diet pills. Back then they didn't have clinics specifically dedicated to drug rehabilitation. Whacked out, strung out, it didn't matter.

Everyone went to the same place. I was a little skeptical at first about her problem being diet pills. I was figuring she was probably hooked on speed or something a little more sinister-sounding than diet pills, but something you learn upon entering one of those places is that the patients (the ones that can talk) usually don't lie to each other. No reason to. A bond of trust is built up rather rapidly when you're institutionalized with people who are all crying out for help. (Besides, who knew what they put in diet pills back then, or where the hell she was getting them?)

Bad trips, guilt trips, diet trips—whatever the reason, we all had one thing in common—we couldn't cope with life. We couldn't even cope with our own minds, and we had no idea how to fix ourselves. Yeah, we bonded. We looked out for each other. After Randy or I would get shocked, our institutionalized brethren would lend a sympathetic hand or ear, trying to console us. Randy and I were the only patients being sent to the shocker machine while I was there. They liked to shock the bad-trippers, I guess: "You think that was a bad trip? Try this one on for size." I'm sorry. As ugly as they were, and they were extremely ugly, those seven shock treatments didn't add up to one bad drug trip—they paled in comparison, in fact.

We were on the "A" side of the psych ward. (I never did like settling for lower grades.) There was a big, old, thick padlocked steel door that separated us from the "B" side, where they housed the seriously whacked out—the major players—the gone and ain't never coming back, *truly* insane people. Randy and I would be allowed to go over to the other side to play ping pong once a day. We never could figure out why they put the ping pong table on the "B" side. There wasn't a single one of them over there that could hold a paddle, let alone hit the goddamn ball with it. Maybe they just wanted an excuse to send us over there, to show us where we might end up if we weren't careful—a friendly little warning of sorts.

One afternoon the four of us were playing pinochle, which had become a daily event. (I learned to play pinochle in a psych ward—not everyone can say that. I crafted a crude ceramic ashtray and an equally crude woven wall hanging while I was in there, as well.) Without provocation or warning, I was suddenly thrust into a full-scale panic attack (although I had had a number of these episodes in prior months, I still had no idea what they were or why I was having them). I instantly became extremely frightened of the very people who had become my closest confidants. I got all flushed, sweaty, shaky, my heart

43

started palpitating, and I felt like I couldn't speak or that if I did it would sound like I had a vibrator stuck in my throat on account of being so terrified all of a sudden. And I was too scared and embarrassed to let them know what I was feeling. The only option became flight, so I high-tailed it to my room. The twenty-year-old girl followed me and tried to console me. I truly appreciated the gesture, but I had to ask her to leave. I couldn't face anyone—that social paranoia thing was showing its ugly face again. I had started freaking out inside my mind—it's difficult to explain unless you've visited this particular state of mental paralysis. "Drug flashback" was still the only explanation I could come up with for any of these attacks, though even that didn't seem plausible to me. They didn't feel quite the same, for one thing (nor did anyone in the psychiatric world think they were flashbacks). The fear wasn't quite as intense—or maybe it only seemed less intense because I knew there would be a sooner end to it—all I had to do was get away from people, and the fear would gradually subside.

Whatever these episodes were, that particular night's attack broke the camel's back. I called my parents and told them I had to get the hell out of that place right then (too crazy for the psych ward—that'll boost your confidence). They tried to talk me out of it. They came down the next day in an attempt to calm me, but I was adamant. I won. (We addicts are very convincing people when we want to be: "Shock me, damn it!" "Okay, now stop that and get me out of here, damn it!" "Convincing," I said, not necessarily sane—but then we've already established my credentials, or lack thereof, on that one.) The bottom line—I was allowed to check out early.

My psychiatrist wanted to know what had happened in there when I saw him next. Well, I sure as hell didn't know. That's what my folks were paying *him* for, I was thinking. But I couldn't blame the doctor. He was trying his damnedest. It's just that nobody had figured out that much about how a normal human brain functions. One certainly couldn't expect anyone to decipher this particular jumble of fried and confused synapses. At least not in this lifetime.

Over the years, there have been a handful of (un-credentialed) people in my life who have proposed a simple explanation for my periods of mental duress. They've suggested that I think too much, and, as I like to say—I've given that a lot of thought. The truth be told, if there's something I haven't given a lot of thought to, it's only because I haven't thought of it yet. But I take some solace in the knowledge that a good many people in society are tortured by this affliction, a fact that I have become more acutely aware of in recent years. The Indian sage, Ramana Maharshi (1879-1950), has been attributed with saying that spiritual progress is measured by the "degree of reduction of thought." As I have gained more understanding of certain schools of "thought," this statement has become more profound to me. I speculate that Ramana may have been referring to the reduction of negative, non-constructive thought forms, which, I am told, often take up a preponderance of our mental activity. But then again, I'm no sage—and there I go, doing that thinking thing again. Not very damn spiritual of me.

In any case, I wish I could remember their names. I wish I could remember their faces—my troubled, but kind-hearted, psych ward cronies. They were good people.

THE MADNESS OF INSANITY

Being in that psych ward had really set some disturbing parameters for me early on in life. I was forced to learn at the tender age of nineteen that "crazy" wasn't that far off for me. It's a hell of a thing to discover about yourself, especially at that age. It's tough to live with knowing that you've gotta dodge *that* bullet for the rest of your natural born days, which just happens to statistically constitute about three-fourths of your life expectancy and *all* of your adult life. I hadn't even made it to legal drinking age, and I was already certifiable. Worse yet, I was aware of it. I wasn't even granted the mercy of delusions about my own sanity.

The six months or so before entering that woeful ward had been a nightmare, an unending, horrific nightmare. It was more than three decades ago—seems like another lifetime. I cried myself to sleep most nights—when I could get to sleep, that is. I spent the biggest portion of those nights lying in anguish. Depressed like a zombie during the day, chock-full of anxiety at night. I couldn't shut my mind off. I couldn't block out the thoughts, the fear—the terror, actually. I don't really know what it was exactly that I was afraid of. Afraid of going nuts, partly. Hell, if that wasn't nuts I don't know what would be.

Much of this anxiety seemed to stem from worrying about having panic attacks (the social paranoia thing), that I had begun experiencing soon after my bad trip. Paranoid about being paranoid. And being afraid of people finding out how I felt added significantly to my angst. I couldn't face anyone I knew anymore. Although I had a great group of close friends, I was ashamed to tell them what was going on with me, about my anxieties and confusion. Ironically, not seeing them only added to my anxieties and confusion.

The onset of my social paranoia had occurred at another party, just a couple of weeks after I had experienced my bad trip. I don't recall the exact circumstances—I just remember feeling horribly out of sorts at some point. All

I remember is that it was initiated by something someone said. Someone poking clean fun at me, I'm sure. Nothing serious, I'm quite certain. But I went from feeling a little embarrassed to feeling terribly uncomfortable to feeling utterly petrified somehow, all in a matter of seconds. It was downright maddening. I didn't understand it then, and I don't understand it now.

The only thing I know for sure is I wanted to get the hell away from that party. I wasn't high at the time, and it was at that moment that the notion of having a flashback from my bad trip first began to haunt my psyche, and it scared the holy hell out of me. I began to fear that somehow my mind would get "stuck" that way. The fear caused my heart to race wildly, I broke out in a cold sweat, and my hands began to tremble as if I were ninety-five years old rather than eighteen. In hindsight it's easy to see that this episode was indeed what they have since labeled a panic attack. But putting a label on something doesn't cure it, alter it, or improve it in any way. In my mind it became simply "the fear." All I know is that prior to that experience I had been a very outgoing and fairly confident human being. Suddenly I found myself in the early stages of an anxiety disorder that would plague me in one way or another for many years to come. It was the beginning of an extremely long dark night of the soul.

I had several more such episodes over the next few months. These attacks were so unnerving that I began to worry more and more about it happening again, until the anxiety of it happening again became as debilitating as the actual event. It was then that I began to avoid social settings of all kinds. I started reclusing more and more. I ended up spending a lot of time in my room at my folks' house. It's called psyching yourself out, and I had become a Jedi master at it. The more shut-in I became the more depressed I got. And the more depressed I got the more anxious I became about what was happening to my life. I had gradually traded my public fear for my own private hell.

The madness in my mind became so unsettling and so unbearable that I started to commit suicide at one point. I swallowed four anti-depressants and had twenty more in my hand cocked and ready to go. Most people would figure that fear was the reason I didn't go through with it. Crying myself to sleep at night but didn't even have the guts to end my own pain. Not enough nerve to "pull the trigger." If they only knew how badly I wanted to. Most people can't understand getting to such a final point of despair. For anyone that hasn't been there it's perfectly understandable that they would have trouble comprehending it. I pray they never know that state of mind. But anyone who has knows. I would have given anything for the anguish to be over—anything, even my own life. So what stopped me? Well, it sure as hell wasn't fear. Hell, I had so much fear in my own life, one more little blast of fear was nothing if it would end all the other turmoil. No. The reason I didn't go through with it had nothing to do with my "shuffling off this mortal coil" giving me pause. In truth, my supposed lack of guts was probably the single-most selfless moment of my young life. I stopped short of swallowing the rest of those pills because, for a brief instant, I felt the pain of those I was about to leave behind, and I couldn't do that to them. That's all. That's the sole, simple reason I'm here today. And I can live with that.

The medical professionals proposed that the drugs, and in particular my devastating experience on the mescaline, had somehow triggered an underlying anxiety disorder that had been mostly dormant prior to this time and might have remained mostly dormant had I not chemically altered my brain. Once it had been brought to the surface it took on a life of its own, fueled by genetic predispositions as well as my own thoughts and imaginings.

This appears to be reasonably sound theorizing. Whether hypothesizing of this nature can lead to resolution is another matter. In my case, it didn't. In my unprofessional analysis, I was born with or developed certain insecurities that became extremely magnified at an early juncture in my life, and whether they were biological, psychological or chemical in origin is of little significance to me. You can blame problems of this nature on biology, bad trips, broken hearts, or anything else you want. The fact is, whatever equipment I had been assigned in this life was evidently woefully inadequate in dealing successfully with this particular crisis. Not an excuse. It's just seems a logical interpretation of the situation. Since one obviously wouldn't consciously choose to suffer to the point of being suicidal, it stands to reason that this suffering was unavoidable and that a solution was not immediately within the grasp of the sufferer. End of analysis.

FROM DELUSION TO ILLUSION

A couple of months after I had the shock treatments at the institution, I was still a virtual recluse in my parents' home. It was now summertime, a year after having graduated from high school. Although I had completely stopped seeing my friends from school, my younger brother had friends who would come by that I would occasionally see. They didn't pose as much of a threat to me, because they were really there to see my brother. The social pressure wasn't as pronounced. I wasn't the focus of the visit. Over the years, some of these friends of my brother's had become my friends as well. A couple of them I had come to know quite well. But because the origin of the friendship emanated from my brother, it psychologically allowed me to visit with these people briefly from time to time without much fear of a panic attack setting in. These "dual friendships," with both my brother and me, eventually served as a springboard for my jettison back into society.

One such dual friendship was with Luke—the same Luke who years later would die of a heroin overdose. He made a habit of coming by to see me during my sickness, often under the guise of seeing my brother Tim. However, his intentions became quite transparent as he began to pester me about coming to work with him at the service station that his stepfather owned. His first such overture was met with great incredulity on my part. How the hell could I go to work anywhere? I was a lunatic. I was quite a few bricks shy of a full load. My elevator was stuck in between floors with no repairman in sight. My lights were off, and I *was* home—but nobody was coming in. How could he even broach such a subject? Couldn't he see that I was severely disturbed?

Well, either Luke couldn't see it, or he was being compassionate. I know in retrospect that he knew I was sick, and he wanted to help me. So, he pestered me and pestered me until gradually the idea of going to work with him wasn't a complete fantasy. It was still definitely terrifying, but it began to loom as more of an actual possibility, something I might be able to do *someday*. It would be a simple job—pumping gas. It would be just the two of us working swing shift together. No boss, no other employees. And, most important, it would be at a service station way across town where the odds of my seeing someone I knew would be remote.

You see, I wasn't afraid of strangers or of going places where I didn't know anyone. Yet, I was definitely terrified of going to the store or other public places out of fear that I might see someone I knew. On those occasions when I would venture out in public my antennae were so attuned to my environment it was incredible. I was constantly on red alert, watching intently for signs of anyone I might know. There was no way I could talk to these people if I were to run into them, particularly any of my old friends. I would have a full-blown panic attack, and I was not about to allow that to happen. Compounding my social paranoia was the dread of having to explain to someone where I had been "lately." The longer I remained in this state the more intense this dread became. (This seems surreal to me as I write this, being so long removed from this anxiety. But I held onto this fear for many years, even after I had started seeing friends again. The power of that conditioning had been so intense that for years my heart would palpitate and I would start sweating profusely if I ran into someone I knew at the store—long after I had become "normalized" back into society. This same panicked reaction would set in immediately whenever the telephone rang as well. It became like a Pavlov's dog response. So terrified had I become of having to talk to someone I knew during my recluse period, that the mere sound of a ringing telephone haunted me, even many years after I had started answering the damn thing again.)

For weeks Luke continued to badger me and pressure me about working. He had a very strong and persuasive personality in those days. One day he simply stood up and literally screamed at me:

"YOU CAN'T JUST SIT HERE FOR THE REST OF YOUR LIFE!"

Something snapped in me when he spoke those words, and I knew he was right. It woke me up. It was time to do or die, and I knew it. If I didn't do something to shake up my world, I would be doomed to lasting depression and eternal hermit status. So, gathering up every fiber of courage in my being, I agreed to go to work with Luke at the station.

In many ways, Luke saved my life that day. I only wish I could have returned him the favor twenty-six years later.

FUELING UP AT THE STATION

Going to work at the service station with Luke was the onset of my resurgence back into society. It was the beginning of my "cure." The seed of mental health was planted that day (or at least surface mental health).

Another seed was planted in the early months of working at that service station, or re-planted, I should say. It was at the service station that I eventually became reintroduced to alcohol, and my active addiction to drugs began a new and extremely lengthy journey. Paradoxically, it was the alcohol that contributed to a more speedy reentry into society, relaxing my inhibitions enough that I eventually began to see old friends. So, in a way alcohol saved my life, and I often contemplate the irony of that, since in later years it was alcohol and drugs that all but took my life.

I was nineteen years old when I went to work at the station. I enjoyed it for the most part. Luke and I had a pretty good time, but there continued to be something missing in my life. I knew that although I was feeling more normal and appearing more normal (at least from culturally accepted standards), I was still not well. I couldn't feel well until I began to see old friends and do the things I used to do. And although I had had enough sense to quit taking drugs soon after my bad trip, the thought of drinking alcohol (which I now know *is* a drug, and one that can be every bit as debilitating) didn't alarm me. So, although I had sworn never to take psychedelics again (or any drug that might induce paranoia), when alcohol showed up I found a much-sought-after relief there. This seemed to work for a great number of years (although at the core of my being I knew I was still hiding from something). I donned this newly discovered alcoholic mask because it was at least more comfortable than the one I had been wearing for the last year and a half of my life.

It was shortly after Rick Owens came along that I rediscovered the great calming effect of alcohol. Rick was a college graduate going for his master's in sociology. He attended night school and began working at the station during

51

the day. He was an extremely intelligent and affable man with a great sense of humor. He was interested in world affairs and people. I had never met anyone like him. I found myself mesmerized by his intellect and his passion for discussing the plights of the world. But what Rick and Luke and I had most in common was a love of laughter. Each of us had our own sense of humor, and we could readily make each other laugh.

Still, the urge to get high was slowly calling me back—the desire to loosen up a bit. "Reality is only a crutch for people who can't handle drugs" was a popular saying in the early seventies. A long way from the days of, "This is your brain on drugs," but it's all we had to work with. The truth was, I couldn't handle drugs *or* reality. That's a bitch of a dilemma to come to terms with. Then I found booze—or it found me—and I thought it was different from other drugs. It took many years to discover that for me, at least, it was no different, no different at all. It only served to camouflage my true self, the me that was desperately wanting to reveal itself but somehow lacked the nerve.

Luke had always enjoyed tipping a few beers or shots of booze, since his early teens, actually. And alcohol was no stranger to Rick, either. And so it was that I became reintroduced to alcohol in the fall of 1972 at the Exxon station on NE 82nd and Prescott in Portland, Oregon. It was a second marriage for me (having visited with wine on occasion in my early teens) but I would conjecture that alcohol has been conjoined in this manner somewhere numbering in the billions over the millennia. I was just another notch on its infinitely massive headboard.

When I was fourteen years old I drank wine a few times with my best friend, Jeff Carson. We would each toss down a quart of wine, throw up a few times during the process, and then proceed to have a grand ol' time. (We just assumed that throwing up was part of the deal. It never occurred to us that it might have something to do with the amount or quality of the wine we were drinking. Of course, we had to steal the wine, being underage and all. And having some apparent inability to grasp the concept that if we were stealing the stuff we might as well steal something of higher quality, we would knock off some of your finer table wines—you know, names like Tokay, Bali Hai, Spanada, Ripple. Maybe we thought we would feel less guilty about the theft part if we stole less-expensive wines. Who knows what lurks in the minds of fourteen-year-old would-be winos?)

Aside from that one summer of indulging in fine wines, I touched alcohol only once between then and the time I went to work at the station. That once was at a high school dance of some kind. The fact was, I just couldn't get by the taste of the stuff. I came to realize early on that chugging alcohol and then barfing my guts up was probably not going to be socially acceptable for long. Not to mention it just wasn't a whole lot of fun.

But at the station I was older and discovered I could acquire a taste for beer. The very first night I drank beer, I consumed fifteen bottles of it. I don't know how many my drinking partner, Rick, had. We definitely got drunk, though. We drove separate cars that night for some reason—Rick in his purple Dodge Challenger and me in one of the countless junkers I owned in my youth. We raced each other down Powell Boulevard at one point. ("Please don't drink and drive" wasn't even in its embryonic stage yet—and no, we probably wouldn't have listened anyway.) We ran a red light doing about eighty miles an hour through the heavily traveled intersection of 92nd and Powell. Christ, that was nuts. (Every time I think of that night or any of the countless other nights I drove drunk, I thank God I never killed or seriously hurt anyone.)

We ended up the night at a massage parlor. We paid twenty bucks apiece for a "massage," which is about all it turned out to be (although I'm quite certain that your licensed professionals aren't naked while they're rubbing you down)—fifteen beers was a little much for this pup. I enjoyed the "rub down," though. I had gone in first and when I came back out Rick was having pangs of guilt on account of he was married (he wasn't even Catholic—maybe we're *not* the only ones up there), so I went in again. I wasn't about to waste Rick's twenty bucks, since they wouldn't give it back to him.

And so began my reentry into the world of alcohol.

In the initial years the beer appeared to be a good thing. I was able to cut down fairly significantly from the quantity of that first night and still attain a decent level of relaxation—enough to be sociable, at least. I was actually able to go out with a couple of old friends a short time after Rick and I had gone out. My cousin, Mike, and our mutual friend, Drew Olsen, stopped by with some beer one night, and we had a couple and then went out to the dog track.

With careful and patient experimentation I was able to locate a hard liquor that was palatable enough to ingest on a regular basis—rum. And so rum and beer became my temporary saviors. They enabled me to relax enough to go out and meet the world, and meet the world we did, my friends and I. We golfed and traveled and partied. Alcohol simply proved, at the time, to be my most productive therapy, at least from the standpoint of enabling me to develop the ability to conform to cultural depictions of normalcy. It was my "pharmaceutical" relief. And I was able to gradually reduce my doses, self-monitoring my consumption until I was eventually able to return to a mainstream life without over-indulging every time out.

Being single and in our twenties, my friends and I partied extensively in those years. Most of my friends didn't marry until they were thirty or older, me included. I would be misrepresenting the truth if I was to say I didn't have considerable fun during that time. However, the fun was interspersed among many debilitating hangovers and a number of anything but fun events. In later years, as the severity of my addiction progressed, the fun would become altogether absent. But initially alcohol supplied me with the courage, albeit a false courage, to return to the planet Earth, to "society America"—if only for a while.

It was a new beginning for me. But as fun as it may have seemed in those years, it was only a piece of my journey—a necessary piece, but still only a piece. In retrospect, none of my escapades over the next twenty-six years of active addiction resulted in the discovery of anything overly profound, yet they were all integral steps in a lifelong journey, a road I still travel. This brings to mind the Zen inquiry, *Which step in the journey of a thousand steps could you eliminate and still reach your destination?* In recent years I have been led to realize that all are equally important.

MEASURED LUNACY

As the years passed, though I was engaged in some entertaining moments, I was also developing a sense of slowly losing contact again with the normal world. I was fading out, gradually drifting into this new, undefined dimension. It was as if everyone else was maintaining their status quo in life, and in doing so they simply assumed that everyone else (including me) was doing the same thing. They had no idea that their universe, their dimension, was slowly fading out on me. They couldn't see that it was becoming harder and harder for me to focus on their world. They could only see the world from their perspective, just as I could only see the world from mine.

It became more difficult as the years went by to see and hear what was going on in that normal universe. It was getting quieter and quieter out there. That normal world was sounding more like a distant crowd—becoming fainter and more indiscernible as my life passed by them instead of with them, an unintentional, uncontrollable, undesired separation from their world. Helpless to stop it—wanting to, but not knowing how.

One day, although it would be many years later (in my early recovery from drugs and alcohol), I had a so-called "moment of clarity." It became clear to me that perhaps a separation, at least from an illusory sense of the universe, somehow *was* necessary and desired. At about six months clean and sober I penned the following:

For the world had painted me a picture of what I should want in life
And I had allowed myself to stare at it for far too long,
Until the picture became real to me,
And I became mesmerized by it
And felt I could no longer escape its embrace.
Then one day it became clear to me that I must put the picture down,
For I discovered it wasn't the picture that was holding me in its grasp,

But rather I who was clutching the picture.
And this "I" that was clutching was not my True Self,
But rather the self that I had allowed the world to paint for me as well.
My True Self had never been attached in the first place.

However, it would be many more years before I was given the courage to examine my life and the world in greater depth. For more than three decades my primary goal was simply to make it through each day with my sanity still (at least partially) intact.

In my twenties, thirties and on into my forties, both during my years of active addiction and for several years thereafter, whenever I did stop to ponder my existence, I would wonder if I could ever truly find peace in this world, under any circumstances. Today I know that I can. (Well, *most* of the time I know I can.)

But, I digress.

FROM ROSARIES TO PRESIDENTS

There were no tell-tale signs in my youth pointing to any reason for deviation from the norm. All signs pointed, instead, toward success and fulfillment. I was relatively intelligent (again, by societal standards). I seemed to be popular, always having a diversified set of friends. I wasn't physically revolting or anything. In my mid-twenties I actually had a woman tell me I looked like Robert Redford. I kept shouting at them to let her talk as they were dragging her out of the bar. I don't think the fact that she was grossly inebriated made her a totally unreliable witness. Of course, that's my opinion.

Other than my five-year-old birthday party, I can't remember much of anything before second or third grade. I was devoutly religious my first five or six years of grade school. I went to Mass and Communion nearly every day. That was back during the days when you were supposed to fast three hours before receiving Communion ("the body and blood of Christ") or else you weren't eligible or worthy or something like that. Nowadays you only have to fast an hour (or maybe it's five minutes; I really have no idea—it's been awhile). There was a Mass every morning at 8:00, and those of us kids who were going to receive Communion were allowed to bring our breakfasts to school and eat them after Mass during class time.

In third grade I was into saying the rosary (which consists of fifty *Hail Mary* prayers, the *Lord's Prayer* seven times and seven *Glory Be* prayers) fairly frequently. One day during study period my teacher, Sister Marion Loyola, saw me moving those beads along my fingers and praying under my breath and asked me what rosary I was on. She knew I prayed every day in class and knew I took Communion every day. (I was getting pretty much straight A's and always did my homework so I guess praying during class was permissible. That, and Sister Marion had taken a liking to me, too, I suppose.) I told her I was on my third rosary, and she asked me if I would come to the back of the room and pray with her. So, we went to the back of the room, and she sat in a chair because of her bad back and I knelt on the floor beside her, and we started softly saying the rosary together. I don't know what the other kids were thinking (at least we were in the *back* of the room) but I was feeling pretty good on account of how I felt about Sister Marion. She was my first real crush, to tell you the truth. I thought she was just about the greatest thing in the world and the prettiest, too—nun or no.

At the end of that third grade year Sister Marion asked me if I would do her a favor and say a little prayer for her every day. I don't remember the prayer, but I said it for her every day like she asked, way past when I had stopped being real religious and all. I stopped saying it when my mental illness hit at the age of nineteen, but I began praying for her again about four years later. I had forgotten the prayer by then so I started saying the *Hail Mary* prayer for her instead. I continue to pray for her to this day.

So even though I had eventually given up on the communal worship thing, I still believed in God or in some sort of spiritual power that was greater than the individual. It didn't matter much to me at the time what it was since I couldn't prove it one way or another. I just always sensed (usually sensed) that there was some supernatural essence that defied human explanation and that didn't require group worship by more-often-than-not-hypocritical Homo sapiens. I don't have anything against anyone who wants to worship their God in any way they so choose—just allow me the same tolerance to do (or not do) my thing.

I continued to get almost straight A's throughout grade school. I was always pleased that I never seemed to be labeled with the nerd moniker on account of getting good grades. (I know what you're thinking—do nerds really know if they're being labeled as nerds? Great point, but it's my perspective here, delusional or otherwise.)

In fifth grade I entered the annual poetry contest, which meant reciting something in front of the class. (It didn't have to be poetry.) Winners would be selected from each classroom, and those selected would then have to perform at an evening function in front of all the teachers and parents from the school. My mother mentioned to my teacher one day (my mom was the school secretary at the time) that I wanted to recite President Kennedy's *Inaugural Address* for the contest. My teacher responded that she thought it was too old for me. My mother informed her that I already had it memorized. The teacher said, "All righty then."

I won the contest for my grade and gave the speech in front of the student body and then again in front of the parents and teachers one night. I received a standing ovation from all those adults, I am told. (I regret that, save for a few lines from the speech, I remember absolutely nothing of this experience— possibly a side gift from those "therapeutic" shock treatments that I begged for later in life?)

I was voted president of my class three years in a row in sixth, seventh, and eighth grades. I was president of the Altar Boys as well. I was the first one in my class to memorize the Mass in Latin.

I don't really know why or how things went awry in later years. It's not like I didn't have a decent foundation. I went from saying rosaries with Sister Marion in third grade to reciting Kennedy's *Inaugural Address* by heart in the fifth grade to President of the damn Altar Boys to slamming heroin into my body thirty-five years later. Something missing here somewhere. I guess there were a few years in between.

CATHOLIC SCHOOLS, THE SEVENTH COMMANDMENT, AND BABY FOOD

I went from St. Peter's grade school to La Salle High School in Milwaukie, Oregon. It was the only co-ed Catholic high school in the Portland area at the time. My older brother Joe was in the first graduating class in La Salle's history. I ended up being in the second—the class of 1971. The school was run by Christian Brothers, who also comprised much of the faculty (along with a smattering of nuns and lay personnel).

Those Christian Brothers were fairly strict. Really strict, I suppose, by today's standards, but just your "regular strict" for back then. We had a dress code we didn't much care for. And I always had somewhat of a rebellious streak, as did my friends. We ended up organizing the first protest in La Salle's history. Hell, it might very well be the only one in their history, I don't know. (Haven't exactly kept in close touch.)

The dress code prohibited jeans. We had to have shirts with collars. Hair for the boys had to be above the ears and above the collar. The girls couldn't wear pants, which would have been okay with us, but they made them wear skirts and dresses instead—and those couldn't be more than two inches above the knees. The vice principal of the school those first couple of years was a nun, and she would stop girls in the hall if she felt their skirts were too short. She would make them kneel on the ground and then she'd pull out that tape measure she carried in her habit. She would measure from the floor to the skirt. If the skirt was more than two inches off the ground the girl would have to go home and change.

The school actually sent my parents a letter (which my mom was cool enough not to bother me with because even she thought their protestations were a little frivolous—she didn't even mention it to me until years later) telling them that they thought "Gary and his friends" were trying to set a trend because we were wearing our pants too long. Pants too long? Hell, I suppose they were a little too long, and isn't that a damn sin? God forbid we have any freedom of expression whatsoever. Same old story. Kids wanting to be different, to be individuals, to express themselves. It never changes—probably never will. At least I hope not. One of the great things this world has going for it is young people with some heart.

After high school I really let loose with the pent-up rebelliousness I had been forced to repress during my adolescence. I grew out my beard and let my hair grow several inches past my shoulders. People would call me Charlie Manson at times because of my looks. But kids do the same type of thing every generation. I suppose our generation had the most visible rebellion in a while, what with the anti-war demonstrations and the rock festivals, the long hair and beards, and flower children and communes and all. I bet those parents of ensuing years wished their kids with the Mohawks and pierced lips and noses would have just let their hair grow long like we did. Not to appear smug or anything, but at least our expressions were natural. We mostly just let our hair grow out. We didn't shave it in odd fashion or spike it or pierce all of our body parts or anything. Of course, once we'd done all the things we'd done in the way of rebellion it didn't leave too much in the way of cool for future generations to be expressive about. Poor kids.

Our demonstration was fairly amusing. Four of my friends met at my house (my parents were decent about it and didn't bother us) and made plans to hold a protest against the dress code. We made fliers announcing that there would be a demonstration regarding the dress code at noon the following day in the courtyard outside the cafeteria. We made copies the next morning and passed them out to everybody in school. Everyone showed up for this thing, and when they did my friends and I stood there wondering what the hell we were supposed to do next. Obviously our plans were somewhat lacking in depth. People were staring at us, and I remember my girlfriend Sarah whispered to me that she thought they were all expecting one of us to address the gathered masses. We kind of looked at each other and then at the several hundred staring students (*and* staring Christian Brothers with their arms folded and faces frowned), and finally my friend Matt Larson got up and said something like: "If you don't like the dress code, well, keep on thinking about it, and we'll meet again and do something about it." Classic oratory.

We were unprepared, but everyone seemed to think they had taken part in something meaningful, so we were pleased. The very next day the Christian

Brothers passed around a questionnaire asking all the students what they would like to change in the school's dress and grooming code. They had established new parameters of their own choosing, but at least we had gained ground. We had spurred them to action. We had caused change, and we were proud.

That was junior year. It was back in freshman year that I had fallen in love with Sarah Mathis—the only problem being she already had a boyfriend. I had to wait until our sophomore year for her to break up with that guy, only then I didn't move fast enough. She had another one very quickly. But he didn't last long. I finally won her over at a school dance. The girl of my dreams. She was pretty, she was smart, and she loved to laugh. What more could a guy ask for? She was an honor student and cheerleader all through high school. And she was as popular with the girls as she was with the guys. That said something. She was voted senior prom queen, and although they didn't vote on the guys back then, I've always kind of laid claim to the king title. Hell, how can you have a queen without a king? Well, I don't rightly think you can.

I guess it was in the summer between freshman and sophomore year that I kind of shed the last of my good-guy cocoon. Not that I turned into a bad guy; it's just that what was left of that third-grade kid kneeling next to Sister Marion reciting rosaries was, from all outward appearances, pretty much gone. Oh, I still had my inner beliefs buried somewhere. I still believed in the *Golden Rule* and all, but I was into being a juvenile now, into sowing some oats.

That summer my best friend from grade school, Jeff Carson, and a couple of new friends from high school and I became engaged in shoplifting. Though we were each fully aware of the Seventh Commandment, *Thou shalt not steal* (having, after all, been partly raised by nuns), we somehow managed to block out that piece of our ritualistic brainwashing, at least for the few months we were involved in petty larceny.

We worked in pairs for some reason, and more often than not Jeff was my partner in crime. It wasn't that we couldn't live without whatever it was we were stealing. It was more out of an urge for excitement that we acted. We didn't feel like we were being evil or anything. In fact, we never stole from Mom-and-Pop type stores. We had *some* scruples. We only hit the big chains, the ones we felt could afford it. It was our form of rationalization, our ethical reasoning, if you will. (Or unethical reasoning, depending on your perspective, I suppose.)

Fred Meyer—they're a large, regional "one-stop shopping center"—was a frequent target. Eastport Plaza, one of the first shopping malls in Portland, was another. We didn't realize we were contributing to escalating insurance premiums to cover shoplifting costs and to the subsequent consumer price increases that resulted. It never dawned on us that they *had* shoplifter insurance, for God's sake. We didn't have shows like *20/20* to tell us these things. We'd of just rationalized it anyway, I'm sure—just like we were doing—figuring that these big stores could afford it because of all the money they were making. We were paying them back for some of the pricing we felt wasn't justified. Justification of injustice—we had it all covered.

We stole everything from expensive pens to tennis shoes to record albums. Tennis shoes were a little tense. One under each arm beneath our jackets— our *Sir Jack's*. For record albums, we'd go buy one and then head back into the store with the album in a sack and put five or six more in the bag. They didn't have those funky little bar codes or tags or any security stuff that had to be removed before you could exit the store back then. I guess it was people like us that forced them to develop apparatus like that. Sorry.

We even stole a few things for Jeff's older brother and then sold them to him. (All the berry picking that Cliff had done while Jeff and I screwed off every summer hadn't gotten him very far. Here he was, just a couple of years later having to save some money by buying discounted stolen goods.) I suppose our biggest claim to infamy was the fishing rod and Mitchell 300 reel we stole for Cliff.

Cliff had wanted this certain rod and reel for fishing, and of course, couldn't afford them. So Jeff and I said we would steal them for him if he'd pay us. Cliff thought we were nuts. He asked us, "How are you guys going to steal a fishing pole, for Christ's sake?" We told him he shouldn't concern himself with how we were going to do it—we just wanted to know if he was willing to pay us for it. The rod and reel were going for about twenty bucks apiece at Fred Meyer, so we told him we'd sell them to him for five bucks each. He agreed. We obviously weren't into this thing to make a killing. We were in it for the challenge, the thrill.

We had become fairly proficient at this shoplifting scenario, I am now sad to admit. We knew how to scout around for onlookers or security-type people. We knew there were plain clothes security in those places, so we never let *anyone* see us take the goods (at least to the best of our knowledge we didn't).

We also knew they couldn't arrest you for shoplifting unless you actually took the goods out of the store. We'd get ten or fifteen feet from the exit and then casually stop to look at something, all the while checking out the situation to see if there was anyone nearby who looked like he or she didn't really have a plan in life. Then, if everything was cool, we'd casually leave the store.

So we went to Fred Meyer and began checking out the rods and reels like we were browsing. Jeff looked out for me while I jammed a Mitchell 300 in my armpit under my Sir Jack. Then I watched for Jeff while he grabbed a full-length fishing rod, broke it down, shoved one end of one half down one pant leg and the other half down the other pant leg. He zipped up his Sir Jack so the tops wouldn't show. Then he started to walk toward the front of the store like Frankenstein after a bad night's sleep, with me following behind him. I was wondering how he was going to leave (they didn't have "courtesy exits" back then). I was getting more nervous than usual. Normally we would find an empty check-stand and cruise through there, but they were all being used. So Jeff headed to the turnstile, which of course was only for entering the store, and proceeded to back up to it, using his arms to hoist his butt up on top of it. I took the cue and started spinning the turnstile for him, trying my damnedest not to laugh as he spun toward the other side with his legs fully outstretched like they were both really glad to see me. Jeff didn't have my self-control (or fear), and in spite of the rather compromising situation we had placed ourselves in, he began to giggle uncontrollably. Now, whenever Jeff started laughing, I had to follow suit. It was an involuntary reflex—like when the doc whacks you on the knee, ever since we had met each other at the age of five. He just cracked me up. So, here we were stealing this stuff, and now we're both walking as fast as we could for the door doing our best to stifle our laughter, me with one hand in my pocket to keep the Mitchell 300 from sliding out from underneath my Sir Jack and Jeff walking like he had no goddamn knees.

We got back to Jeff and Cliff's house and Cliff told us that we'd done great except that I had stolen a left-handed reel. (I didn't even know there was a right and a left way to fish, for God's sake.) Cliff wasn't about to pay us for a left-handed reel and the pole didn't do him any good without a reel. I told him there was no problem—I'd go back and get a right-handed reel if that would make him happy. So I did.

I guess I must have been the most careful shoplifter among my friends (or the luckiest), on account of I was the only one of my friends that never got caught. Each of the four of my friends that I knew were shoplifting got caught eventually. We had only been doing it for a few months, but we had done a lot of it. I took the cue from their mishaps and retired. (I always felt bad about stealing all that stuff and always meant to make restitution someday. In the last few years I told myself that some of my volunteer work in prisons and hospitals could be used as a trade-off, but somehow I felt it wasn't sufficient. So, several years ago I started sending a little money every month to one of Fred Meyer's charities, and hope to continue to do so until I've finished with my tour on this planet.)

It would be easy to relate my shoplifting sprees in the context of addiction. My friends and I, but particularly Jeff and I, didn't stop at just the candy bar or two that perhaps a fair section of the population chalked onto their slate of transgressions while growing up. We always seemed to carry things one step further—always going to the next level. They have a saying in recovery circles that "one is too many and a thousand never enough." And that was how it came to be with most things I engaged in over the years. It should come as no surprise, I imagine, that Jeff and I would both end up one day as "people in recovery." For Jeff, that positive step in his life occurred quite a number of years before mine did.

After that summer of sin I developed sort of a surly attitude around authority figures, including some of the Christian Brothers at high school. I still liked most of them, and most of them liked me. However, I developed this tough-guy demeanor on occasion just to let them know who I thought was boss.

Brother Timothy was younger and a little more liberal than most of the other Brothers. My friends and I thought he was pretty cool. One day he and Brother Anthony happened to be riding in a car behind the one I was in (the dad of one of my friend's was driving a couple of us home from school). The not so sane part of me thought it would be amusing if I turned around and flipped him and Brother Anthony off.

It turned out that Brother Tim didn't think it was all that damn funny. The next day at the beginning of English Literature class, Brother Timothy called me up to his desk and said he wanted to see me right after school. Talk about your pissed-off dudes. This guy was baked. I spent the rest of the day pretty much scared shitless. I thought he was going to kill me. Back then if they felt like it they'd whack you one, too. It didn't happen often, but it did happen. Old Brother Charles—I pegged him to be about two hundred years old—had himself a fine temper, for example. I saw him slowly walk down the aisle in Algebra class one day, and right when he got near the kid that was goofing off, right when you thought he didn't know who the hell it was that had been causing all the commotion because he was looking straight ahead and not at the kid, he took his left hand all the way from his right shoulder and backhanded that young man across the face like you wouldn't believe. That bone to flesh contact sounded like an overhead clap of thunder. Hell, *my* knees shook for about an hour afterwards, and I was three rows off.

Anyway, Brother Tim, he didn't kill me. He didn't hit me, either. It was a funny thing—he wasn't even mad by the time I went to his classroom after school. I sure was relieved to see him smile. He just proceeded to have a long talk with me, real concerned like. He wanted to know what had happened to that nice kid from freshman year, the kid with so much to offer. I told him that that kid was sitting right in front of him. I told him that I was the same person I'd always been, just a little older and a little wiser and a little dumber all at the same time. We ended up shaking hands, and I think he could see I wasn't going to end up in San Quentin really soon or anything like that, so I think he felt better.

Then there was the time I told Brother Mark to go to hell. I don't remember why I did that, other than he must have displeased me in some fashion. I'm quite certain that whatever it was he had said to me obviously hadn't justified my response. But I was a cocky bastard at times. I just up and told him to go to hell right to his face and then walked off. He kept yelling at me to get back there while I kept walking, acting cool because other kids were watching, but pretty much shaking in my boots. The next couple of days people kept telling me that Brother Mark was looking for me. I always thought that was a bit odd, considering it wasn't all that large of a school and he knew where to find me, or he certainly could have me called to the office or whatever. And that's what I told whoever cared—that he knew where to find me. (I had to keep up the facade, of course. Consistency is everything when you're trying to convey an attitude.) I ended up having a nice talk with Brother Mark, too, just like with Brother Tim. I suppose those authority figures liked me even though I could be a pain in the ass sometimes.

Brother Ernest was Vice Principal my junior year. He was an intelligent man. He was also quite a disciplinarian, into that control stuff, but he had a fairly decent sense of humor as well. Of course, it was my job to see just how good a sense of humor some of these old boys had. I was walking down the hall one day with my arm around my girlfriend when Jeff's brother, Cliff, called out to me. I smiled and casually extended the middle finger on the hand I had on Sarah's shoulder. I didn't know Brother Ernest was looking. I probably wouldn't have cared if I *had* known. Anyway, he called me over and proceeded to ask me if I was going to be crass and flippant all of my life or was I going to learn to be a gentleman? Well, I sure as hell didn't know what those "crass" and "flippant" words meant so I just measured him up trying to figure out if this was a trick question or something. I couldn't discern their meaning from looking at him, however, so I cautiously replied, "Hell, I don't know, Brother." I guess that wasn't the right answer. It seemed to elevate his ire. I don't recall exactly what transpired next, but I do remember looking up those words in the dictionary. Very educational places, those Catholic schools.

I played basketball my freshman and sophomore year until I got kicked off the team for being late to Spanish class three times. Team rule—academics and discipline first. There were some of us that gave our Spanish teacher a pretty rough time, now that I think about it. Jeff Carson, Pat Ryerson, and I found each other quite entertaining. Mrs. Bogsley didn't. But she couldn't control us, so she'd end up calling Brother Ernest. The third time this occurred he hauled all three of us out of class and proceeded to tell us that if we disrupted Mrs. Bogsley's class one more time we'd be expelled. We toned it down a bit and survived the year.

I ended up running away from home during the summer after my junior year to attend a rock festival. Well, I called it running away. Actually, I just took off for a couple of days and a night because my parents wouldn't let me go to the festival. It angered me that they had said no when I was being honest about telling them where I wanted to go. I could have made up a lie and gotten away with it, I was quite certain. I was pretty cheesed about where openness had gotten me. So, I had just taken off.

It was the summer of 1970, the year after Woodstock. There were about thirty thousand people at our rock festival compared to the three hundred thousand at Woodstock, but it was a happening thing, nevertheless. Our festival was called Vortex. It was held at McGiver State Park outside of Estacada, Oregon, about thirty miles southeast of Portland. The park was bordered on one side by the Clackamas River, making it an ideal location for the freedom-loving youth of those years. I say "ideal" mainly because it provided the young women with a place to skinny-dip, and we found this factor alone to be well worth the trip out there. It was a wild, week long event. Girls skinny-dipping in the river, the smell of marijuana wherever you walked, sunshine, LSD, mescaline, overdose tents, live rock bands, hundreds of campfires at night, and everyone welcome at every campsite. Sex, drugs, and rock and roll. (Well, sex for some of them, I imagine.)

It was in this summer of my seventeenth year on the planet that I ingested my first hallucinogenic drug. (My previously mentioned experiences with fine wines had set me on a quest for an easier way to escape reality. I found that swallowing a pill was far more appealing to my stomach than drinking an entire bottle of Tokay.) Yes, it was the era of rock festivals, and we were basking in the ideals of peace, love, brotherhood, and getting higher than a bloody kite.

Jeff's older brother Cliff was at Vortex when I got there. He took his first psychedelic trip the same day I did. I remember spotting him sitting cross-legged under a large evergreen tree eating a can of Gerber's baby food—peaches, I think. I asked him what the hell he was doing, of course, saying something like, "What the hell are you doing?" He informed me that he was eating his mescaline. He had taken the capsule apart and had dumped the powder in his baby food because he couldn't swallow pills worth a darn. Which explained the swallowing part, but not the choice of food. I mean, why not applesauce (the adult variety) or something? It's one of those vivid images that kind of stays with you—a nearly grown man sitting under a tree eating baby food mixed with mescaline. Some sort of hidden irony there, I'm thinking, although I'm not quite sure what it would be. Well, to each his own.

Jeff Carson, Mark Brewster, and Dick Langston met us later in the day. I was shocked, I remember, when I had learned of their mode of transport. It seems Mark's car wouldn't start, and neither of the other two had a car, so they stole one. *Stole a goddamn car to come to a rock festival.* These guys were getting way out of my realm of permissible transgressions now. Shoplifting pens from Fred Meyer was one thing, but stealing a car? I don't think so. Dick's two older brothers had stolen quite a few in their day, I knew. One of them had done some time for it. I wasn't about to get into anything like that. After Vortex I didn't hang with those guys as much. I just didn't want to stray that far off the path, you know? (As far as I know I was the only one of the bunch that ended up a heroin addict many years later. So much for my straight and narrow, holier-than-thou act.) However, I was here to have fun and after calling those guys "fucking fools" a few times, I tried to wipe their little escapade from my mind.

Jeff and I ate our mescaline just before dark and then began wandering around from campsite to campsite doing the hippie, brotherly love thing. In other words saying, *"Hey, what's happenin', man?"* a lot, *"Far fucking out, man"* a lot, and anything else that ended in "man" a lot. And, of course, smoking a lot of other people's dope a lot.

I recall that after leaving one campground, I suddenly came to a halt. Jeff looked at me and asked what the matter was.

I said, "Can't you see 'em, man?" I was pointing at the ground.

"See what, man?"

"All those damn snakes, man!"

"Snakes?"

"Yeah, hundreds of them, man!" In my intoxicated state the blades of grass were swirling around, and I believed them all to be snakes. I was scared out of my wits, but Jeff, as usual, was able to make me laugh.

"It's okay, man. Just follow me." Jeff stepped gingerly out in front of me and then started tiptoeing real fast across the next ten or twelve feet of grass.

His exaggerated mannerisms made me laugh, and the snakes disappeared as suddenly as they had appeared. (I tiptoed behind Jeff anyway.)

Later that same night there were about fifteen people standing around one of the many campfires and I witnessed someone shooting up drugs for the first time. Some guy was handing something to another guy—both of them strangers to us. The supplier was saying, "I think they're reds, man. I don't know for sure. The dude that gave them to me said they were."

The other guy replied, "I need to come down, man. Does anyone here know how to tell if these are reds?" He looked around at the different faces at the campfire.

Here was this complete stranger about ready to fire an unknown substance into his vein and Jeff's brother, Cliff, piped up like he was Dr. Fucking Kildare.

"Yeah, I can tell," Cliff said authoritatively.

Jeff and I looked at each other dumfounded. Cliff knew less about drugs than almost anyone we knew. Nevertheless, he reached over and dabbed his index finger into the crimson-colored powder and then touched it lightly to his tongue. He pretended to ponder the flavor for a few seconds and then with an air of confidence that impresses me to this day, Cliff said, "Yeah, these are reds, man."

Jeff and I can't believe what we're hearing. If this guy had witnessed Cliff eating his mescaline mixed with baby food a few hours earlier he might have asked for a second opinion. But I've got to admit, Cliff was good. If I didn't know him, hell, I probably would have believed him.

Evidently, the shooter did. "Thanks, man," he said to Cliff. Then he nodded at his girlfriend who immediately began to tie him off. Thirty seconds later she was injecting those "reds" into her boyfriend's arm, based solely upon Cliff's professional assessment of the stuff.

I gotta say, the guy didn't croak or anything. At least not as far as we knew. That was Vortex, and my first foolish step into *The Twilight Zone.*

PING PONG AND POLITICS

I played a lot of table tennis growing up. Our junior year in high school, Dale Ford and I were doubles' champions in LaSalle's annual tournament. A ping-pong table was one of the few luxuries we had at home. My older brother Joe and I played many thousands of games. We used to fight after about every third or fourth one. Whoever lost would usually be the instigator of the ensuing battle. The preferred method of attack was an airborne paddle aimed at the victor's head. We were applying our geometry and physics lessons to real life—the shortest distance between two points is a straight line, and the least amount of friction is through space. Very competitive, Joe and I. Looking back on it, I'd have to admit it was probably I that started most of these fights, on account of he won more games than I did. (I can't quite bring myself to say he was better than me. He just won more games than I did.)

My younger brother Tim brought his new friend from high school, Steve Barton, over to our house for the first time one day. Steve didn't know about the ping-pong rivalry between Joe and me. He was upstairs watching TV while Tim was reading the newspaper. They could hear us playing ping pong downstairs. Suddenly Steve heard all this loud banging, crashing, yelling and cursing. He looked at Tim with alarm in his eyes. "What in the hell is that?" Steve asked.

Tim, of course, knew what was going on and was unaffected by the commotion. However, sensing Steve's concern, he calmly looked up from the paper and said, "Game must be over."

Steve always found that incident amusing.

Senior year I was voted class vice president. I didn't campaign for it like the other candidates. I just put my name on the ballot. Most everyone else seemed to be into making posters and fliers and talking to people about what they were going to do if elected to their respective positions. I felt all of that campaigning was just a little too much trouble to go to (after all, it wasn't like

71

we were going to be paid for our services if we won), but thought it would be kind of cool to be vice president nevertheless. (I had chosen vice president over anything else because I figured the position didn't hold much responsibility.) I won the election. It turned out I was right about not having to do too much. There were other perks as well. I had the good fortune of getting out of class once in a while to attend student council meetings. One of my buddies, Craig Hartford, was voted president (he hadn't done any campaigning, either).

All in all, it looked like a rather proper foundation had been laid in my life, near as I could tell. I had recited rosaries with an ordained nun in the third grade, had that Kennedy-speech thing going, was president of the Altar Boys, pulled good grades through high school, was vice president of the senior class, self-proclaimed king of the damn prom, for God's sake, and yet I was diverging somewhat radically from what would be considered a mainstream path in life. Some of this path was infused with self-indulgence, some of it was garden-variety soul-searching, and some of it was just plain confusion run amok.

It was shortly after high school that my decline into the dark period accelerated. My bad trip on the mescaline and hashish had been toward the end of my senior year. My break-up with Sarah had been shortly after graduation. I managed one term in college in the fall of '71 before quitting to complete my submersion into that horribly ugly world of total isolation and madness. The shrink and the psych ward showed up at this point in my life, along with those expensive shock treatments. (It seems even more criminal that they actually charge you for whacking your brain with juice like that.) It was a few months after my exit from the psych ward that I started working at the service station with Luke.

EARLY JOBS

I didn't work at the station forever. Although I had some good times at that job, it turned out I got fired for evidently having *too* good of a time. That shocked me. Not that I didn't deserve to be fired, because I did. It's just that I'd never been fired before. Yes, it was only my third job, but it still shocked me.

Well, my third job of any note, that is. First off, I'm not counting berry picking as a job on account of in my estimation it only counted as cruel and unusual punishment, and if it was any indication of what working for a living was all about, then my best grade school buddy Jeff Carson and I weren't planning on attending this adulthood thing. Every summer we'd last us an average of two and a half days at this strawberry-picking, sweat-shop precursor crap, and then we'd end up hitchhiking home. We'd either get fired for berry fighting or just up and leave because it was too damn hot, and we'd plain had enough. For some reason our older brothers had that gene that Jeff and I were evidently missing. They would end up picking all the way through the summer—strawberries, raspberries, and then the big money-maker, beans. They'd make a ton of dough (well, to us it was a ton of dough) working their butts off for three straight months. We'd make about seven or eight bucks apiece in two and a half days, and near as I could tell they came out on the short end of the stick. We didn't see them saving enough money over the years to buy them a frickin' Ferrari when they turned sixteen or anything (hell, Jeff's brother couldn't even afford a fishing pole, for God's sake). The fact of the matter was, we had a helluva lot more fun spending the summer doing what we'd always done—goofin' off. That's what twelve- and thirteen-year-olds are supposed to do, isn't it? There'll be plenty of time for work later on, doesn't everyone know? Yes, our older brothers were much more practical than we were, and we had us a grand old time while they were being much more practical than we were.

My first sort-of-real job was as a caddy at Waverly Country Club, an exclusive old-money golf club in the Portland area. I was fourteen years old in the summer between grade school and high school. That Catholic high school I went to wasn't cheap. A lot of the kids that went there had parents who were pretty well off. It turned out that some of these parents belonged to Waverly. I had played summer basketball for LaSalle High School between my eighth grade graduation and the start of freshman year. It was there that I had met some of these rich kids (hence, my "in" for the caddy job), only I didn't know they were rich. They just seemed like fourteen-year-olds to me. Anyway, my parents sure as hell didn't have any money. They both worked full time to make ends meet (long before it became the norm for both parents to work outside the home). We lived on SE 86th and Woodstock in a Portland neighborhood that is commonly referred to today as Felony Flats. My brothers and I had to ride a bus ten miles to high school.

In spite of a lack of economic wealth, my childhood was great as I remember it. I don't recall wanting for anything. We didn't have much, didn't need much. Baseball glove, bat and balls, a basketball, a one-speed bike (I didn't even know there were ones with more speeds until I was older), and enough pop bottle change to go to the Saturday afternoon movies once in a while. Thirty-five cents for two full-length feature films, previews *and* cartoons. Who needed money?

Anyway, I caddied that summer for rich, and sometimes, miserly people. I was caddying for one elderly lady (the other three in her foursome handled their own clubs) and at the turn she handed me a dollar. She directed me to go get them four Cokes and as an afterthought told me that if there was any money left over to go ahead and get myself one. The overwhelming generosity and thoughtfulness of this gracious human being had me all choked up, but I bit down on my young smart-ass tongue and headed for the beverages. It turned out there ended up being enough to get myself one, but she obviously hadn't known whether or not there would be.

In truth, most of the people at that country club actually were pretty nice. Hell, the parents of my friends that belonged to the club were beyond nice. Duane Keaton's parents had bucks, and they were great. I spent almost more time at their house than I did at my own. They treated me like a member of the family. It was pretty cool for me, coming from the other side of the tracks, to hitchhike up to the exclusive Eastmoreland area to visit my buddy Duane at his family's five-bedroom, three-bath, two-story home. Hell, in my neighborhood if you had two stories it meant you varied tales about your upbringing; if you had more than one bathroom you were either lying or you were counting the back yard; and if your house had more than three bedrooms it meant your parents had thrown a curtain up in the room you shared with your brother and told you that you each had your own bedroom now. The Keaton's had a frickin' piano in their house, for God's sake, and a bunch of fancy-looking colonial-style furniture to go with it. We had a couch with three-inch pads for seats and back cushions that looked like foam rubber spray-painted orange, and it was the nicest piece of furniture in the house. Don't get me wrong—Mom and Dad busted their butts to get us what they could. It's just that not everyone gets dealt the same hand in life. That's just the way things are. The fact is, though, I felt like a damn king when I spent the night or had dinner over at Duane's house.

My second job was at McDonald's. I started off at a dollar ten an hour. By the time I quit a year and a half later my pay had escalated to a whopping buck-thirty-five. (Of course, hamburgers were only twenty cents back then, to put things in perspective.) But it was a good job that I enjoyed, for the most part. In 1968, McDonald's employed only males (things have changed). My manager was twenty-five years old. He voted me as having the best-looking girlfriend (Sarah) in the place, I remember. We were sixteen at the time. He also gave me my first three joints of marijuana. Actually, they had been given to him by another employee. My manager hadn't wanted them, so he asked me if I did (evidently I had that look). I had never done drugs before (other than alcohol), but I had been curious for quite a while. Marijuana was becoming fairly popular by this time. So when my boss asked me if I wanted this dope, I simply said, "Sure."

I brought the joints over to my friend Duane's house. I smoked all three of them myself because we had heard that's what it would take to get high the first time you imbibed. (Potency increased astronomically over the ensuing years.) Back then the going rate for a "lid" (an ounce of marijuana) was ten bucks. Cheap. Of course, you practically had to smoke half the damn bag to get off. Anyway, I didn't feel much, but that was my initial journey into the world of drugs. Turned on by my boss at the All-American hamburger joint.

So the station was my third real job. And I got fired. It started out that Luke and I were in a bit of a disagreement over a certain matter. You see, for quite a few months, Luke and I worked swing shift together. And come supper time, every night we would decide on which fast food place we wanted to procure our meal from, and one of us would go there to get it. That was all well and good, until Luke one day decided he was tired of his food getting cold when we had to pump gas for customers. So he simply stopped pumping gas during our dinner time. Luke had worked at his stepfather's station in one capacity or another since he was eleven years old. I could understand why he felt certain privileges, but quite frankly, fair was fair. Why should I pump gas and let my food get cold while he sat feeding his face?

After a few days of this I was getting more and more upset. At least when both of us were pumping gas, we could *both* get back to our dinners sooner. Now, I was doing twice as much work, and it was taking twice as long, and my food was getting twice as cold. There was no self-serve in Oregon, so I was stuck. I told Luke my feelings on the subject, but he refused to give in. He suggested that we shut down the station during dinner. For some reason, my addled brain saw this as the only logical alternative.

So, the next night at supper we shut her down. We put barrels out blocking the paths to the pumps on both islands. Not only that, but Luke had picked up a six-pack of beer and had brought a thirteen-inch television from home and set it up in his dad's office. *Star Trek* reruns were on at six o'clock. This was great!

So, there we sat, drinking beer, eating Arby's roast beef sandwiches and watching *Star Trek*, and this customer had the nerve to get out of his car and come in looking for someone to service him—at a service station. What was he thinking? We explained to him that we were closed for dinner, but if he would come back later we'd gladly pump his gas for him. He evidently didn't comprehend. He asked us again if we were going to pump his gas. We told him no, using the shorter English word "No," in order that this time he could maybe come to grips with the fact that he wasn't getting any gas at this particular moment in time.

The guy had the audacity to tell Luke's stepfather, Tony, the next day. When I got to work that afternoon, I could see that ol' Tony was really fuming. He simply asked me for my key to the till, his face puffing up with some sort of anger as he spoke.

"Your services are no longer required at this station," he said to me, without looking up. That was the longest sentence he had put together in the two years I had worked for him. I asked him if he would mind telling me why, knowing the answer, but just wanting to make sure.

Tony said, "When you guys have to close the station to eat dinner, that's going too far."

He was right, of course. It seemed funny after some of the other shenanigans we had gotten away with—drinking on the job, closing up early, etc.

I hadn't felt all that much loyalty to Tony, anyway. At least not since the week I had worked seventy hours, including a sixteen-hour shift, to help cover because Luke was out of town. At the end of that week Tony had handed me a check for one hundred and forty dollars. My pay was minimum wage, two bucks an hour. I knew Tony didn't believe in paying overtime (illegal or not), but I expected *something* extra, for God's sake. He did thank me for putting in the extra hours. For Tony, that was huge.

Yes, Tony was a crusty old codger. I couldn't help but like him, though, even if he didn't pay me overtime. And even if he did make me work Thanksgiving Day, Christmas Day, New Year's Day, and Easter Day. Besides, with him doing things like that, I didn't feel quite so guilty about some of the crap we pulled.

If Tony had known about some of our other behavior he'd have fired me long before he did, more than likely. There was more than one night that Luke and I would drink an insane amount of alcohol and then close the station up early and head out for a night on the town. On a couple of such occasions we each drank an entire fifth of booze. This was a lot more than I was used to drinking, and it was more just to see if we could do it and what would happen if we did. One night we each drank a fifth of Scotch, and another time we each drank a fifth of tequila (mixed with a fifth apiece of liqueur). On the scotch night we left the station early in search of the newly constructed Fremont Bridge—just to check it out. It turned out that we crossed the thing four or five times before we realized we were on it. We were cussing up a storm the whole time wondering how the hell come we couldn't find the biggest, newest bridge in Portland.

Yes, Luke and I had quite a penchant for getting high. And it would be nearly twenty years later that we would hook up again to pursue getting high. Only then it wouldn't be booze nor would it initially be street drugs, and the depths to which we sank in order to procure this form of escape would not sit well with most normal peoples' minds.

But that would be many years after getting fired at the station.

MINI-MARKET MUSINGS

After getting let go by Tony at the service station, I took a job at Plaid Pantry, a successful, local convenience store chain. Though short-lived, it was probably my favorite job of all time. I truly enjoyed it. You see, at a convenience store you only have to deal with people for like three minutes at a time, max. Not hardly long enough for you to develop any sort of deep-seated hatred for them. They barely have time to irritate you and I considered this a major plus. They aren't after anything real life-altering, either. You aren't selling them anything that they're going to pay an arm and a leg for and then maybe go postal if something goes wrong. And back then, clerks like me didn't have lottery machines to take care of, or all of this hot food to go you see in today's mini-markets. It was a lot less complicated, the way I liked things.

For the most part, it was a gravy job with very little hassles. Of course, there was still the robbery risk, and working next door to a tavern in Southeast Portland wasn't the greatest location for a risk-free environment. But I survived. I had a couple of nervous encounters when I worked the graveyard shift. Guys pulling up in an old wreck of a car at three in the morning and strolling in wearing long overcoats in the middle of July will make the hair on the back of your neck stand out some. But they just bought juice.

I did have a guy come in around eight o'clock one Sunday morning asking me if he could do some work in exchange for a bottle of wine. He was in pretty sad shape. I told him I didn't have any work for him. He kept bugging me, saying he'd do some sweeping or any other kind of chore to earn his bottle. I repeated that I had nothing for him to do.

So he said, "If you won't let me work for it, then I'm gonna have to steal it."

"Well, whatever you gotta do," I replied.

The guy walked over to the wine section and stood there staring at it for at least five minutes, like he wasn't sure what particular brand of wine would suit his palate that morning. Suddenly, he reached out, grabbed a bottle of Mad Dog 20/20 (a classic choice for true wine connoisseurs), walked up to me and said "Thanks" as he tapped the counter with the bottle.

"No problem," I replied. I wasn't about to stop someone with a two-buck bottle of wine. That was the big robbery of my tenure at Plaid Pantry.

I had a guy show up one night with his face covered with blood—a very gory scene. He had these deep crescent-shaped cuts all over his face. He wouldn't let me call the cops or an ambulance. He was bleeding badly. I asked him what had happened and he said he had been hitchhiking and two guys had picked him up and cut him up with a broken beer bottle. I wasn't buying much of his story on account of he wouldn't let me call the police or anything. I got him a couple of rags and he took off. I never saw him again.

There was a good-looking blonde girl in a white Porsche who came in a few times during the summer months. She'd smile at me, and I'd talk with her a bit when she came in. One Saturday afternoon Steve Barton was in the store visiting with me, and this same blonde came in, grabbed a bottle of pop, and sashayed up to the counter in her usual free-spirited manner. An older lady got in line behind her.

The blond put the bottle on the counter, looked at me for a few seconds and suddenly said, "Do you like me?"

I'm a little slow, so I said, "What?"

She repeated, "Do you like me?"

I cleverly responded, "Well, yeah. Sure."

"Well, why don't you kiss me then?"

I'm not the only one that's caught off guard. Steve and the older lady in line are a little taken aback as well, as evidenced by the expressions on their faces. Of course, at this point I have zero options. I may have been a little slow on the take, but I wasn't brain-dead. So I leaned over the counter to kiss her. She threw her arms around my neck, pulled me in and we kissed rather passionately for thirty or forty seconds. That's a relatively long time when you're a convenience store clerk and you have customers waiting in line. I glanced at the elderly lady out of the corner of my eye, and she was grinning at Steve.

The blonde then paid for her soda and with a big smile on her face said, "Thank you!" She walked out without saying another word, while I stood there dumbfounded.

I have to admit, I was pretty damn pleased with myself. I proceeded to tell

Steve that this sort of thing happened to me all the time. In fact, it got a little old after a while, I told him, but I had somehow learned to live with my curse. I'm fairly certain Steve wasn't buying into that one.

Eight years of Catholic grade school, four years of Catholic high school, one non-denominational bad trip, one broken heart, one term of college, a side trip to bonkersville with a seventeen-day bonus stretch in a psych ward, seven shock treatments, a stint at the service station, a few months at Plaid Pantry and where was I? In any sort of meaningful, spiritual sense, who knows? But physically and mentally I was on my way to college again.

STILL CRAZY, BUT "FUNCTIONAL"

FROM PSYCHO TO SELLOUT

From October of 1973 through December of 1976 I was back in college. I spent two years at Mt. Hood Community College acquiring a 3.84 cumulative GPA (in spite of my shenanigans and alcohol abuse). Then it was on to Portland State University for another three terms before calling it quits. Forty credit hours away from graduation, and I threw in the towel.

I told everyone I was quitting because I was tired of being broke. That was certainly at least partly true. I told myself that I had to get a job *now*. I couldn't wait another nine months to get my degree, I said to myself. I was tired of the classes, tired of my major—my fourth major.

Late in high school I had decided that my career was going to be in psychology. Ironic choice, in retrospect. Well, "The shoe salesman always needs shoes," they say. From early on in life I had always felt a calling to help people in some way. To do something good for society, for the world. To make a significant contribution. I had felt I could do that in the field of psychology. After high school I had enrolled in college with a major in psychology. But that particular scholarly effort lasted just one term before the madness that was descending upon me completely took over, and I had to leave school. A few months later I was in the psych ward getting those shock treatments. Rather than becoming a successful student of the field, I had dropped out and become a highly successful *subject* in the field. Went bonkers. Lost my cookie. It wasn't until after my "dark period" and my jobs at the service station and the Plaid Pantry that I returned to college, three years almost to the day after I had initially enrolled. Upon my return I had actually entertained the thought of majoring in psychology again. After all, I now had insider experience in the field. And I still held onto the dream that I was going to do something really constructive in this world. However, I was also aware that it required far more than the basic four years of schooling to make a good living in that field. And after all, I wanted to help people, sure, but I now wanted to make some decent money while doing so. I had evidently established new priorities in life. Capitalism had infiltrated my ideology. Materialism had become a part of my vocabulary. I had begun my cop-out. I suppose that because it had been awhile since I had actually felt good mentally, I had convinced myself that increasing my material wealth would somehow enhance my well-being. I know today that nothing could be further from the truth. However, at the time, I could take some solace in the knowledge that there were countless numbers of people in the world pursuing a similar course. That is, they were looking to attain a sense of fulfillment through the same empty monetary means.

Since becoming a psychiatrist meant too many more years of school, and becoming a psychologist meant not enough payment for my services, I made a conscious choice to stay away from any field beginning with "psych" or "psycho" (a rather Freudian move, I think).

Due to what was, in retrospect, a patent lapse in logic, I chose sociology as my second major. Though the field possessed the same lack of lucrative employment potential, I evidently opted to ignore this obvious similarity to my previous major. I was stubbornly holding onto the delusion that I was going to be of real service to the people of this world. But that wouldn't last long. I was soon grappling with the same issues, allowing myself to recognize and admit that there was little chance of making a decent living in the field of sociology, either. It wasn't the only reason, however. The fact was, by then I was figuring out it was tough enough to help myself, let alone start a career where I would be attempting to help others.

So, I would drop that major as well, my last link to my selfless self, my last connection to a free-spirited, peace-love-and-brotherhood era, whose basic ideology had been a part of my soul since well before the terms had made their appearance in society. I sold out, at least to my way of thinking. This lack of fulfilling my life-long dream of doing something significant for the world would continue to haunt me for many years. A lingering, torturing self-knowledge, ever-present in the back of my mind. "Sell-out. Cop-out."

Math became my next choice for a major. Although I was consciously aware that I was selling out my dreams, I convinced myself it was only temporary. I would get a job at Boeing or wherever, and make enough money to be able to do what I *really* wanted to do someday. I wasn't copping out from saving the world—I was merely postponing it. This was my rationalization. Besides, I was still too fragile from my dark period, I told myself. I would take a little time to grow stronger, and in so doing I would be better able to serve the world.

The math thing wasn't too insufferable the first couple of years. I had always done quite well in the subject. I'd been in the top one percent of the nation in the math section of the SATs, so it seemed a reasonable choice. For a while that logic seemed well-founded. I pulled straight A's through three terms of calculus and two upper division terms of Probability and Statistics.

Then it happened. Out of the clear blue I ran head-on into the *"What in the hell is this all about?"* senior-year Differential Equations class. Two weeks staring at the blackboard from hell wondering what class I had missed that would have logically preceded this one and perhaps given me some clue as to what the professor was babbling about up there. Sitting there watching all these brains with their black horn-rimmed glasses (at least in my mind they were all stereotypically "nerdish"), vigorously waving their hands like Horshack clones from *Welcome Back Kotter,* just itching to answer a question. Or even more nauseating, wanting to point out a mistake that the professor had made on that unnerving mass of confusion on the chalkboard. They were blowing my mind (what was left of it). I understood absolutely nothing. I mean, nothing. Zero. Nada. Zilch. Way less than something. It was like Chinese to me. And me with this supposed high I.Q. (maybe they had misread those tests). I became thoroughly convinced that this subject had only two possible uses: one obviously had to do with some futuristic concept of proposed intergalactic-space-flight theory and the other was, of course, teaching this very subject to a roomful of friendless nerds.

I dropped the class and the whole math thing.

I settled finally on a business major. I chose it as a last resort only because I had fulfilled more requirements for it than most other majors that fell into my pool of possibilities. As it turned out, it was the worst choice of all: Systems Analysis, Business Administration, Accounting. The fact that I at least understood what they were talking about was of absolutely no consolation. I'm sorry. I know it's me. I'm the one that's missing a link here. I think I've established that. But I've gotta say, this was the most boring collection of tripe bullshit ever perpetrated on an individual since *The Ins and Outs of Needlepoint: A Comprehensive Analysis of the Stitch,* by Purl Knitwit. I just couldn't handle it. I know it must've been me, though. I must've still been certifiable.

The fact of the matter is, business represented the complete opposite of everything I had ever wanted to do with my life. And I simply couldn't come to grips with that. At least math had somehow seemed removed from that awful word, "business." And psychology and sociology at least had the potential to fulfill those altruistic dreams of saving the world, of contributing in some significant manner to the betterment of society. But business just didn't, at least not to my way of thinking at the time.

One would have to read a rather thick notebook I had filled during my brief sojourn into sociology to completely understand my disenchantment with the business world. In it, I formulated my opinion of how mankind, once it had satisfied the basic animal needs of food and shelter early on in its existence, instead of then aspiring toward more spiritual goals, continued to refine its levels of creature comforts. Enhancing luxury became man's primary goal. Spirituality took a back seat. Technology became our god, and "business" was the thriving force behind technology. We took a wrong turn ages ago, and we have never found our way back. *Certain members of society make occasional gestures in the right direction,* I wrote, *but there's far too much resistance from the masses.* We had strayed too far off the path, it seemed.

The very word, "business," represented to me everything I had pledged to avoid in this world. This was (at least on the surface) my personal motivation for leaving school at that point. I just couldn't allow myself to fall into the trap I had been avoiding all my life. And when it became evident that this was happening, that I was heading in what I felt was the wrong direction for me, I had to take a rain check. Even after I had dropped psychology and sociology, deep down I had felt I would do something far removed from the world of suits and ties. A photographer or a journalist, perhaps. Anything but business. So, I left—dropped out so I wouldn't completely sell out.

But I've gotta come clean. Although this whole cop-out scenario was the truth, it wasn't "the whole truth, and nothing but the truth, so help me God." The fact was, there was another very powerfully motivating force behind my decision to leave college. A very familiar friend of mine was knocking at the door—Mr. Anxiety. Yes, anxiety had a *lot* to do with me wanting to leave school. The truth of the matter was that I absolutely dreaded being called upon in class. The very thought of it raised a blinding fear in me (producing the same panic sensations that had plagued me during my dark phase just a few short years prior) that I finally became unwilling to live with anymore. I hadn't quite risen above that particular malady.

In my mind, I tried to rationalize why it was okay for me to run from this fear rather than facing the fear (as I learned to do many years later). I told myself that I was there to learn, not to become a public speaker, for God's sake. I would have majored in speech and communications if that had been my goal.

It's funny. I used to talk my fool head off in high school in front of anybody. I even voluntarily got up in front of the entire student body at a rally once on the afternoon of the basketball season opener and gave a light-hearted pep talk that I had written myself in the preceding class. I used to get up in front of the bleachers at home games and lead everyone in cheers. I'm not sure when and where I lost my nerve, but I do know for sure that that damn shocker machine hadn't brought it back. (I enjoy Jerry's Seinfeld's bit about the fear of speaking in public being the number-one fear in America. He goes on to say, "The number *two* fear is death. That means at a funeral most people would rather be the guy in the box than the guy up there giving the eulogy.")

The fear of speaking in public remained a constant for many, many years. As my disease of addiction progressed, so did this fear—so did all my fears. The more I hid behind the masks of alcohol and drugs, the more pronounced my fears became. When I got into recovery some twenty-three years later, I became bound and determined to overcome (or to at least face) my fears. And that is what I have done, to the best of my ability. When I was in rehab, several outside guests came and spoke to us about recovery. I wanted more than anything to be able to do that someday, but at the time I couldn't even imagine such a possibility. Nevertheless, I held out hope that someday, some far off day, I would be able to do that—to give back what was so freely given to me. (With determination and a whole lot of support, I was able to go into a hospital and talk to addicts about recovery *one year to the day* that I had gotten clean—it hadn't been so far off after all. I continue to try to bring a message of hope to addicts in hospitals, jails and prisons to this day.)

But back in the seventies, I had no such support. I had no specific guidance. I had no tools, no idea whatsoever as to how to combat my fears, other than with my own willpower—and that wasn't nearly enough to do the job. So, I booked. Quit. Exit, stage left. Bored, broke, bummed-out, so I dropped out.

"Can't handle it—then get out!" That was my motto of the day.

COPS AND COOLERS

In my early twenties I spent a lot of after work hours with Steve Barton and my brother Tim. They were a couple of years younger than I was, but before I was twenty-one the three of us were getting into bars periodically. We found a place or two that rarely carded us. As far as being able to buy alcohol in stores, that was always a crap shoot. We never knew when I was going to be successful, but the closer I got to legal age the higher my hit ratio was.

Steve and Tim had been best friends all through high school, and they continued to hang out together as the years went by. Steve was always one of my favorite people to party with. When he got going he could really make me laugh, and he had a great laugh himself. He was about my height, five foot nine, and had dark wavy hair. He was a good looking young man who got along pretty well with women, yet more often than not he was spending time with his friends. That seemed to be the way it was with most of the guys I knew back then. I suppose, for whatever combination of psycho-babble reasons, it was easier at that point in our lives to hang out with other males than to be in a relationship with a woman.

One evening, before I had yet turned legal age, the three of us were drinking alcohol up on Mt. Tabor, a small, inactive volcanic mountain resting in the middle of the city of Portland. Mt. Tabor boasts several different park settings. There are also a few residential areas tucked into the sides of the mountain. As you wind your way up to the peak on a wide, paved road, there are various areas one can pull over and enjoy the view or stretch out on the groomed grass that the city keeps mowed.

It was on the side of one such hill that Tim, Steve and I decided to situate ourselves, along with our cooler of beer and wine. Steve and I had each bought a twelve pack of beer while Tim had selected three bottles of Mad Dog 20/20 as his drink of choice that evening. Normally, one bottle of Mad Dog would do the trick, but Tim liked to "obliviate" from time to time (as did we all).

Since some of what I'm about to relate focuses on my brother, allow me to digress for a moment so that I don't completely disparage his character—which is truly of the highest caliber. (Disparaging my character is one thing, but I'm trying not to take any innocents down with me.) My brother Tim stands five inches taller than me at six foot two. He has a wiry build, fair skin, curly brown hair, brown eyes. A nice looking and normally very quiet and shy young man who seemed to have developed a propensity in his youth for breaking out of his shyness at just the wrong moments, God bless him. Tim rarely drinks now and *never* gets drunk. He appears to be one of those people who could party hearty on occasion in his youth and get away with it. He is an awesome father to his four children and an equally awesome brother to me and brother-in-law to my wife, Judy. He and his ex-wife Lisa have given us four of the greatest nephews and nieces in the world. I truly admire him as much or more than any man on this planet. Okay, now that I've practically canonized my brother, I feel freer to continue relating this incident that occurred slightly prior to his sainthood. We were, after all, much younger.

There was hardly anyone on Mt. Tabor on this dark summer night, and we were enjoying the effects of the alcohol along with the solitude and the cool evening air. Steve and I were probably into our seventh or eighth beers when a police car suddenly pulled up behind my '64 Chevy Impala. The two of us were still pretty much under control, even after that many beers, but Tim was on a completely different path that night. He was well into his third bottle of Mad Dog and was not hiding the effects of it at all. He had been making quite a bit of noise that evening, whooping it up, doing the drunk-cowboy routine or some damn thing. Unfortunately, of the three of us, Tim was the closest to the cops when they pulled up. Steve and I were well back up on the hillside enjoying our suds, probably seventy or eighty feet from the road. My brother, however, was only about ten feet from the road—and the police.

Two cops stepped out of the car and looked over at Tim. They said something to him about complaints of noise while he stood there staring at them, drunkenly swaying from side to side with that third bottle of Mad Dog in his right hand. Suddenly (or as suddenly as Tim could move at this point), he rotated toward us and at the top of his lungs yelled out: "STEVE, GAR'—*THE PIGS!*"

We were far enough up the hill that we weren't sure what he had said (or perhaps couldn't believe what he had said). So I turned to Steve and said, "What did he say?"

Steve looked at me and said, "I'm not sure. Something about 'the pigs.'"

What we saw next will be eternally etched into our visual memory banks. After yelling "STEVE, GAR'—*THE PIGS!*" once more, my "little" brother turned away from the cops and started running up the hill toward us (the term "running" being used very loosely here—if it's possible to stagger while running, Tim was accomplishing it). He went a mere fifteen feet or so from where he had started "stagger-running" and suddenly did a head-long, arms fully outstretched, belly dive onto the ground and then rolled over a couple of times, like he was in the army and dodging an array of bullets. (In his mind, I'm sure he thought these guys were going to open fire on him at any moment.)

I can just imagine the ensuing conversation between the two cops, probably not much different than the brief one Steve and I had just had:

What did he say?

I don't know, something like "Steve, Gar', or Bar', the Pigs."

In any event, the two officers watched right along with Steve and me as Tim continued his G.I. Joe drop and roll every twenty feet or so in a nonsensical zigzag pattern. In spite of the potentially severe consequences of the situation, we couldn't help but start laughing. That is, until the cops finally decided that they had seen enough and started heading toward us.

Steve and I looked at each other and immediately took off running, going further up the hill where there were more trees and shrubs. We each found a bushy area to disappear into and then lay there panting as quietly as we could.

Five minutes or so went by and I called out in a hoarse whisper, "Steve!"

I heard Steve a few yards away let out an audible, "Shhh!"

So, I waited a few more minutes and then whispered loudly, "I think we're okay, Steve."

Steve and I crawled out from our respective perches in the forested hillside, quickly looking around for the police and then for Tim. No sign of either. We called out Tim's name and seconds later saw him stumble out from behind some bushes further down the hill.

"Damn!" Steve said suddenly as he looked around. "The cooler's gone!"

The cops had evidently taken our cooler and then left the scene.

We got in my car and started bitching about our lost beer as I drove off. Like I said, it wasn't always that easy to procure alcohol, being underage and all, and we weren't done drinking for the night. Getting into a bar was no cinch, either. So I began speculating about what we could do regarding the situation. It dawned on me that if we had been of legal age and had been peacefully drinking beer in the park (at the time, anyway, it was legal to do so) and the police had come by and taken our cooler, it would be the same as theft. At least, this is my theory, and my obsessive brain wouldn't let go of it. (Never mind the fact that we *weren't* of legal age—I had a drunk plan, and drunk plans don't require a basis in logic.) In my fortified state I was feeling pretty brave. I told Tim and Steve that the cops were probably still in the vicinity and would be coming back to see if we had come out of hiding. I suggested to them that I would stop the cops and see about getting our cooler back. Then I decided there was no sense in all three of us getting thrown in jail so I told Steve to drive and if we ran into the cops I would get out of the car.

Steve got behind the wheel and less than a minute later the cops came around the upcoming bend. I told Steve to stop the car and let me out. He asked me if I was sure, and I gave him an emphatic "Yes!" Steve let me out and then drove past the cop car as I flagged it down.

The police stopped their vehicle and the driver put his window down. I began the conversation with a friendly "Good evening, officers." From there I proceeded to go into my spiel as diplomatically as I possibly could. I spelled out the exact scenario I had mentioned to Tim and Steve, wondering aloud to the police what would happen if three adult males of legal drinking age were peacefully having a few beers and then the police came by and grabbed their cooler. "Wouldn't that somehow constitute an illegal confiscation?" I asked them.

The police told me they had received a complaint about some noise in the area. I told them that we had been laughing some, but there was no way we had been a disturbance. At this point I continued with my poetic license and mentioned that we *had* seen some younger people earlier and they were making quite a commotion near where we had been. I said that these *kids* really sounded drunk and their noise had been bothering us as well. I added that they didn't sound very mature and they had taken off just a few minutes before "you guys showed up."

Now, I didn't have the greatest gift of gab in the world, but I did have my moments. This had evidently been one of those moments. The alcohol had greased my tongue enough to where I was half believing my own lie (As George Costanza once said to Jerry Seinfeld: "Remember, Jerry—it's not a lie if *you* believe it."). One of the officers looked at me and asked me if it was my cooler they had taken. I responded that it was.

The driver got out of the car and went around and opened the trunk. He looked at me and said, "Well, you seem to be okay. If it's your cooler, go ahead and take it."

I immediately became suspicious, wondering at what point they were going to ask me for my I.D. So I shook my head and said, "You're going to ask me for my I.D. as soon as I grab it."

The officer assured me he wasn't going to.

Internally, I was baffled, ecstatic, and suspicious all at once. I measured the look on the officer's face and decided I believed him (or at least wanted the beer badly enough that I decided to believe him). I reached into their trunk and grabbed the cooler. To my elation it felt like the beer was still inside. I set the cooler down on the side of the road and thanked the officers and wished them a good evening. To my complete and utter dismay they said goodnight to me and then got into their vehicle and drove off.

A few minutes later Steve and Tim came driving up and when they saw me standing there with the cooler next to me their faces were overcome with astonishment. I was still in shock myself. Every single beer remained in the cooler.

I got behind the wheel, and we celebrated all the way down the mountain. We ended up driving to Laurelhurst Park a few miles away to finish off our beer. (Portland has more parks within the city limits than any place in the country, which we were very grateful for at the time.) This was a relatively unbelievable episode in our young lives. I mean, we were having a hard time believing it ourselves, and we had been there. Cops actually giving confiscated alcohol back to underage kids? I have sometimes hesitated to tell this story, or to write about it, because it reeks of improbability, youthful fantasy, and literary hyperbole. But, on my father's grave (and I loved my father more than anything in this world), the events of that night occurred exactly as I have described them.

I attained a certain level of hero status for a while after this incident. Unfortunately, as with anything else, this badge of honor eventually wore off, and it was just like on the job, as in "What have you done for me lately?" But I lived happily off of my coup for a while.

That became a pattern with me in my twenties, trying to impress friends with various escapades, most of which occurred while under the influence of alcohol. Not an uncommon thing for young men, but a particularly dangerous mind set for addicts of my persuasion. It also made it more difficult to "top" the last scenario, as the precedent-setting stakes grew larger.

INTOXICATION INTROSPECTIONS

Not all of the events in my life between the ages of twenty and forty-six (when I got clean and sober) involved alcohol and/or drugs—just some of the more colorful episodes, I suppose. There were memorable moments that occurred in sober states as well—climbing Mt. Hood with my brother Tim, getting married to Judy, going to kids' ball games, among a host of others. There were also events involving drugs and alcohol that were much more mundane than the ones I may be relating, but I doubt that anyone wants to read about someone sitting in a recliner swilling rum and clicking a remote. Besides, they say addiction is a progressive disease, and I believe that this progression can be more readily seen through an overview of some of these more colorful episodes in one's life. Some of these events involved things I can't believe I actually did, or "we" did, depending upon the story.

My attitudes and my thinking have changed dramatically since the days of my drinking and using. I have my pre-sober mentality and my post-sober mentality. Not that some of my pre-sober thinking hasn't crept into my head from time to time (and sometimes more often than not), but today I make a concerted effort not to let the negative thinking and attitudes of my previous life take over. And not that all of my pre-sober mentality was bad or negative or without merit. It wasn't—anymore than my post-sober mentality is all good and positive and meritorious. It is not.

Some of the attitudes and actions of my past can be, in retrospect, somewhat embarrassing to me, such as: shoplifting; vandalism (I had a seemingly uncontrollable glass-breaking fetish whenever I consumed too much tequila); hitting objects with various motorized vehicles (on way too many occasions); as well as my attitude toward getting severely intoxicated (an attitude which was, at the time: "I'm for it").

From an analytical point of view (not as a defense), I remind myself of the potent inhibition-reducing quality of alcohol. Although this quality was predominantly responsible for facilitating my resurgence into society, it was also the catalyst behind the destructive episodes in my life, namely, breaking glass and smashing objects with my cars. In other words, the same quality of alcohol that produced a supposed therapeutic effect (relaxing me enough to socialize), also at times released a wildness within me that culminated in destructive acts, foolish acts, potentially dangerous acts. This over-the-top release of inhibitions was, not surprisingly, directly related to the quantity of alcohol that was consumed.

That said, I wasn't an angry or a mean drunk. It was more of a release of pent-up frustrations, as I see it now. Frustration, perhaps, with the insane workings of my mind and/or disappointment with where I was at in my life. It was as if the feeling of something missing was buried beneath the surface and too much alcohol would sometimes prompt me to express this turmoil in unhealthy ways. This baser self, if you will, can be triggered by alcohol or drugs in many people, sometimes in the form of a mean drunk—*or*—as it would occasionally come to light in my case, in the form of smashing things.

Although these destructive episodes of mine were relatively rare, I think that revealing the scope of them is pertinent to an honest overview. To avoid or to deny the past is pointless as well as fruitless. And as my dear wife said to me when I expressed hesitation about including potentially embarrassing subject matter, "If you're going to sugar coat your story, why tell it?" Indeed, why at all?

And if I tend to repeat apologies due to my remorse over some of these attitudes and incidents ad nauseam, please forgive me. I simply want to emphasize that I am neither proud of these things nor do I wish to promote or condone them in any way. I most assuredly do not relate these stories in any effort to glorify drug or alcohol use—that is the furthest thing from my mind and the last thing I would ever wish to do. Drugs and alcohol have taken the lives of some people that were very, very close to me, as well as almost taking my own life. I have seen the disease of addiction destroy countless individuals and innumerable families.

Regardless of any shame or guilt I may have felt, these past incidents and perspectives are a part of my life story, and as such have their place in my history. I do not regret my past. I have made my amends where possible. I can only work on making myself a better person *today*. As I have stated, I believe that everything comes to serve a higher purpose and if we can learn from our mistakes, then we can continue to grow and evolve.

In spite of the semi-serious and reflective nature of the preceding paragraphs (it just comes over me from time to time—I'm a veritable dichotomy, a plethora of severely conflicting mental patterns), some of the upcoming stories are of a light-hearted nature—or certainly bear the capacity to be viewed in a light-hearted manner. An elderly lady I knew in my early recovery used to say that "laughter is God's voice." It is my belief that humor comes from the same sacred place as do compassion, kindness and love.

But then, again, I'm relatively insane.

ROGER MILLER AND CLARK KENT

In the spring of 1974 I was twenty-one and back in college. One Friday night, without advanced warning, Dale Ford and Don Dryden showed up at my door. I had gone to high school with them both. They were two of the nicest guys around and they could both readily make me laugh. I opened the door wondering what they were up to.

"Get some things together, Gar—we're going to Reno!" Don announced exuberantly. Don was a country boy, raised on a farm (which gave him a considerably different upbringing from the rest of our gang of friends), but he and I meshed really well. Don loved to laugh more than anyone I knew, and that trait alone was enough to endear him to me. He was about my height, five foot nine, but stockier than I was (marathon runners were stockier than I was), with jet black, wavy hair and a youthful grin that added friendly to a face that already naturally was.

Dale was about the same height as Don and I. His curly black hair was beginning to recede already. He was a handsome man (although not quite in the category as his younger brother, Joe—"Angel Eyes," as the girls referred to him). Dale had a great aura about him, one that somehow successfully mingled confidence with humility.

I was a little stunned at Dale and Don's sudden arrival, as well as, of course, their departure and destination plans, and reacted accordingly. But they would have none of my hemming or hawing and insisted instead that I get ready so we could embark upon our journey (Reno is a ten- to twelve-hour drive from Portland). Being just twenty-one, none of us had ever been to Nevada as legal adults before. It didn't take much prodding for me to agree to this impulsive trek. The only gambling I had ever done was at our weekly poker game. I was anxious to see how I could do at the tables in Reno, even though nothing in my life so far had indicated I would be successful at gambling in other venues. I rarely won at our poker games, for example, mostly because I would never fold a hand (or at least not until even the remotest of mathematical probabilities of winning had been exhausted). I just couldn't bear to sit idle while the action was going on. (Gambling became one of my many addictions over the years. About the only addiction I didn't ever really take on was over-eating, and that never became a problem, I suspect, only because I was blessed with "thin" genes and a high metabolism.)

In any event, a mere ten minutes later we were on our way to Reno. (Ah, the spontaneity of youth.) Although I had finals coming up at college the following Monday morning and hadn't studied for them, my compulsion to have fun overtook the logical portion of my brain (which happened more often than not in those days). We were meeting a few other friends down there as well.

On the way to Reno I remember occasionally taking what I explained to Dale and Don were "wolf naps"—fifteen to twenty minute rest periods. (I had recently read that wolves only slept fifteen to twenty minutes at a time.) In truth, I had started practicing Transcendental Meditation (I did endeavor to do some healthy things over the years to quell my unhealthy compulsions) and hadn't felt like divulging this fact to them. The reason for my secrecy was that one of my friends who I *had* told I was meditating in an effort to learn to relax more, had responded with, "Hell, when I want to relax, I just drink a six pack," and I wasn't seeking any further discouragement on the subject.

Upon arriving in Reno we began gambling immediately, of course. Later that day we found out that Frank Sinatra was playing at one of the casinos, and my friends became obsessed with seeing him. Granted, we were young people from the sixties and seventies—and most of us were definitely more about rock n' roll than easy listening—but Frank was Frank. Everyone but me bought tickets for the Sunday night show (the only show that wasn't already sold out). I had finals Monday morning and was flying back Sunday afternoon, so I couldn't attend the concert.

We stayed up most of Friday night and most of Saturday night, drinking and gambling. I got on a winning streak Saturday night at the blackjack tables. I ended up going from just a few dollars in chips to over three hundred dollars in about three hours. Now, three hundred dollars certainly wasn't a king's ransom, even in 1974, but it was a lot of money to a twenty-one-year-old college student. Then the oddest thing happened—I started to lose. I lost so many hands in a row at one point that I was, in a very short period of time, back down to fifty dollars. (I had more money in the motel room, but that was the last of my stash for the night. I had *some* restraint in those days, although my stash never remained at the intended levels for long.) I finally gathered up enough willpower to pick up my chips and walk away from the table.

It was about four o'clock in the morning, and I was feeling pretty rummy (the fact that I had been drinking rum and cokes all weekend may have contributed slightly to this feeling). A bizarre thought came into my head as to how I might perk myself up a bit and I suddenly dropped down and began vigorously doing pushups in the middle of the casino floor. Surprisingly enough, a uniformed security officer was soon looming over me. Spotting his shiny black shoes from my carpeted vantage point, I quickly jumped up, extended my hand, and said, "How you doing tonight?" in an overtly friendly fashion. A smile came quickly to his face, and I knew we were good. He was just checking on me to see how I was doing.

My buddy Dale decided that my streak was over, and that I shouldn't gamble anymore, but that it would be a good idea if *he* took my money and gambled it for me. (Dale had been out of money for quite a while by this time). Somehow I saw the logic in letting someone who had already lost *all* of their weekend money take *my* money and gamble with it. Dale sat down with my last fifty bucks and lost it all in about three minutes. Just one more genius move in a lifetime of genius moves.

I experienced an embarrassing, but nonetheless rather amusing moment later that same morning. After a couple of hours of sleep, a few of us were heading to breakfast when I spotted an open craps table. I had always thought it would be fun to roll dice on the big tables in Nevada, but knowing next to nothing about the game, I was a little intimidated by the whole scenario. However, when I spotted this table with just two croupiers and no players, I gathered my nerve and approached it. I asked one of the guys what I needed to do. He suggested that I place a bet on the "pass line" and then roll the pair of dice that he handed me. I placed the bet and with sweaty hands (I was still a little tense, being a virgin roller) I shook the die and let them fly. And "fly" they did. I was so nervous and shaky that my sweaty palm released the pair of dice a little late. The die flew off my fingertips to the right—they never even came close to hitting any part of the table—and seconds later they crash-landed underneath separate barstools about twenty feet away. After a brief second or two of disbelief (and rapidly reddening cheeks), I slowly and sheepishly trudged over and retrieved the pair of dice, then brought them back to one of the croupiers and dropped them into his awaiting palm.

He stared at me for a few seconds without saying anything. His muted mug was deafening. And then, initially, just two simple words: "Fifteen years." He paused, both to keep me guessing and to drag out this agonizing moment, I suspect. "Fifteen years and I've never seen anyone do that."

As if I wasn't humiliated enough already. I looked back at him and all I could think of to say was, "Did I win?"

My comment forced a smile upon him as he shook his head no. I rolled the dice again (using the table this time) and thank God I "crapped out" quickly, bringing my torture to a relatively quick demise.

Around noon that day it was time for me to head to the airport. By this time we were all sitting in one of our motel rooms (no one had much money left to gamble with). After saying my good-byes to everyone, I went downstairs to get a cab. I had been gone from the room maybe five minutes when it suddenly hit me that I simply couldn't leave while everyone else was still in Reno. It just wasn't in me (anymore than folding at a poker game seemed to be).

So I made a couple of phone calls. I called the airline and switched my return flight to seven o'clock the following morning. Then I called my dad to see if he could pick me up at the Portland airport at about 8:30 a.m. and drive me directly to Portland State University so that I could take my first final exam at 9:00 a.m. He said he would. (I was grateful at the time that my dad had answered the phone rather than my mother so that I didn't have to listen to her read me the riot act about drinking, gambling, the importance of a college education and a good night's sleep, and about how the world would undoubtedly shift off its orbital path if I didn't come home that evening, etc., etc. Dad just said, "Sure.")

I arrived back at the motel room to a mass of rather startled faces. With each expression searching for an explanation, I simply threw out my arms and acting as if I had no choice in the matter, exclaimed, "Could I miss Frank?" Laughter and hollering ensued.

Frank was pretty good—nothing to write home about—but it *was* Frank. It didn't matter whether he was "on" that night or not (as if I'm any judge of that). Actually, the best part of the show to me was when Frank introduced another singer who was in the audience that night, Roger Miller. (I loved some of his songs, particularly "King of the Road.") I think Roger got a bigger hand than Frank had. After the show, my friends and I were walking out when I asked them to wait a minute, that I had to go say hi to Roger (like we were close). They laughed as I walked boldly up to the table where Roger was sitting (I was feeling very little pain at this point) and said, "Hey, Roger."

Roger rotated in his chair toward my voice and one look into his bleary eyes and it was rather obvious that he was feeling very little pain himself. He looked at me and said, "Hey, how ya' doin', babe?" and then extended his hand.

I smiled, shook his hand, and then walked away. *What a great guy*, I thought, as did my friends. He hadn't needed to acknowledge me (I had interrupted his evening with his friends), let alone be so gracious about it. "Hey, how ya' doin', babe?" He truly was King of the Road in our minds, God rest his soul.

That night I stayed up all night drinking and gambling. I managed to stay on enough of an even keel at the tables to survive monetarily until it was time to get to the airport. (I had never been on an airplane before—I was getting a lot of first experiences that weekend.)

So there I sat on the plane, not yet far enough removed from the consumption of alcohol to be feeling hung over but beginning to feel the effects of no sleep. A voice from the cockpit came on and announced that he was the pilot of the aircraft and that his name was Captain Clark Kent—I am not making this up! My first flight ever, I had been drinking and gambling all weekend with very little sleep, and I was on a Boeing 707 with a guy who thinks he's Superman in street clothes. But his name apparently really was Clark Kent and he got us to our destination safe and sound (without having to don the cape).

My dad picked me up at the airport as planned and drove me directly to PSU, where I took my final exam. I got a C on the test and a B for the class. I could live with that.

That was my first trip to a big gambling city. I got to see Frank Sinatra and shake Roger Miller's hand and had my first plane ride with Clark Kent as the pilot.

Although on the surface this appeared for all intents and purposes to be a fun weekend, deeper probing reveals signs of a foreboding nature: my seeming inability to stop gambling or drinking when it would seem reasonable to do so, as well as my impulsive decision to stay for Sinatra when logic and prudence would have encouraged otherwise. These traits would continue unabated for two and a half more decades.

BROKEN GLASS

In my early twenties, whenever I happened to partake of the evil spirit tequila, I would, through some sort of chemical misunderstanding, became a one-man glass-seeking missile. The good news is that once I had shattered glass of some kind, the urge seemed to be quelled for the evening. Unfortunately, it seemed to be plate glass windows that I preferred breaking (rather than something of a smaller stature) and usually my right foot was the irresponsible party. I feel remorseful about these incidences to this day, of course, but they occurred nonetheless.

I recall a gas station window on Powell Boulevard one night. It was a pyramid of oil cans in the window that had caught my eye. I was the driver that night. (I was the driver a large percentage of the nights we went out in those days. As I stated, I have thanked God a thousand times that I never killed or seriously hurt anyone in all the times I drove drunk over the years. I have met a number of people who *have* killed or seriously hurt someone while driving drunk, some of them in prison, and they are endlessly tortured by it). Being the driver of the vehicle I was able to do a quick U-turn upon spotting the irresistible sight that had stabbed my peripheral. However callous, inconsiderate, or wrong it was, the anticipated sight and sound of breaking glass and falling oil cans took precedence in my drunken stupor. I always felt badly about these incidents after sobering up the next day, and assuaged my guilt by telling myself that these people all had insurance. Of course, I obviously didn't feel badly enough (or wasn't brave enough) to offer these places any recompense at the time. (I've never expected to be canonized.)

On another night it was my right foot crashing through a large plate glass window of a store in downtown Portland. I had had too many shots of tequila (*two* was too many for me) and was way out of control (which is why I rarely drank tequila, and, in fact, stopped drinking it altogether sometime in my mid-twenties). Steve Barton and my brother Tim had done their level best to stop

102

me. They had taken my keys from me a few moments prior (we had at least a modicum of sense back then) and then they saw me heading toward a window. Fully aware of my penchant for breaking glass after shooting tequila they both grabbed me from behind and held me. After getting me to calm down and making me promise that I wouldn't break the window, they let go of me. Two seconds later the window lay shattered.

On yet another night it was a beer bottle sailing into a bank window in downtown Portland. It's relatively amazing (and a little sad, actually) that I've never spent a night in jail in my life (I was arrested once for singing in a bar and taken to a drunk tank, but that's another story). Nor in twenty-six years of drinking and driving did I ever get a D.U.I. (I did get a "concealed open container" citation a few months before I got clean and sober, but that's another story as well.)

And on one very insane night, on the occasion of the bachelor party of my best high-school buddy Duane Keaton, I put my foot through a downtown photo store window after having had a few shots of tequila. My friend, Ken Matthews, was with me that night. (There were others in our group from the bachelor party as well, but they were already at the bar where Ken and I were heading to meet them.) After I kicked in the window, Ken and I ran down the street as rapidly as our intoxicated states would take us. We made it about half a block before our lack of endurance decided we were well out of danger. Being exhausted from our marathon fifty-yard run, we decided that lying down would be beneficial. So there we were, having just committed a crime of vandalism ("we?" Ken's foot had been nowhere near that window), lying flat on our backs on a sidewalk in downtown Portland, acting as if this were a normal thing to do. Seconds later, a homeless person walked by and began staring at us. He asked us what we were doing. I don't remember the exact conversation, naturally, but whatever we said shook the fellow up enough that he dropped the brown paper sack he was carrying as he walked away from us (reminiscent of the bum in the *Star Trek* episode, *City on the Edge of Forever,* dropping his sack when he saw Doctor McCoy being transported out of thin air). *Maybe we cured him,* I remember thinking at the time. (Which of us was in more need of a cure was highly debatable at that point.)

Later that same evening—well, actually about three o'clock the next morning—we were all in a downtown restaurant having breakfast. After eating our meals we went out to my car and discovered, after several minutes of drunken deciphering, that my car had run out of gas while we were in the restaurant. Evidently I had not only left my keys in the ignition, but I had left the motor running. So we did "odd man out" with quarters to figure out which one of us would begin a search on foot for a gas station. In keeping with my gambling prowess, I lost.

I wandered around downtown Portland for probably forty-five minutes looking for an open service station. At one point, I spotted a police car parked on the street. My brilliantly intoxicated mind decided that it would be a good idea to ask these officers for directions (and hopefully a ride) to a station. They seemed to be preoccupied as I approached them. I explained that I had run out of gas and was wondering if they knew where there was a station open.

One of the officers looked up at me and said, "I don't really know." And then nodding behind him, added, "As you can see, we have a little situation here."

I turned around to see a broken photo store window. "Yeah, I can see that," I muttered, as I wandered off. *What were the odds of that?* (Impressive response time, though, I must say. I had only broken the window about five hours earlier.)

I eventually found a gas station, and we made it home without further incident.

Many of the places belonging to the windows I destroyed either no longer exist, or their names no longer exist in my memory. As I've stated (*ad nauseum*), I feel bad about those incidents and hope I have made (and will continue to make) restitution through other means. It is often impossible to take things back in life (as a gentleman once said, "I've given up all hope that my past will get better"), but we can do our best to learn from our mistakes as we progress on our respective journeys. In some small way, I hope I have been able to repair some of the damage.

BROKEN CARS

I made mention of "hitting objects with various motorized vehicles." Although many of the collisions I had in the first few licensed years of my life were not my fault, most of the later ones were. This is also something with which I have harbored guilt and I retain the same hope that restitution is being made as I mend my ways.

My first automobile accident was just nine days after getting my driver's license. I was sixteen years old. It was also the first of several windshields that I would shatter with my head over the years, which could explain a lot. (A friend of mine, Ben R.—who happens to be the same friend that is amused by the fact that I begged people to electrocute my brain—has often remarked to me, "You got hit in the head a lot as a child, didn't you?")

The next nine wrecks weren't my fault, nor were alcohol and/or drugs involved in any of these accidents. (Yes, I said *the next nine*, and unfortunately there were many more after that.) In any case, I began to feel as if I had a huge target painted on any vehicle I drove.

After number ten, alcohol did become a factor in most of my remaining collisions. To this day I'm not sure exactly how many accidents I compiled, but I do know it was well over fifteen and somewhere less than twenty-five. I'm including parked cars, guard rails, fences, fire hydrants, and roadblocks. As horrendous as the numbers might seem, I am truly grateful that many of the later alcohol-induced collisions were with unmanned objects.

The fence incident occurred somewhere on the low side of the double-digit mark. My brother Tim, Steve Barton, Ron Carver, Eddie Schultz, and I were at a drive-in theater on Foster Road. We were in my '64 Chevy Impala convertible, my favorite car of my younger years. I had purchased the Impala for $140.00 at a car lot (they had been asking $195.00). The driver's side rear quarter panel was all smashed in and the back window of the convertible top was rusted so bad you couldn't see through it, but everything worked on it, and the 327 engine in it was strong. (It lasted over three years before the tranny malfunctioned.) Our nickname for the Impala was simply "the '64."

Playing at the drive-in that night was *White Line Fever* with Jan Michael Vincent, a movie about a truck driver who goes a little nuts on the highway. After it was over, some of the motorized insanity in the movie channeled itself into my being, taking over my better judgment (the beer may have had something to do with it as well). As soon as the credits started rolling, I began wildly bouncing the '64 over the drive-in's gravel humps, riding them like a bucking bronco with everyone in the car whooping and hollering. As I rounded back toward the exit there was a line of cars that I apparently didn't feel like waiting for. I saw an opening and maneuvered past all the cars, heading toward the closed and chain-locked cyclone fence which was to the right of where people were exiting (properly). I punched the '64 as I approached, easily smashing through the locked gate, flying crazily past everyone else. About twenty feet beyond the newly formed exit my car died. In a panic, after trying to start it several times to no avail, all five of us jumped out and started pushing the car out of the drive-in onto Foster Road. We continued frantically pushing the '64 for what must have been ten blocks, taking a right on 104th Street, our adrenalin serving as impetus. We stopped to catch our breaths and when it seemed clear that no one was on our tail, we examined under the hood. We discovered that the force of crashing into the fence had cracked the distributor cap. I don't remember how we got the car the rest of the way to my brother Tim's house (where I was living at the time), but it was only another fifteen blocks away. Maybe we pushed it, maybe we towed it later with someone else's car. In any case, I had once again struck something with a motorized vehicle, and this time alcohol was definitely involved.

A year or so later I was with the same four guys in the '64. We had just left the lounge at the airport (no one had flown anywhere—we had just decided to go have a drink at the airport bar). I was driving the '64 toward one of the exit parking booths. About a hundred feet from the booth I evidently decided it would be a good idea to crash the gate. Obeying my irrational impulse, I floored the '64 and began heading toward the roadblock (the black-and-white-striped arms that come down to hopefully keep you in until you've paid for parking). I had no idea at the time what those things were made of, and apparently I didn't care. Fortunately (for us, not the airport), they were made of plywood and only about a half an inch thick. The bar splintered into a surprising number of pieces, I must say, several of them careening off my hood and windshield as we screamed through the exit. I took just enough of a glance to inspect the expression on the face of the guy in the parking booth as I flew by. His mouth was agape, and his eyes wide as his head mechanically turned, following the path of the '64. My friends were as shocked as he was, but nevertheless seemed to be entertained by my spontaneous combustion.

Incredibly, (and somewhat regrettably), I never got caught or cited in any of these driving irregularities. I had other collisions in my twenties (too numerous to enumerate or to accurately recall), but my very last crash as an operator of a motorized vehicle occurred in 1981. It would also be the last time I shattered a windshield with my head (knock on glass). I was twenty-eight years old and had just met Judy, my future wife-to-be, a few weeks prior. We were leaving The Grove (the same bar where I had met her). It was two-thirty in the morning, and I had been drinking for a couple of hours after having been to a movie earlier with Judy. It was also one of those relatively rare instances in my twenties when I had smoked marijuana (it was definitely not my drug of choice). I was rather blitzed.

We were no more than two blocks from the bar when I slammed into the rear end of a van that had stopped to make a left turn. I had not seen the van (not because I was loaded but because I hadn't been looking at the road—instead, I had been engaged in tom-foolery with Judy and not paying attention). I consequently hit the other vehicle without applying any brakes, doing about forty miles an hour. Neither of us had been wearing seat belts. Both Judy and I hit the windshield (my third, her first). My side of the windshield was not nearly as damaged as Judy's side. After I bounced back into my seat, I looked over at her and immediately panicked. Her face was literally covered with cuts and her eyes were shut tightly. I quickly asked her if she was all right and she replied that she wasn't sure. She said she didn't want to open her eyes because she was afraid there might be glass in them.

People immediately began pulling over. The first person on the scene was a nice man in his twenties who assured Judy and me that she was going to be okay. I was an emotional mess at this point, feeling terribly guilty that I might have blinded her or been the cause of disfiguring facial scars. In an effort to assuage my concerns, the kindly man remarked, "She's going to be okay. Her wounds are all superficial." I had absolutely no idea what the word "superficial" meant in this application, but I could tell by his tone that it was a good thing, and I immediately loved this man.

Two ambulances and two police cars arrived on the scene within minutes. My brother Tim and our friend Steve Barton had also been behind the van, but they had gone around it because the driver had been driving erratically. (She had been at the bar as well.) Except for a bruised wrist, she was uninjured. Regardless of her intoxicated condition or erratic driving, the accident was clearly my fault. Our friends, Tom and Beth, had been behind us. Everyone was trying to console us after we had finally exited the vehicle and gone over and sat on the curb. Tom and Beth were very comforting, I remember. And Tim and Steve did their best to convey information to the police.

Judy and I were taken to the hospital in separate ambulances. I had wanted to ride with Judy, but the paramedics insisted that I ride in a separate ambulance. I was practically hyper-ventilating out of concern for what I had done to her. I also had a gash on my neck, various bruises, and a large knot on my head. They strapped me to a Gurney, and on the way to the hospital the paramedics told me they were going to put me on oxygen if I didn't calm down. I managed to take some deep breaths and relax enough to satisfy them.

A couple of officers interrogated me at the hospital. They asked me if I had been drinking, naturally. I told them that Judy and I had been to a movie and we had stopped at a bar to see a few friends, where I had had a couple of drinks. I was evidently sobered up enough by the accident to be believable.

Judy ended up being all right, although for several weeks minuscule shards of glass would work their way to the surface of her face—not a pleasant experience for her, to say the least. Insanely enough, I was not wearing a seat belt during any of my collisions. They really didn't start stressing the safety-belt thing until after I was done running into things, it seemed. (And I obviously wasn't intelligent enough to figure it out on my own. I tell you, I'm just not all that bright.) Fortunately, the last two-plus decades of my life have passed by collision-free. This is in spite of the fact that I irresponsibly drove drunk on hundreds of occasions during many of these years. However, I toned it down somewhat as I got older, not taking as many chances or driving quite as recklessly, although there were times I obviously had no such control due to my level of intoxication. The bottom line—I was truly very lucky.

Perhaps if I had had more frequent or more severe repercussions over the years for my various transgressions, I might have sobered up sooner. But I try now to no longer second guess things. As I have shared, I believe things happen the way they do for a reason. Each of us are on a path in life, and it is my belief that at different points along these paths we have opportunities to recognize certain basic things about the nature of the universe. If we take advantage of the insights we are offered, we can then begin to change in positive ways as a result, and in doing so, make the world a slightly better place as well (or at the very least, a little less dented).

TRAINS

My friends and I took numerous road trips in our twenties. Since most of us remained single until we were thirty, or close to it, we had quite a lot of freedom and independence—and we did not appear to be bashful about utilizing these gifts. There were many weekend nights, for example, when my brother Tim, Steve Barton, and I, would impulsively decide to take a trip to the Pacific Ocean at midnight or even later (the beach is an hour and a half away from Portland). We even had our favorite little cottage at Seaside, Oregon. We became regulars there, and dubbed it "The Old Man and the Sea," because of the elderly gentleman that ran the place.

There were many trips to Reno in those days as well. They always seemed to be the most exciting and alluring of road adventures, partly due to the ten-to twelve-hour drive, I'm sure, but also because of what awaited us at the end of our journey. Namely, a chance to win large sums of cash. Unfortunately for me, I gambled the way I partied, "balls to the walls" (I have no idea what that means), which is why when I got clean and sober my wife was kind enough to suggest that I was done with gambling, also. And for her sake, initially, I stopped. (Within a few months of her "suggestion," however, as I began to have an occasional moment of clarity, I recognized how right she had been and have not gambled since.) For me, going to Reno to break even (or to win just a few dollars) wasn't in the cards. I always said I would rather lose than break even (the sad thing is I was actually serious). Breaking even was unacceptably boring to me. If I still had money in my pocket when we were ready to leave Reno or Lake Tahoe or Vegas, and it wasn't enough cash to cause me to stoop from the weight of it, than it was time for one more trip to the tables (I never left Nevada doubled over from anything other than alcohol poisoning).

To make clear this point: On one such trip to Nevada there were about ten of us—all guys in our twenties. Everyone but Ken Matthews and Jim Foxx had flown to Reno. These two had driven down in Ken's new Datsun 240Z. When our stay was over, and most of us were taking cabs to the airport for our return flight home, I got a wild urge and suddenly shouted out to the driver: "Stop! Let me out!" I told the guys in the cab that I was going to go gamble my last ten dollars (this did not shock anyone). The taxi pulled over to let me out. "If I can quickly make some decent money," I told them as I got out of the car, "I'll get another cab to the airport and meet you guys there—otherwise I'll try to find Ken and ride home with him."

The ten dollars was gone in about thirty seconds. Fortunately, I had a plane ticket which was partially refundable (casinos will take almost anything). I got sixty dollars for that ticket, I remember, and proceeded to lose it all in about ten minutes.

Riding home for ten hours in the back of Ken's 240Z with a full length cast on my right leg (I had broken my leg skiing a few weeks prior and had been on crutches the whole trip), was far from the most comfortable way to travel. But the point was, in my sick mind at least, that I could have parlayed that sixty bucks into thousands. (Logic never visited me in these moments.)

There was also that little problem of mine that I mentioned earlier—the fact that I just couldn't stand to leave when there were friends of mine still in town. I was always one of the last to leave a party or the bar, as well. (Today I practice a slightly healthier habit: I'm often one of the last to leave a Twelve Step meeting.)

In any event, another one of the more memorable trips to Nevada that we had over the years involved my brother Tim and four other guys—Steve, Luke, Ron, and Eddie, along with me. All six of us slept in the same room, using the two beds and sleeping bags (*no sense wasting precious gambling money on extra accommodations* was our thinking in those days—we rarely spent much time in a motel room in Nevada anyway).

During this trip we were treated to a telephone monologue from Luke that would have made Bob Newhart envious. It occurred on our first night there. Each of the six of us had stumbled into the room to crash at various moments during the night. We were staying at a relatively small hotel situated directly adjacent to the railroad tracks that run through Reno. We had all ingested enough liquid sedative to put us into relatively deep states of slumber. However, these railroad tracks were being frequently visited by incoming trains. Trains with extremely loud whistles. Trains evidently run by people who enjoyed blowing these extremely loud whistles for extended periods of time.

As such, none of us were sleeping very well. When we did manage to fall back to sleep, it wasn't long before we would be rudely jarred to consciousness by one of these whistles.

About five in the morning, Luke suddenly grabbed the phone and called the front desk. One cannot possibly do justice to the ensuing conversation we were lucky enough to be privy to on that day. It was one of those situations where you definitely "had to be there." But Luke, in his twenties, was at times nothing short of hilarious, and it wouldn't seem right to begin this book with the dark narrative of his demise without at least attempting to portray a lighter side of his being—the side of Luke that drew us to him in the first place. Luke was definitely not one-dimensional. He was a very skilled restorer of old autos, he played the piano, was one of the best pool players I've ever seen, and was an awesome pitcher in baseball. He had even tried out for the Portland Mavericks once—a semi-pro baseball team. He also loved exploring and discussing different philosophies of life. Unfortunately, as Luke began to consume more and more drugs in his twenties they gradually began to consume him, and his interest in other things subsequently dwindled with time. But he could always make me laugh.

"Yeah, this is Luke," he said, matter of factly, into the phone, as if the person on the other end had been a friend of his for years and would know who he was.

"Yes, well, it's five o'clock in the morning and we've got trains." He spoke in a calm tone of voice, stating a simple fact, yet at the same time managing to convey his bewilderment over the situation.

There were short pauses in between each of Luke's sentences as the conversation progressed, undoubtedly filled with "uh-huh's" and "I'm sorry's" and "yeses," "no's," "I don't know's" and, after a while, a lot of giggling by the young lady on the other end of the line (judging by the demeanor and continuance of Luke's little dialogue).

"Yeah, trains—we're talking trains. Evidently passing right through the hotel lobby."

"Uh-huh. Well, I was wondering if you could maybe tell us why that is." The five of us were already in stitches.

"Well, I don't recall anyone mentioning it to us when we checked in."

"Yes, well, you see, we've been up half the night drinking and gambling as you can imagine, and now—we've got trains. These are really *loud* trains, and their whistles are all apparently stuck, and they seem to be coming from just the other side of our bathroom wall."

"Well, we were wondering how necessary it was to blow the damn whistles all the time. I mean, it's not like the people down there can't see them coming. They're *trains,* you know. Large—*extremely* large things."

"Uh-huh. Well, you're certainly not going to fall asleep on the job—maybe the railroad has something going on with your boss. But we'd enjoy catching a little sleep, frankly."

"Yes, well, we were all pretty set on getting up early for Mass."

"No, I'm serious. We're all very religious."

"I imagine the owner probably didn't pay a lot for this piece of property."

"Uh-huh, well, maybe they could have put a warning in your brochure or something. You know, about the trains and the whistles. Something like, *'You can store your shit in our rooms, but don't count on getting any sleep here.'* Something along those lines. And what is your name, young lady?"

"Well, Katie, I'm sure you understand. Right now we're all caught between being extremely drunk and extremely hung over, and we've got a lot of gambling to do in the next couple of days if we're going to make up for last night—and we could really use a little rest."

"What is it that they're hauling into this town every ten minutes, anyway—more craps tables or what? Whatever it is, don't you think this town has enough of a supply that they could maybe do this during the day? Is it really that urgent that they have to do this in the middle of the night?"

"Yes, I understand, Katie, that you really have no control over any of this, but I was wondering if maybe you could get a hold of the mayor or something."

"Yeah, that's right—just give him a buzz and tell him we're trying to sleep here."

"No, I think he's probably a reasonable man. If you told him there were some guys in room 143 that were having trouble sleeping, I'm sure he would get a hold of the appropriate authorities down at the terminal and ask them to knock it off for a couple of hours so we could get some rest."

"Well, okay. Yeah, if you could just let your boss know, that would be great."

Like I said, impossible to do it justice, but Luke had us holding our guts that morning. I remember choking, I was laughing so hard.

Certainly a lot of memorably amusing times in the early days, but as we got older, so did the hangovers, so did the empty morning wallets.

Yet, it became all I knew. I guess back then I did have more than a decade of respite from the severe forms of anxiety and depression that had plagued me earlier in my life. But as it turned out, it was only a respite. They came back with a vengeance once the drugs and alcohol began to reveal the other edge of their swords.

MORE GUILT-RIDDEN JUSTIFICATION

I suppose after experiencing the depth of turmoil and angst that befell me relatively early on in life, that once I found some legitimate relief in the form of alcohol and certain other drugs, it was only natural that I grab onto them with all my might. I remember my older brother Joe asking me once, sometime in my mid twenties: "Gar', how come you drink so much?"

I had replied, in my arrogant tone of the day, "Well, Joe, I'm just trying to kill enough brain cells to lower my intelligence down to that of the average human being so that we can have decent conversations."

He had replied, "Well, you can stop anytime now."

It wasn't like I was loaded 24/7 during all the years I spent in active addiction. Although it was true that, as the years progressed, I imbibed in drugs and alcohol more and more frequently, it wasn't until my forties that my use during daylight hours increased. During my twenties and thirties I managed to stay sober during the day, for the most part. And it wasn't until my late thirties that I started heavily abusing pain medication, which I indulged in regardless of the time of day. And although using cocaine (which began after I left college) during the daytime over the years was certainly not out of the ordinary, the greater percentage of my working hours were spent in a clean and sober state. But when five o'clock hit (or whatever hour my shift ended over the years) it was more often than not party time, particularly on the weekends. The weekends were always party time. And these patterns would continue for many years, until the spring of 1999, when at last I got clean and sober.

But I digress.

ACCEPTING STEEL

Shortly after quitting college I got my start in the world of steel. I was twenty-four years old. My parents were managing an apartment complex at the time. One of their tenants, Joel Madsen, worked at National Steel, located in the industrial section of Northwest Portland. I happened to be in my dad's office when Joel came by to pay his rent. My dad mentioned to him that I was looking for work. Joel told me that they were always bringing new blood through the warehouse, and that I could use his name if I liked. So I went to National Steel and applied.

The personnel that did the hiring reviewed my application and then went to Joel and asked him about me. Joel said, "Who?" Then he thought for a minute and said, "Oh, Swoboda! Yeah, well, I know his dad. Kid seems nice."

That was my "in." They called me for two interviews. One was with the current plant superintendent, and the other was with a guy who would become superintendent a couple of years after I was hired. Their only concern was that I might be over-qualified. They couldn't understand how I was going to be content working in a warehouse when I had all of this education along with a high grade point average. (Four or five years after I was hired, the superintendent would call me into his office and say, "Swoboda, you're an eight cylinder running on four. When are you going to get your act together?" In his mind I'm sure this would have justified his initial interview concern had he recalled it.) I wanted to tell him not to worry about it, but I came up with a bit more of a diplomatic response and the rest, as they say, is historically unalterable. I believe I told him I was just looking for a decent-paying job and that I wouldn't let them down. (The truth was that my plan was to work one year and then quit and collect unemployment for a while. Talk about your heady life ambitions. That was the mind set I went in with anyway. I ended up working for them for almost nine years, and for many more years in the steel industry after that. So much for plans and goals.)

I was hired in April of 1977. Within ninety days I was making $8.00 per hour, which was a lot of money to me. (Minimum wage was $2.30 per hour in those days.) A guy earned more starting out in the warehouse then he could in the office. It *was* hazardous work. The cranes in the shop picked up to fifteen tons of steel at a time.

National Steel was a service center, as opposed to a steel mill. That meant we sold steel products, rather than manufacturing them. Wide-flange beams, angles, flat bars, channels, tubing, pipe, and steel plate were the main commodities. I spent eight and a half years in the warehouse at National Steel, four more in the warehouse at Sanford Steel, a year and a half working for R & S Steel, and about six months at Unity Steel (later bought out by GOM Steel) before moving into the office there. Fifteen long winters in cold, steel warehouses bearing one name or another before I slipped into office work (which I've done for fourteen years and counting as I write this).

Due to a variety of circumstances, I gradually moved into the office (initially splitting time between the warehouse and office). I learned to program parts for burning machines on a CAD system, which meant drawing pictures off of blueprints or sketches onto a computer screen and then downloading them to a burning machine computer. The burning machine torches would then follow the pattern I had drawn and cut the shape from whatever thickness and grade of steel plate the order called for. My employers eventually had me concentrate more on sales as the years progressed, and that's where my later years were focused.

Starting out my first career job in a steel warehouse may have seemed far removed from the business world that I had wanted to avoid, yet I still felt like I was missing something. I had sensed somewhere deep within myself that I was going to feel that way, too. Right from the get-go. At first I ignored it. I was making good money like I had wanted. It seemed like good money to me anyway. Hell, I was twenty-four years old and single with a decent paycheck. From my perspective, I was rich. I could buy anything I wanted, it seemed. I was in hog heaven for a while. But eventually you learn that no amount of money is ever enough. There's always something else you need or something else you want. There always will be until you face the music, I'm thinking. At least with me that's the way it was. I was getting trapped in the very materialistic world I had longed to avoid. It didn't matter that I wasn't wearing a suit and tie. It maybe looked better that way—it looked like I wasn't falling into the trap, but in reality I was.

There was a certain gnawing lack of fulfillment in my life for many years. Whether I worked in the warehouse or later on in the office, I felt like somehow I didn't fit in, like I didn't really belong. And this was tough for me because growing up I had usually felt I fit in. I had always gotten along with all types of personalities, had always been popular with a fairly wide variety of people. But I just didn't ever feel I belonged in the steel world, especially later on when I moved into the office—into the business world. Sales and salesmanship— everybody all excited about dollars and cents and the latest, greatest sale. For a long time I couldn't seem to fully connect with what was going on—but, again, *I know that was just me.* Everyone was contributing something positive to society, weren't they? What was the problem? No problem, it just didn't seem to be for me, that's all. (In later years, I too, became excited about the latest, greatest sale. Well, at least most of the time I did. Well, relatively excited. I have in more recent years been convinced that where I work or what happens in my life doesn't matter nearly so much as does my perception and subsequent handling of these things. We can make a difference and be a positive influence no matter where we are physically placed in this world.)

The hell of it was, I did fairly good in those circles, right from the start. I was able to communicate with customers well. I initially dreaded cocktail parties and lunches and the like, but normally ended up doing pretty well on the social scene. I even enjoyed it for the most part. Yet it still didn't seem quite right to me—it often felt like I was somehow in the wrong room or something. It's difficult to explain. I know I'm not alone. I know many people have felt unfulfilled or out of place in this world, but most learn to accept their lot in life and make the best of it—or at least it always appeared to me that they did. And that's where I fell short for the longest time. I just couldn't seem to do that. And I recognized that this was a shortcoming of *mine*. It was *my* problem. Being aware of that fact somehow made it even tougher to accept. (Self-awareness was not something I usually lacked, and it can be a brutal thing at times.)

I had the same awareness when it came to judging the stress, anxiety, anguish, and depression that overwhelmed me at various stages of my existence. I know that others have suffered these things as well. I know that everyone has had to face hurdles at various junctures in their lives. *No one gets through this life unscathed,* as I heard someone express it. That made it all the more difficult for me to bear the pain, feeling that somehow I was incapable, somehow inadequate because I couldn't handle these internal battles as well as others did.

Yet I also somehow knew that this could not be the entire truth. I sensed that there was no way that everyone on the planet could have experienced the same depth of mental anguish that I had. It seemed inconceivable to me that this could be true. Just as it appears obvious that not all people suffer the same degree of physical pain in this world, logic would dictate that the same must be true of psychic pain. There are degrees of everything in this universe. People on this planet possess varying degrees of physical strength, for example, just as people obviously vary in height, weight, pigmentation and degrees of intelligence. So, too, logic would tell us, must this variety of nature hold true when it came to degrees of mental and emotional pain.

That's certainly not to say that there aren't others who have suffered as much and more than I have—I am not *quite* that self-absorbed. However, I just can't accept that the majority of human beings have undergone similar degrees of mental and emotional anguish in their lives. Not, at least, to the point that their suffering becomes so unbearable and so insoluble in their minds that the only option seemingly available to them is to end their own existence. Suffering to the point where contemplating suicide is not just a passing thought, but the only comforting thought, sometimes lingering for days, weeks, or even months on end.

Whatever the case, I just sensed that not *everyone* had withstood the same level of tortuous thoughts and anxiety, the sadness and depression, and the bouts of anguish and turmoil that had overwhelmed me at various junctures of my journey. For one thing, if they had, I'd have seen some evidence that life was damn near unbearable for most human beings on this planet. There just can't be that many people putting on a happy face most of their damn lives. Can there? What would be the fricking point?

I do have some collaboration, albeit unscientific, for my theory. I have talked to many people who say that although they've certainly felt sad or down before, they have never reached the point where they have wanted to die. The thought of killing themselves, of wanting to end their own existence, has *never* crossed their minds. This is completely mind-boggling to me. What would it be like to have lived a life on this planet for a number of years and not have ever seriously entertained a suicidal thought? Well, I obviously wouldn't know, but I'm thinking it must be pretty cool.

As far as the occupational woes I felt subjected to, why didn't I just shut up or put up? Rather than complain about my situation, why didn't I do something to change my lot in life? *You have to make something happen if you want change,* I would hear from different people. And yet it wasn't like I hadn't pursued other avenues. I had taken a stab at writing, for instance. I wrote because I enjoyed it, and then people began telling me that I had a way with the written word, so I began putting more effort into it. For several years I pursued a career in writing, but to no avail. Several years of rejections from publishers who were unwilling to take a chance on unproven authors (many unwilling to even receive unsolicited submissions, let alone read them) and agents who received most of their clients through referrals, and I began to lose hope as to that particular avenue of escape.

Since I didn't really know what else I wanted to do with my life (when I was growing up I had received a lot of positive reinforcement—people always telling me I had the ability to be anything I wanted to be, not knowing, of course, that I hadn't a clue what I wanted to be), I became more and more discouraged as the years went by. I *never* knew what to do with my life, really, career-wise.

And I had become trapped. Once I was in the steel business for a while, it became all I knew. I didn't know how to gain employment in another field. I certainly couldn't have walked into the same salary doing anything else. My income kept rising with each new job in the industry, and the paying of my bills became dependent upon each new level of income. I became used to a particular lifestyle and later on, after I married and had step-children, felt that my wife and kids were used to a certain standard of living as well. I couldn't let them down.

Knowing all of this, and being aware that I evidently wasn't prepared to change anything about my life, then I should have been mature enough, I know, to accept that this was the course life had laid out for me. Shut up and make the best of it. Face it. Accept it. Stop whining about it. Life is what you make it and all that stuff. Excitement is for race-car drivers and movie stars, and guess what, pal—you ain't neither. Buck up.

At least when I worked in the warehouse there was always the possibility that a cable could break and ten tons of steel could come crashing down around me. That provided some sense of impending excitement. But this office stuff, this business stuff. It just wasn't up my alley. Yet, everyone, various bosses and owners over the years, kept telling me I was good at it. Granted, I liked most of the customers and developed a great rapport with many of them. Some of them I became quite close to personally. And not that I didn't always enjoy the people I worked with in addition to liking most customers. Because I did. I enjoyed them immensely. Whether it was the earlier years in the warehouse or later years in the office, I always enjoyed the people I worked with, and for the most part, *loved* the people I worked with. I developed many close, personal relationships with both coworkers and customers over the years.

But, as I have stated, getting along with people had never been a problem for me. The bottom line is that the work I was engaged in didn't fulfill that sense of wanting to help others that had dug at the core of my being since I was a youngster. Eventually I would begin to fill that void, but it would be many more years before that occurred (and as it turns out, I wouldn't have to leave my occupation to begin doing so).

For years, what I didn't understand was how people came to accept their lot in life. I admired it (or at least envied it, sensing a higher degree of peace in it). I just didn't understand it. The irony was, I had become bored to death in a business job that left me feeling unfulfilled, and twenty years earlier one of the main reasons I had left college was because my business major was boring the hell out of me, and I felt I would never be fulfilled in that field. Talk about your self-fulfilling prophecies.

So, how do so many people learn to settle? How do all these people come to that point in their lives where they say, *Okay, this is it. I accept this as my life?* Is it just maturity? Are they just being realistic, responsible adults? Or is this capacity something that is innate in most people, some part of ordinary human biochemistry that I had evidently missed out on? When they were handing out that "acceptance gene" had I been out getting high or something? Because I was always good at that, I know.

I didn't have any answers. I still haven't reached any definitive conclusions, these many years later. But I did eventually come to believe that I wasn't the odd one. And that's not to say that everyone else was—I just came to believe that for me, personally, it was important to find something in my life that would provide a sense of fulfillment *to me*. And I came to learn that there is a vast difference between acceptance and settling.

Although, in time, I would gradually learn to be much more accepting of my daily place in life (most days, that is), I would also come to know that, armed with the proper desire and motivation, I could effect positive change in my life as well.

TEAMSTER TALK

Those fifteen years working in steel warehouses made for some interesting times. Most of the steel warehousemen in the area belonged to Teamster's Local 206. Working in a building full of Teamster employees could be quite entertaining. My very first morning on the job, I was standing at the supervisor's desk waiting for instructions. Nervous as hell, of course. A very large man came sauntering up to the desk two or three minutes after the start of shift. The supervisor, Jon Lancaster, looked at this guy and said, "Jim, why don't you start loading #11 over there?"

"Fuck you, you rummy cocksucker," replied Jim in a surly tone, then looked over at me and winked. I was rather shocked. This was the first decent-paying job of my life. I figured that things would be pretty serious around there for the kind of money we were being paid. I mean, this was no two-dollar-per-hour mini-mart job. I'm thinking this guy Jim is in big trouble.

"That's *Mister* Cocksucker to you, Jim," the supervisor calmly responded.

Jim grabbed a clipboard from Lancaster and lumbered off, feeling pretty smug, I imagine, about impressing the new kid. And I *was* impressed. *I should have gotten this job a lot sooner,* I was telling myself. *This just can't be too tough a position to hold onto if you can walk around calling your boss a "rummy cocksucker." What a country.*

I ended up having a lot of good times at National Steel. Eight and a half years working with mostly the same guys out in the shop. There were over a hundred workers total on three shifts. I became good friends with quite a few of them.

I met a guy on day shift by the name of Bret Turner who should have been in show business. He was one of the funniest people I had ever met. Everyone knew Bret. He had quite the outgoing personality. At six foot one, he was a tallish, good-looking, thirty-four-year-old man, with light-brown hair and blue eyes. He was ten years older than me and could have passed for my age. Aging like young Dick Clark, he was, on a diet which included fairly regular consumption of alcoholic beverages along with a couple of other substances that can't be found at your local grocery store. Bret's mind was as sharp as a tack, and he had probably the quickest wit I'd ever had the pleasure of sharing atmosphere with. I don't mean to insinuate for even one second that mind-altering particulates may have contributed to his youthful looks, quick wit, or sharp mind. Some people are just quite obviously born with better genes (or more brain cells) to begin with, and some are evidently born with a higher capacity to withstand bombardment of these cells, I suppose.

Regardless of genetics and brain-cell theories, Bret became my best friend at National Steel. Our senses of humor meshed really well. We car-pooled together and partied together. For me, this meant abuse of alcohol as well as other substances, which included cocaine. I obviously hadn't, as yet, learned my lesson about drugs. (I had never claimed to know what was good for me and what wasn't.) However, after my earlier disastrous experience with drugs, I had become very cautious (well, as cautious as one can be, I suppose, when experimenting with uncontrolled substances) about what sort of drug I would take into my system. "Cautious" meaning I wouldn't ingest any substance that might induce paranoia. And cocaine, at least for me, and at least with "just" snorting it, didn't produce symptoms of paranoia. It didn't mess with my mind the way psychedelics did. It just made me feel alert and good. Well, "good" for a while, anyway. Eventually it did get to me, of course, but in the beginning it seemed like relatively harmless fun. I'm certainly not recommending it—in fact just the opposite. Some people try it and never like it. They're the lucky ones. Because if you like it the way I did, it gradually begins to rob you of your life, your freedom. You can hardly think about anything else (and this, I found out after many years of dedicated research, was true for any drug, including alcohol—if you're an addict of my nature). Even if you go a few weeks without it, it's always in the back of your mind, a subtle (sometimes not so subtle) gnawing in your subconscious: *Sure would be nice to do a little line about now,* you're thinking, whenever you're tired or whenever you're out on the town, or sometimes just whenever. You start to think you need the crap to have a good time—and as long as you're thinking like that it's going to ring true. And then there are the physical side effects: lying in bed trying to sleep with your heart pounding at an insane rate, the unceasing drum of it resonating furiously in your ears, each maddening pulse a reminder that once again you had gone too far. Enough to drive you crazy. Nights like that got really old after a while. Really old.

The first time I tried coke was at a party with some friends. I made everyone convince me several times that the stuff wasn't like LSD or mescaline or any other mind-altering drug before I finally gave in and tried it. They were right. At least in the beginning it doesn't mess with your mind. Sure, it alters something—why else would anyone pay that kind of money for it? It was a deceivingly mellow alteration, is all. The fact of the matter is when we first started using cocaine there were actually magazine articles coming out saying how it might be the safest street drug around. As if we didn't already have enough trouble resisting the junk.

I had a neighbor who dabbled in distribution of the white powder and that kept me in supply. He also worked down the street from National Steel and would car pool off and on with me over the years. He had spent time in a federal prison for a drug-related offense, and although the statute of limitations on this sort of crime has long since expired, he shall remain nameless. (No one need be unnecessarily implicated here.) We made all kinds of trips to the bathrooms in bars in those days, but more often than not we were brazen enough to do a line of cocaine on whatever happened to be nearby: pool table rails, bar counters, tables, etc.

There were a number of us at National Steel that abused drugs, some more than others. I did coke once in a while at work, but for the most part saved it for recreational use. It was the same with alcohol—there were days I drank my lunch, but those days were relatively rare compared to some of the other guys (particularly on the night shifts).

After my initial month of training on day shift, I was transferred to graveyard. I spent a year and a half on that shift before having enough seniority to take a vacant day-shift position. During my stint on graveyard I worked with a couple of guys who smoked quite a bit of dope on the job. They were in their early forties, army veterans who had served together and were from the same small town in Eastern Oregon. Harold and James. They were good guys with great senses of humor. I'd been on the job only a few weeks and had gotten to know them pretty well. I learned to love those guys almost from the onset of our meeting.

One night James came back from lunch having just smoked a joint with Harold. Now these two were peas in a pod in a lot of respects, but when it came to drugs, Harold had a natural affinity for them, whereas James wasn't quite as adaptable. He came back from break on this particular evening and started running the crane. (They didn't like the rookies to run the crane because we were too damn slow. Of course, we could never learn to be quicker if we didn't get some experience with the damn things. I became the same impatient bastard with new guys after I had been there awhile. Never-ending cycle.)

There were about fifteen thousand pounds of steel floating near our heads as James ran the crane. He reeked of pot, and his eyes were reddish and glazed over. After a couple of minutes of maneuvering this load, James suddenly turned to me and said, very earnestly, "Am I doing okay?" His fingers had stopped working the buttons on the crane box. "Because I'd sure as hell hate to hurt anybody."

Now, I'd only been around steel and cranes for about three weeks, and I was still pretty much in awe of the amount of tonnage being moved around in these buildings. And here's some guy who'd been there fourteen years asking me, the rookie, if he's doing okay.

"Hell, I don't know, James," I replied. "You're doing fine, I guess." Nothing seemed to be falling. Yeah, I felt pretty safe.

But all things are relative. Some of the guys on swing shift were *really* into their drug use at work. There were a few of them that made any of these other guys look like amateur imbibers. I had been on day shift for almost four years when circumstances beyond my control got me bumped to swing shift, where I became a first-hand witness to this drug abuse. After I'd worked at National Steel for about five years they acquired another steel company, Gifford Steel. National bought them out and dovetailed the seniority from both shops. "Dovetailed" meant that instead of putting people from the acquired plant on the bottom of the seniority list, they allowed them to retain their seniority and mixed it in with ours, year for year. Now, seniority was *the* sacred cow in unions. It was what had allowed me to get to day shift (which was, by far, the most popular shift) after a year and a half on graveyard (a comparatively short period of time). We thought the dove-tailing was highly unfair, since we were, after all, the mother company, but we also sympathized with the Gifford employees and knew it wasn't their fault the decision had been made.

When I found out that I was being transferred to swing shift, I thought it was the end of the world. I was devastated. When I was first informed of my shift move I immediately broke down and lit up a cigarette. (I hadn't smoked a cigarette on the floor of the shop in almost two years. It had been a self-imposed restriction to help cut down on my smoking. During that time I only smoked at breaks. It had been quite an achievement, quite a test of willpower for me, and I had been very religious about my floor-time abstinence.)

There was an older guy named Burt Rice working with me when they came and notified me of my shift transfer. Burt watched as I whipped out a cigarette and lit it. He started grinning—that sly, silly grin of his. "You crack pretty easy, don't you, son?" he quipped, and threw back that big head of his and started laughing. As upset as I was, Burt's remark made me chuckle. (I agree that laughter *is* the best medicine. Trust me on this; I've tried all the others.)

So, off I went to swing shift, cigarettes in tow. Now, I thought I had met some real druggies in my days, but apparently I hadn't even come close. I had heard tales of their insanity but had never witnessed it first hand. There was a group of five or six guys on swing shift that really liked to party. I mean *really* liked to party. They were animals—in fact one of them was nicknamed "Animal." They were great workers, every last one of them, but good God, they were out of control.

My very first night on swing shift I was coming back after first break, and I saw Animal coming from the parking lot, the preferred break venue for the gang. He came walking up to me, his eyes all red and bugged out, and blurted, "I just had two shots of whiskey, a beer, two pink hearts (speed), half a joint, and a bowl of hashish." This is in less than fifteen minutes! He started walking away and then suddenly whipped his head around like Linda Blair on crack and said to me, "Coke's comin' at eight!"

I was appropriately impressed and decided to steer clear of those fellows for a while, at least while any of them were running a crane. As it turned out, the plant manager got to spying on these guys one night. He perched himself on the roof of the company next door sporting his 35 mm Pentax.

The next day the plant manager had a meeting with both "days" and "swing" at shift change. He was actually pretty cool about it for him. He told everyone how shocked he was at what he had seen. He said someone from swing shift had complained about a group of guys indulging on the job. He reminded everyone how dangerous it was to be intoxicated at the plant. He said he had pictures of guys drinking beer, peeing on the side of the building, and smoking stuff that didn't look much like cigarettes. He said he had a 400 mm telescopic lens on his camera and that he could tell us not only what brand of beer these guys were drinking, but where it had been made. He ended up the meeting by saying he was moving a couple of the night shift gang to day shift in an effort to disband the offending group.

I never did find out how well that worked. Soon after that, I ended up getting transferred to the old Gifford plant in the Willbridge industrial area a few miles away. Or "Swillbridge" as we liked to call it. Damp, dark and dirty. "The Toxic Waste-pit of Oregon" one magazine article had actually termed the area. There was a battery manufacturer on one side of us with a fluorescent green pond sitting between our properties where old batteries had been dumped for years. A chlorine manufacturer directly across the street from us had some sort of spill every couple of months or so (an alarm would go off and we would run from the warehouse into the office, which was more enclosed. Chlorine is invisible and odorless—and deadly). Directly to the south of us Shell Oil had a ton of those mammoth gas tanks all lined up nice and pretty. And last, but not least, was a plant that manufactured *Sevin,* a pesticide produced from methyl isocyanate gas (the very same chemical that had killed over three thousand people at the Union Carbide plant in Bhopal, India in 1984, not too long before I was transferred to Willbridge).

In spite of the toxicity surrounding us, I didn't mind working at Willbridge. It was much more laid back over there. Everyone got their work done, but the atmosphere was looser. All the bigwigs were at the other plant. I got to know a lot of people that I hadn't known very well and developed as deep a comradery with them as I had with the guys at the other plant. And, of course, we partied a lot together.

SINGING WITHOUT A LICENSE

One of the things that I consider a positive aspect (on most occasions) of my drinking days was the unabashed willingness of some of my friends and me to sing whenever the mood struck us. Although there were several Christmas seasons where a group of us became engaged in door-to-door caroling, it wasn't like we needed a holiday setting to spur us to sing. Yuletide songs, Irish songs, contemporary songs, songs from the old days—we didn't care. We just liked to sing. And though we may not have sung particularly well, we sang with great passion.

There was the time, somewhere in the mid-seventies, that six of us decided to go to a University of Oregon football game being played in Seattle. We thought it would be fun to take the train up to the Emerald City—a nice three-hour ride on the rails. We had a friend who lived in Seattle and had agreed to pick us up at the depot when we arrived. So Drew Olsen, Gabe Unser, Ken Matthews, Dale Ford, Mick Evans, and I bought tickets, and away we went.

The first thing we did after finding our seats, of course, was head straight to the lounge car. We befriended the bartender for a few minutes, telling him we hoped he was ready to go to work because we aimed to do some serious partying. We sensed that he was looking at us as if we weren't your average sort of Amtrak clientele, but he was amicable nonetheless.

As we were conversing with our newfound close friend, Dale asked him how many Budweisers he had on board. He opened a door underneath the counter and counted up his cases. He gave us a tally: "One hundred and sixty-four cans." I remember Dale asking him if he'd ever run out before. The bartender chuckled and said, "No." Dale told him to get ready because he was going to run out on this trip. The guy laughed like Dale was either kidding or crazy and went back to wiping down the bar.

Ten minutes outside of Seattle we meandered back to the lounge car for the umpteenth time and Dale asked the barkeep how many "Buds" he had left. A big grin came to the guy's face when he saw what was left of his stock.

"Six," he said with a smile.

"We'll take 'em!" Dale shouted out, somewhat proud of the accuracy of his earlier prediction.

Now, of course, the six of us hadn't drunk all those beers. We most certainly had help. We drank more than our fair share, mind you, but we'd also been at least partially responsible for helping to put the entire train in a partying mood that Friday evening.

Because I had figured we would probably "break into song" at some point during this commute, I'd brought copies of the words to "Hey, Good Lookin'," a song from my dad's era. (I'd gotten the lyrics by playing an old 78 record of his.) My friends and I had sung the song before, loving how it started out, but we had never gotten very far because we didn't know many of the words. I had taken the initiative to listen to my dad's record and copy them down.

We sang this and several other songs on the train, getting the people in our car involved before we moved onto each of the other cars, starting a sing-along in every one of them. It's amazing how complete strangers will join in with you if you're enthusiastic and cheerful, which we were. Most of them were quite a bit older than we were, but the spirit of youth can be contagious. Our "golden oldies" musical selection didn't hurt either, I'm sure. All in all, I'm confident that the party atmosphere created by our singing contributed significantly to the consumption of those 164 cans of beer.

As can be seen, my friends and I enjoyed a good sing-along well before this Karaoke stuff came into vogue. In fact, Mick Evans and I were actually arrested once for singing in a bar. Well, at least that was the initial reason for the cops showing up in the first place. There were a bunch of us sitting around Patty's (a relatively nice bar in downtown Portland) one night, and about one o'clock in the morning we started singing songs. For the most part, our group of friends' musical tastes leaned toward rock, as I have mentioned—Stones, Dylan, Beatles, Clapton, Cocker, Skynryd, Hendrix, etc. Most of us didn't mind a little country now and then as well—Willie, Waylon, and the boys. And, of course, you've got to throw in The King and Ray Charles and, well, we liked most kinds of music, truth be known. But the music best suited for "singing along" has to be those golden oldies from my dad's era: "You Are My Sunshine," "Hey Good-Lookin'," "My Wild Irish Rose," etc. Of course "God Bless America" was a good one to really belt out and always a crowd pleaser.

So here we were in this bar having a good ol' time when the manager came over and told us we couldn't sing in there. In a bar, for God's sake (and singing some Irish songs in an Irish-named bar, to boot). Well, we pretty much informed him that not only *could* we sing in the bar, but that we actually *were* singing in the bar and that we were going to *continue* singing in the bar on account of this was the United States of America, and we were free to do as we pleased as long as we weren't bothering anyone. And we weren't. A few ladies had joined us at our tables and were singing along with us. The rest of the people in the bar were either laughing or clapping for us when we finished a song. It was after one o'clock in the morning, and it *was* a bar, for God's sake, lest we forget where we were.

So we kept singing. About twenty minutes later two uniformed policemen came into the bar. They looked over at the manager, and he nodded toward us. The cops walked over and informed us that the manager had requested we stop singing.

We couldn't believe that this guy had actually called the cops on us for singing in a bar. And when we couldn't believe something we usually let our feelings be known in one manner or another. So Mick Evans and I impulsively jumped to our feet and arm in arm started blasting out the best damn rendition of "God Bless America" ever sung in a Northwest Portland bar at one-thirty in the morning. The policemen stood there with scowls on their faces and actually let us sing ninety percent of the song. Truly. We were really getting into it by then.

"God Bless America, land that I love.
Stand beside her, and guide her,
With the light that shines from above.
From the mountains, to the prairies,
To the oceans WHITE WITH FOOOOOOOAM!"
(You really have to whale on "WHITE WITH FOOOOOOOAM!")
"Go—

Cut us off right in the middle of "God"—how rude. They didn't even have the decency to let us show off our rousing finale. They looked at the manager, who had been standing next to them, and when he nodded, the two cops, like puppets on a string, reached out and grabbed each of us by the arm. They grabbed us by our biceps and squeezed hard (hard enough to leave bruises the next day). They dragged us out of the bar while everyone in the bar proceeded to "boo" them. They got us outside on the sidewalk, and Mick and I started mouthing off to them a little bit—okay, maybe a little more than a little bit—okay, maybe quite a bit more than a little bit. After a couple of minutes of our rebellious back talk, which included us threatening to sue them for police brutality, they decided that they had heard enough from us.

One of them finally exclaimed, "Okay, boys. That's enough. You're under arrest."

"You can't arresht us…"

Well apparently, they could.

We were protesting all the more vehemently as they were cuffing us, when we were suddenly interrupted by a huge chorus of *God Bless America.* Everyone in the bar had filed out onto the sidewalk, and they were all standing arm in arm crooning the most beautiful version of "God Bless America" we'd ever heard.

"Look at that! You can't arresht us—the people are behin' us!" Mick cried out, sounding quite a bit like Foster Brooks (I never said we were sober).

As they were leading us to the squad car, the crowd stopped singing briefly, as if they couldn't believe that we really *were* going to be arrested for singing "God Bless America" *in* America. But they started right back up again as the cops were putting us into the car.

Well, Mick and I just didn't know when to shut up. (I had been told that once or twice before in my life.) In the car we kept after them, Mick going with the police-brutality approach, and me suddenly thinking that telling them about my college education would be a good idea. (Ah, the sharp intuition of a rum-soaked mind. It's a beautiful thing.)

"Lookie here, partner! We got us a college boy in the back seat."

"Wow! Maybe we should let him go," the other cop replied, as they broke into laughter.

Very funny.

They ended up merely taking us to a drunk tank facility in Northeast Portland. They told us if we could get someone more sober than we were to drive us home that we wouldn't have to spend the night.

"That shouldn't be too tough," I told them.

We called Gabe, knowing he was probably home because he had gone out with his girlfriend, Molly Lorenzo, that night. They were in bed asleep when we called. Gabe showed up at the facility looking like death warmed over, shaking his head in a gesture muddled somewhere between irritation and amusement, and shouted out to the police officers on duty, "Where do I sign for these boys?"

Arrested for singing "God Bless America" in a bar in America.

All things considered, we didn't think our singing had really been that bad.

And our singing wasn't always bad enough to land us in jail. Although we tested our careers in a number of places, bars and wedding receptions seemed to be our most frequent venues. There were times that a couple of us would end up on stage with a friendly musical group who'd humor us long enough to let us join them for a song or two.

My best friend from high school, Duane Keaton, was one of the first of our group to get married. His and Kathy's wedding took place in her home town— Coos Bay, Oregon. The night before the wedding there was a large group of us in the lounge at the Thunderbird Motel where we were all staying. The parents of both the bride and the groom, everyone in the wedding party, a lot of Duane's friends, and a smattering of locals filled the lounge to capacity that evening. There was a one-man-band playing that night. The guy had an organ and a guitar and was very entertaining. Duane's dad kept buying us drinks from across the room, so we were toasting him all night. Everyone appeared to be having a good time.

The musician took a break around ten o'clock, and suddenly Mick Evans was up there on the microphone starting a chorus of "Kansas City." We began singing along, and the next thing you know Ken got up there behind the organ. He didn't have a clue how to play that thing. It didn't matter—Evans didn't know how to sing, either, and that wasn't stopping him. I looked over at the musician, and he was grinning from ear to ear as Matthews and Evans began their little duet. Well, what they needed up there was someone that didn't know how to play that guitar, either—to kind of blend in with them. So I sauntered up to the stage, slung that guitar strap around my neck like I knew what I was doing and started strumming that sucker. Sounded pretty good, too, I thought, and then the musician came over and turned it on for me.

A motley trio we made, for sure. Evans started making up a song, belting out, "I saw my baby walkin' on down the street." At which point Matthews and I would hit equally off-key chords on our respective instruments. And yet,

I don't think we sounded all that bad, at least not to a roomful of drunks. People in the lounge seemed to get a kick out of our short-lived musical careers.

And we didn't get taken to the drunk tank that night.

GUNS AND AIRPORTS

Speaking of wedding weekends, it was a memorable occasion when my good friend Don Dryden married his girlfriend, Linda Davenport, in Toule Lake, California. But as much fun as I'm sure we thought we all had in Toule Lake, the most memorable event came on the return trip. (Well, for me, at least. I'm sure Don and Linda have different high points.)

Jack and Drew Olsen, Pam Letterman, Jerry Foxx, and I had flown to Klamath Falls, Oregon (the closest airport to Toule Lake) from Portland. Upon arriving at Klamath Falls Airport for our return flight, we were all pretty hung over. Okay, again—*really* hung over. So, while waiting for our plane, we sat in the lounge, and the others had some "hair of the dog" in an attempt to alleviate a portion of their pain. I was feeling *so-o-o-o* bad that I didn't participate in the "dog hair" that morning. It made me ill to even think about it.

When it came time to board the plane we hobbled into line to go through security. As we approached the gate, I noticed that they were opening everyone's bags. This seemed highly unusual, but then again, we had never been to Klamath Falls Airport before—maybe this was routine. However, we weren't concerned because we had nothing to hide (at least not on this particular occasion).

That is, until a thought struck me. I turned to Jack, who was standing behind me and whispered, "Jack, I've got a gun in my suitcase."

Jack looked at me with a silly grin on his face (as only Jack could do with such a statement) and said, "You've got a *what*?"

"I've got a cork gun in my suitcase, lying smack dab on top of everything."

"What in the hell are you doing with a cork gun?" Jack asked, starting to laugh that great laugh of his.

"I don't know. I won it in a carnival recently. I saw it in one of my dresser drawers as I was packing and thought it might be fun to shoot someone at the hotel," I replied with chagrin.

Jack, deadpan: "Let me go first."

This cracked me up. "Okay, but stay close. I may need you." Jack was (and is) an attorney.

As we drew nearer to inspection I was getting more nervous while Jack was becoming more amused, as were the others now. (I had whispered to them my dilemma.) Jack got through the inspection and then stopped and waited for me. He was not about to miss this for anything.

What could I do? The expressions on the security staff were priceless as they opened my suitcase. Talk about your Kodak moments. It was right out of a Seinfeld episode as I stood there with a sheepish Kramer grin on my face. The man slowly—I mean *very slowly*—picked up my "gun" with two fingers, holding it gingerly, as if he were handling nitroglycerin. He was having a bit of fun with this one.

"Sir?" That was all he could get out. Evidently, his first red-and-black pirate-dragoon-cork-gun experience.

"Yes, sir?" I replied with all the intelligence and sincerity I could muster.

"*What*—is this?" And as if this wasn't humiliating enough, he glanced down at the I.D. that I had handed him and added with great audibility, **"Mr. Swoboda?"**

I cleared my throat. "It's a cork gun." There was a cork sticking out of the end of it to prove my point.

"Yes, I can see that," he replied. "But *why?*"

"I don't know." (Jack was now beside himself, I was catching out of the corner of my eye. His hand was over his mouth in a vain effort to hide his glee, and I was thinking that he had never had this much fun witnessing the pain of another.) "I just thought—well, just for fun." Saving face was now out of the question—that was long gone. "It's just a cork gun. Is that really a problem?"

He looked at his side-kick. "What do you think, Louise?" (Or whatever her name was.) Louise must have been the resident cork gun expert.

"I'm not sure," she replied, as I was holding up the line of people, all of whom, of course, were undoubtedly staring at me and my cork gun with mixed feelings of amusement, bemusement, pity, disdain, etc.

"Maybe if it was *all* red," Louise finally surmised.

"Yeah," replied Al (or whatever *his* name was).

At this point I made a tactical decision. I would give up the cork gun. I *really did like that cork gun*, but I was willing to give it up to get out of there and get the line moving again. "You guys can keep the gun," I said. "Really—I don't need it." (That was a very obvious remark, in retrospect.)

"That's okay, **Mr. Swoboda**," Al said. (He kept having to repeat my name loudly.) "We can have it checked out."

"No, really," I protested. "It's okay! You guys can keep the…"

It was too late. Al had whispered to another guard, who was now carrying the "gun" toward the gate. "He's going to ask the pilot if it's okay," Al said to me.

Oh, my God! These people were actually serious. They were honestly going to run this red-and-black carnival cork gun out to the plane and ask the fricking *pilot* if I could keep it. I was twenty-five years old—I honestly felt I could survive without it, sad though that thought was to me (I didn't say I was a mature twenty-five-year-old). Man, these small airports are very accommodating, but I'm done with this.

"Really, this isn't necessary," I pleaded. But it's in the works. I can't stop the entire Klamath Falls Airport Security Staff single-handedly. After all, there must have been two or three of them.

But the guy never made it past the gate. The uniformed cop at the door stopped him and looked at the cork gun. (Everyone wanted in on the action.) After a brief discussion (thirty seconds that seemed like an eternity to me, standing there red-faced while Jack and the others were no longer attempting to stifle their amusement), the guy headed back toward us, cork gun in tow.

"He says it won't fly," the guard said to Al. (A little airport humor?) "He said if it were all red, it might work. But the pilot would never allow the black handle. Might panic someone."

"Honestly, I wasn't going to brandish my cork gun," I said in my defense.

"**Mr. Swoboda**," (a littler louder with the name—the people on that incoming flight may not have heard you) "we can't allow this on board," Al said. "But if you let me jot down your address, we could have it sent to you."

Very accommodating, these Klamath Falls people. "No, seriously—it's okay," I replied. "I'll just say my good-byes to it and let it go." They finally accepted my willingness to part with my toy.

So, the cork-gun saga was over. We were allowed to board the plane unshackled.

The only other thing I remember about the trip home was asking one of the stewardesses if they had anything that would help a hangover. She returned a minute later, sashaying down the aisle cheerfully singing, "Plop, plop, fizz, fizz! Oh, what a relief it is!"

Yes, very friendly and accommodating in Klamath Falls, Oregon.

I've never been back.

I do wonder from time to time how Corky is doing.

BAR STOOLS AND BACHELOR PARTIES

My friends and I, for the most part, all had similar philosophies in life. We were of the peace-loving hippie era—live and let live. (In spite of my penchant for occasionally inflicting pain on inanimate objects, which ceased altogether sometime in my mid-twenties, I was almost always kind to *living* beings.) It seemed to be a much friendlier time back in the seventies, which is when our decade of fun and debauchery took place. I was in my twenties from '73 to '83, as were most of my friends. We had a wide circle of comrades, very close and very loyal and very peaceful for the most part.

But harmless, friendly, peace-loving people that we normally were, it got dull out there sometimes, and once in a while one of us felt compelled to take steps to eradicate that cancer of boredom. Sometimes it was my turn, sometimes it was someone else's. And, yes, for better or worse, it usually involved alcohol consumption.

Although I was primarily interested in peace, on occasion my mouth would get me into trouble. Sometimes, it was completely innocent—like when I got thrown off of a bar stool (from behind) at the Sandy Jug tavern in Northeast Portland because a man felt my language wasn't appropriate for his wife's ears. I mean, after all, it *was* a tavern, and you just don't use foul language in taverns. (It was taking me awhile to figure out the rules. Okay, so no swearing or singing in bars or taverns.)

At other times my getting into trouble wasn't completely innocent. Like I said, there were nights when the boredom just didn't mingle appropriately with alcohol, and it was up to someone in our group to liven things up a bit. Though we would at times push the envelope just to see how close we could come to getting smacked by some innocent victim; the real goal was to talk our way out of these things before that happened. Yes, this is called "sick behavior." However, in our defense, it was an extremely rare occasion when something like this occurred. Out of the thousands of nights we went out over the years, this particular form of pushing the envelope only transpired on a handful of occasions. For one thing, I personally didn't find getting hit in the face by another man's fist all that pleasurable. (During all those fights with my older brother as we were growing up, though they were fairly vicious at times, the face hitting had generally been off limits, but it did occur once in a while, and I found that I wasn't all that fond of it.) And although I seemed to be really quite adept at avoiding this fist-to-face calamity as an adult, I didn't want to push my luck *too* often.

In fact, I've only been hit in the face once in my adult life. And this "once" was by someone I knew, at a bachelor party many years ago. A guy we went to high school with, Billy Buchanan, possessed a different attitude than the people I normally hung with. He didn't seem to mind getting hit in the face. Nor, evidently, did he mind striking other humans in this manner from time to time. Usually this would occur with complete strangers—but since there were only one or two people at this party that Billy didn't know, when he found himself "in the mood" that night, there were very few targets to lash out at. (Billy liked to hit multiple objects when he got in the mood.)

Billy was six-foot-five, two hundred fifty pounds of pure, iron-pumping muscle. Not exactly the best guy in the world to be the only person to hit you in the face in your adult life. But it was primarily an accident. (Billy might be reading this, or having someone read it to him, and I don't want to tick him off again.) He got into a little scuffle with someone who actually was a stranger to him—Dennis Price, a friend of the groom, who happened to be one of the gentlest souls in the world. When people attempted to calm Billy down, he just started swinging, like a windmill run amok. Making full use of my impaired judgment, I was one of those who attempted to be a calming influence. I simply looked at him as he was going berserk in the front yard where the party was being held and said, "Hey, Billy! Cool it!"

He moved very swiftly for a man of his size, I must say. I had been intelligent enough to remain a good (what I thought was safe) distance from Billy when I had yelled out to him. But he covered that ten or twelve feet in less than two seconds, and the next thing I knew my body was literally flying through the air. I did a one and a half gainer, landing on my side on the lawn (about a "nine point five," I'm thinking). And that had been his *left* hand. I started to get up and then thought better of it. Playing dead seemed a far better decision. Within seconds the father of the groom was hovering over me and saying, "Are you all right, son?"

I assured Mr. Nelson that I was fine. A mere five or ten minutes later, shortly after the melee had ended, Billy had his arm around me, contritely remarking, "I hit you too, didn't I, little buddy?"

I nodded in the affirmative, unsure of where he was going with this. Billy proceeded to apologize, saying that when things get going he kind of loses it. Well, that much I could agree with. I accepted his apology, of course. The man *was* a giant, after all.

As the years went by, the hangovers from these alcohol-related episodes were becoming increasingly tiresome. As I began to combine cocaine use more frequently with my alcohol use, the physical after-effects became even more debilitating. Though I rarely missed work because of my drinking and using, I spent many a shift feeling as though I'd almost rather be dead than to be feeling like I was. There were many days at work that I had to manage on very little (or no) sleep and was hung over like a dog. (Where do they come up with some of these expressions? I know very few alcoholic canines.)

After I got married, my hanging out with the gang diminished greatly, as did most of my wild behavior. However, I was still drinking at home and still abusing the evil white powder. During my five years on swing shift, I spent many a night after work at Red's Sidetrack Inn or the Blue Owl, the local watering holes. It was surprising how inebriated one could get in a period of about two and a half hours (before the bars closed). Although swing shift afforded me the opportunity to sleep it off the next morning, I still reported to work many an afternoon feeling downright lousy.

My addiction gradually progressed over the years—but addiction is such a subtle foe that one hardly notices this progression. I always had a good job, kept the bills paid, had decent cars, eventually bought a home, was a good husband and a good father to my stepsons. On the surface, things seemed pretty good. But the fact of the matter is, there was always that part deep within me that knew I was covering up, that knew I was wearing a mask that would eventually have to come off, or that would eventually kill me.

Although I kept up the surface image, as addicts are often adept at doing, I was ever so slowly unraveling. And although I was a pretty good husband, I could have been a better one without the drugs and alcohol. The same thing could be said about my parenting. I treated my stepsons as if they were my own, but my drinking and using sometimes caused me to be neglectful of my fatherly duties. Not to any great extent (and when, in my early recovery, I made amends to my sons for any neglect that might have occurred, they appeared to not know what I was talking about), but I know it existed to some degree.

It was in the last eight or nine years of my active addiction (after the kids were grown) that my drinking and using became more of a problem. It was my wife, Judy, who was the recipient of most of my neglect. It was in those later years, although I had stopped using cocaine (after 1990 I never touched it again), that I became a man possessed in pursuit of narcotic pain medication. It was in the pursuit of these narcotics that my neglect really gathered momentum. I spent countless hours away from home chasing this particular form of escape. I had simply traded one drug for another—a tactic that never benefits an addict, and most assuredly never benefits those around him. Eventually I would incorporate heroin into my using, a move that would (ironically, I suppose) facilitate the end of my days of active addiction.

But for a few more years, at least, although there were definitely some rough bumps in the road, my life would appear to be relatively normal (a term I'm not sure really exists in this realm). So, on I went with my life, pretending as if everything was cool, yet always knowing deep down that it truly wasn't.

PEBBLE BEACH AND PEPPERMINT PATTY

In the summer of 1979 Gabe Unser and Mick Evans piled into my 1970 Buick Wildcat, and we embarked on a ten-day vacation that included some rather memorable moments. The first stop was San Francisco, where we spent a couple of days hitting the sights.

We had taken a supply of drugs with us on this trip, of course: a fair amount of cocaine, a number of "cross-tops" (speed, so named because the pills had lines etched both ways on the surface), and a bit of pot, of which I no longer imbided in much. (As I mentioned, since having my bad trip the pot made me too paranoid, and I could never figure out a way to enjoy paranoia.)

On our second night in San Francisco we piled into a cab. We had left my car at the motel, leaving the driving up to the professionals that night. As we were making our way to wherever the hell we were going, Gabe (ever befriending strangers, a truly loveable quality of his) decided to ask the cabbie if he would like to do a line. The cab driver, who happened to be black (George Carlin had a humorous routine where he denounced people who used this expression: "How can someone just *happen to be black*? It's not like it's an accident"), grinned and nodded yes.

After we each did a couple of lines, it was decided that the more urgent destination would be back to the motel to get more cocaine (we had left some behind in an ever-vain effort to control our use, hoping to stretch out our rapidly diminishing supply).

I don't recall what happened that night, but I do remember that with great restraint we managed to save enough cocaine to last us through the next couple of days. Gabe, Mick, and I headed to Carmel the next day, where we secured a hotel room, and then went out for dinner and drinks to discuss our upcoming plans. We had brought our golf clubs on the trip and had been debating whether or not to play Pebble Beach. Mick was a pretty good golfer and really wanted to play that course. Gabe and I were hackers (still are), but we wanted to play, too. After all, it *was* Pebble Beach. However, the greens fees back then were $50 apiece. This may seem like a relatively paltry sum now, considering the course, but back then it was quite a chunk of change. (An average public course cost around $12 back then. Pebble Beach greens fees as I write this are somewhere around $400, so adjusting for inflation, you can begin to see how much $50 would seem like back in 1979.) Gabe was just beginning his career in dentistry at the time, and Mick and I had decent-paying jobs, but fifty bucks was still a lot of money. This Pebble Beach thing was a fairly major decision for us.

We sat in The Hogsbreath Inn (a bar situated in the heart of Carmel and owned by Clint Eastwood), discussing the affordability of our golf fantasy. At one point, as Mick was heading to the bathroom, he was hit on by a gay man. As Mick was conversing with him, the bartender confided to us that the man was "queer as a three dollar bill" and was the son of a prominent owner of an NFL team. Gabe and I watched with interest as Mick dealt with his new suitor. Within a couple of minutes Mick was smiling and nodding in our direction. The next thing I know, the guy is heading our way. He plopped himself down on the barstool next to me and introduced himself. We talked a couple of minutes before he asked me if I would like to go to his room and share a bottle of wine with him. I politely declined.

Gabe seemed to delight in ribbing Mick and me about our new acquaintance, that is until the man came over and started putting the move on *him*. It was time to turn the tables on Gabe, pointing out that at least we must have been more attractive since the man had hit on us first. We weren't bringing up the rear, so to speak. (In truth, Gabe is a very nice-looking man, who "happens to be Japanese.") Gabe, ever the good sport, chuckled that great chuckle of his.

A little while later, an attractive older lady (older to us) in her late thirties came up to us and asked me if I would like to dance. I commented that there was no dance floor, but she took my hand and lured me off the barstool and proceeded to put her arms around me. We started slow dancing to the soft music that was playing in the background. She told me she was bored with her older (it's all relative) husband, who was sitting over in the corner of the bar. We were not very far into our newfound romance when the bartender interrupted us to tell us there was no dancing allowed in Carmel. (It really was becoming a problem assimilating all the rules in life. Okay, no singing in bars,

143

no swearing in taverns, and evidently no dancing in Carmel, California.) *No dancing in Carmel?* What in the hell was that?

I expressed my disbelief to the bartender and told him that I assumed he was joking. He assured me he was not. There was actually a city ordinance prohibiting dancing. I, of course, having learned apparently nothing from being arrested for singing in a bar a couple of years prior, told the bartender what a really sad law that was and that we were going to continue to dance. I really hadn't wanted to dance to begin with, given that there was no one else dancing in the place, but now that I was being told I *couldn't*, I felt compelled to continue. Call it maturity, call it gifted insight—call it whatever.

Fortunately, the lady's husband saw fit to come over and irksomely ask his wife if she was going to leave with him *or what?* She kissed me on the cheek before dutifully sauntering off into the night with her mate. Consequently, I wasn't able to test Carmel's little law to the fullest. Although, had the barkeep threatened to call the police, I feel confident I would have backed off given that we were in a strange town with an assortment of illicit drugs in our car. (I was defiant, but not altogether daft.)

The bartender had not been being unfriendly. In fact, the guy had been quite hospitable up to that point. I think he was just afraid one of the other patrons might get upset—you know how upsetting it is to see two people slow dancing in a bar. Well, try to imagine it being upsetting. Anyway, the bartender was kind enough to warn us as we were leaving that we had better be careful driving in Carmel. He said, "The cops hang outside the bars looking for drunk people and will arrest you for *walking* crooked in this town." Hospitable place.

So, in addition to being relatively smashed, we were now also paranoid. Rather than risk being busted for the drugs we had in the car, we decided, in our infinite wisdom, that we should hide them somewhere in town before we drove back to the hotel (which was a few miles south of Carmel). As with most things decided in the heat of the intoxicated moment, this turned out to be a far less than brilliant move. Nonetheless, we hid the cocaine, speed, and pot in a planter on a sidewalk in downtown Carmel.

Hastening back the next morning to reclaim our stash, we pulled onto the street we had remembered hiding them on only to discover that we had stuffed them in a planter directly outside of a fire station. This would have been bad enough, but there was actually a fireman outside on the sidewalk, directly in front of our stash, hosing down the side of the brick building. (The building wasn't on fire, for God's sake. What in the hell was he doing?)

Of course, our biggest concern then became the condition of our drugs. We were intelligent enough to have wrapped them securely in a couple of baggies, but we hadn't planned on the Carmel Fire Department hosing them down for us. We quickly debated as to what we should do and Gabe decided he would exit the car and attempt to retrieve our goods. He said there was no sense in all of us getting arrested—a true team player.

I pulled over a couple of buildings past the fire station to watch how Gabe pulled this off. First, he moseyed into a gift shop where he waited for the fireman to start hosing down a different section of the building. Then he brazenly walked up to the now-soaked bushes in broad daylight and started fishing for our baggies. To our relief he found them, shoved them in his pocket and walked off like he was on a casual Sunday stroll. We checked the drugs when Gabe got back in the car—they were undamaged.

It was time to head to Pebble Beach. (We had decided to play, of course.)

I parred the first hole and immediately began thinking two words: "Pro Tour." My delusion was shattered by the third hole. I stopped keeping score by about the seventh hole.

Next stop was Los Angeles. The first night in town we hit The Comedy Store—nobody famous, but they kept us laughing. The next day was Disneyland. Then it was off to San Diego.

The San Diego Zoo and Sea World highlighted our daytime activities. We had only planned on staying a couple of days in San Diego, but the "car gods" had other plans. It turned out that the brakes on the Buick were shot. We had heard funny, grinding noises as far back as San Francisco but had written it off to *We don't want to hear funny, grinding noises, so we'll just ignore them—maybe they will go away.* They didn't.

Four days and three hundred and seventy-five dollars later (a king's ransom for a front brake job, even at today's prices), we were ready to leave town. Something about "aluminum brake drums"—very expensive. They had to order them special, which is why it took so long.

We had no trouble utilizing our extra time in San Diego. We had chosen a motel in Mission Beach—not a great area, but we didn't mind. It was a block from the beach and had a pool—it more than met our parameters. We beached or pooled it during the day, and explored the bars at night. Our last night there we stumbled onto a lesbian bar (a novel experience for us), where Gabe tried to convert a couple of ladies, unsuccessfully, I might add.

Later in the evening we discovered a bar that had pool tables, topless dancers *and* topless waitresses. They also had live music. We thought we'd died and gone to heaven. It was there that we met a young lady who told us she went by the nickname Peppermint Patty. Peppermint Patty, who "happened to be Asian," was a cute, very petite, young (twenty-two) lady. She must have weighed all of ninety pounds. Peppermint Patty spent the rest of the evening (and night and morning) with us. I'll spare you the details, but we had a fulfilling (at the time) night. Now it's a good thing I wasn't a woman, because Peppermint Patty is probably the kind of woman I'd have been. The truth is, I think a lot of guys would have been. In fact, I worried that maybe Peppermint Patty used to be a guy on account of that very thing. You sure didn't run into many women like her (at least we didn't). I guess that's probably a good thing because I've always maintained that if women were as easy as guys we'd all still be living in caves—we'd never have accomplished anything. (Thankfully, today, I have a much broader perspective on the evolutionary process of humankind. It is my belief that there is an underlying movement amid the insanity of this world pointing toward a higher level of consciousness—one that, among other things, recognizes that being broad-minded does not mean thinking about women a lot. I still have a lot of evolving to do in this, and other, regards.)

Later that morning, Gabe, Mick, and I headed for Mexico. Having done such a good job of it back in Carmel, we made the decision (this time it truly was a wise choice) to hide our drugs in San Diego before we took off for Mexico. And having found such tremendous success with planters, we had hidden what had been left of our sorely depleted stash in the planter box outside of our motel room before proceeding south.

Upon arriving in Tijuana, we settled for a quick self-guided tour before moving on to Ensenada, a small fishing village about eighty miles south of the border. A coworker of mine named Vic had told me not to miss out on a bar there called Hussong's. It was nice to have specific targets. It was two-thirty in the afternoon when we entered Hussong's saloon. An hour after shooting tequila, we were feeling no pain. We somehow managed to get kicked out of that same bar three times in one afternoon. The third time we got kicked out by the *federales* (the local police). We were evidently too drunk to appreciate the potential severity of our actions. We had heard horror stories of Americans getting stuck in jail in Mexico, but apparently the tequila was washing our brains of this knowledge.

At one point I was juggling shot-glasses, some of which were crashing to the ancient hardwood floor. And as sophomoric as it sounds, the three of us did a B.A. pyramid on one of the tables. (If you don't know what a B.A. pyramid is, you've saved yourself an uncomfortable image.) Vic had told me it was a bar where the locals came to be entertained by American tourists, i.e., watch them make fools of themselves. We were not about to disappoint the locals.

At one point in the afternoon, all three of us ended up in the bathroom throwing up together. I must say this was my first, and thankfully my last, tri-puking experience.

After our second forced exodus from the bar, Mick got lost wandering down the street and ended up taking a cab back to Hussong's (a ride that cost him far more than it should have, considering that the tavern was probably less than two blocks from where he had gotten into the cab). While Mick was getting screwed by Mexican cab drivers, I found my way to a phone booth to try to call my brother Tim back in the states. The small portion of my brain that wasn't drenched with alcohol thought it would be a good idea to let someone from home know where we were, in case we ran into trouble. It was a perfectly valid idea, except for the fact that I couldn't communicate well enough with the operator to get through to the United States, let alone, Portland, Oregon. Three years of straight A's in Spanish class (in spite of my behavior in that class) and all I could get out was "Los Estados de Unidos." The operator understood nothing else I said. So much for my plan of Tim and Luke coming down with machine guns to bust us out of jail (a very active, tequila-infested imagination.)

So, I did the only rational thing. I headed back to Hussong's for more tequila.

Coming back into the United States proved to be entertaining. Shortly before we approached the border, Gabe noted that it would be a good idea if he drove, because he "looked more Mexican." I'm unable even at this juncture in my life to key in on the logic of Gabe's remarkable suggestion, but I recall he said something about them not hassling us as much at the border if they saw him behind the wheel. After Mick and I got done laughing—a lot—we decided to humor him. His twisted logic made so little sense that we started thinking he maybe had something there. What the hell did us hung over white boys know anyway?

One look at our "Mexican" driver and we were instructed to pull over to the secondary search area. Evidently Gabe looked more criminal than Mexican. We knew we had hidden our drugs in San Diego, but we were nervous nonetheless. We hadn't exactly combed the car for drug remnants or paraphernalia. They searched the car high and low, even dumping our golf bags upside down, scattering our clubs on the asphalt. Nice people. We found it incredulous, however, that they searched everywhere but the glove box. They must've figured no one was that dense. Especially us, what with our clever placement of a Japanese-Mexican in the driver seat.

Thankfully, they found no trace of drugs anywhere, and we were free to pick our clubs up off the pavement and head north. We fetched our drugs in San Diego without further incident and finished them off in short order as we headed north toward home.

JUDY BLUE EYES

When I met my future wife, Judy, I hadn't had any truly serious relationships since Sarah from high school (which would mean that I had only had *one* ever, now that I do the math). It wasn't that I hadn't wanted a serious relationship; it was more that I just couldn't find anyone I wanted to be serious about. Because of this inability to locate my lifelong mate, I sometimes felt compelled to engage in one-night stands (although they were an extremely small percentage of my nights). And although these occasions were primarily self-centered in nature, the truth is I was pretty honest about my intentions when I met someone of the opposite sex.

In the year or so before I met Judy I was growing increasingly tired of the lonely nights. I longed for a companion, for someone to love. Judy filled that need for me.

As mentioned earlier, I met Judy in March of 1981 in a bar in Southeast Portland called The Grove. It has since changed names, but it was The Grove for many years. It was a country-western bar at the time I met Judy. Neither of us were much into country music, but the place was close to where we each lived at the time and had a certain appeal to it (hard liquor being one of the appeals, in addition to a great country band named The Glen Cass Trio).

There are two versions as to how Judy and I hooked up. One is mine. The other is Judy's. I was at The Grove one night with Steve Barton, and we were standing near the back of the bar, talking and watching people. This much we agree on. But Judy seems to recall coming up to me after Steve and I had been there an hour or two and saying, "Well, are you just going to stare all night, or are you going to ask me to dance?" This is way out of character for her, as anyone who knows her would tell you, but she insists that's what she said. She *had* had a bit too much to drink at this point (she was celebrating her 34th birthday with some friends from work), but it's still quite a stretch. Now, of course, I'm not saying she's making this up—I'm just noting that her memory might be a little foggy regarding that night.

My version is: Judy came up to me and said, "Would you like to dance?" End of story. A much simpler, albeit more boring version. Admittedly, my memory of that night is a little foggy as well. I do recall that Steve and I had an unusual night with regards to women coming up to us and asking us to dance. "Unusual" in the sense that women were coming up to us and asking us to dance. It's not like that *never* happened, but it was definitely the first (and only) night that two of us were asked to dance several times each by different women, and the night was still relatively young. My point being, we were reveling in the fact that for once we didn't have to be the ones to pursue rejection. (We, of course, didn't say no to any of the women who asked us because we knew all too well how that felt.) It wasn't like we were looking desperate, at least not on that night. So if Judy's version is correct, than I would say she wasn't being very observant. I mean, what need would I have had on that night to be staring at any one particular woman when it was obvious that Steve and I were being pursued by a wide variety of the fairer sex (slight poetic license)?

Okay, I'll come clean. Maybe I was staring at Judy every now and then. After all, she *was* the prettiest woman in the bar. And that assessment came not only from me, but from both Steve and Gabe (who showed up at The Grove later that evening). Her beautiful blue eyes were (are) perhaps her most prominent feature. She had gorgeous brown hair and a great figure. She may have been the shortest woman in the bar, at just under five feet, but as they say, good things come in small packages.

I was about a month shy of my twenty-eighth birthday the night I met Judy. Yes, she was an older woman—almost six years older. However, she looked much younger than her age, and does to this day, if I do say so myself (though I don't have to—people have always told her that). When I found out that she had three children and the oldest was to be sixteen in three months, I was amazed. That's when I asked her how old she was. She had had an early start in child-rearing, having given birth to Michael three months after her eighteenth birthday. Judy later had two other boys: Darin, who was two years younger than Michael, and Casey, who was eight years younger than Michael. Darin was thirteen and a half when I met Judy, and Casey was about to turn eight years of age, on the 29th of March.

When I met Judy she was in the process of getting a divorce from the boys' father, Al, her husband of seventeen years. (I have gotten to know Al over the years, and he's a good guy. He and Judy had their troubles like everyone else, and it just didn't work out for them.)

I talked Judy into giving me her phone number, and I called the next day to ask her out for the following weekend. We dated a lot in the first few months and fell in love rather quickly. From that first night, actually, she had me going. Aside from being pretty, her smile and her laugh had me hooked. (I kid her today that she doesn't laugh at my jokes as much as she used to. She tells me that she's heard most of them before. I repudiate that, explaining to her that a lot of my "material" is fresh, and when it's not, it's still funny, damn it—like a *Seinfeld* rerun. She responds by saying that she's "laughing on the inside.") Judy is also an extremely intelligent person (she remains one of the most intelligent people I've ever met and without a doubt, one of the most well-read.) And she's a very caring human being who also happens to love animals the way I do.

I knew early on that I wanted to marry her, but there was a catch. For me, it was a huge catch. Judy couldn't have any more children. She had had all three of her boys Caesarean. The doctor had recommended that she have her tubes tied after she had Casey because of potential complications with future pregnancies. She had followed the doctor's advice. Judy let me know about her condition from the onset of our relationship. It was a major setback for me—I had always wanted children. It seems the majority of men in this world want a son, but I had always wanted a daughter. (I wanted a son as well, but my heart always seemed to long for a daughter.) In any event, I had a decision to make: marry the young lady I had fallen in love with and never have kids of my own (including no daughter *or* stepdaughter ever), or walk away.

Though the decision was excruciating for me, I knew all along what I would decide. I loved Judy too much to let her go. And somewhere along the line we got engaged.

Meeting Judy's children was quite an experience. It's a challenge to meet someone's kids when you're coming into their home as a complete stranger and as a man that's dating their mother, especially when their parents haven't been apart all that long. But even before I knew I loved her, I did my level best to relate to those kids. I truly don't understand the "evil stepfather" or the "wicked stepmother" thing. Why would anyone *not* treat their step-children as they would their own? What fault is it of the children that their parents are divorced (or perhaps departed)? It blows me away. But, like I said, it's definitely not an easy situation to walk into.

Darin, the middle child, was a quiet kid. Very handsome (all three of the boys were good-looking and grew to be handsome young men—and I'm not being prejudiced here, since I obviously had nothing to do with that aspect of their being), but shy and reserved, at least in the beginning. But Darin became quite the talker as I grew to know him. He loved to quote movies and comedy routines—a penchant I share, although my memory isn't anything like Darin's.

Casey was the hardest, at first. He was barely eight and didn't understand any of these relationship things. Not that thirteen and fifteen year olds do (who does, for that matter?), but they at least have a little more maturity with which to deal with it all. To Casey I was simply someone getting in the way of his relationship with his mother—a relationship he very much needed at this troubling time in his life, when his parents were splitting up. And to this day I feel some guilt and regret because I did at times get in the way of the kids' relationships with their mother. That fresh love stuff is hard to resist. I certainly wasn't selfless enough to always put the boys' well-being above my own desires. I tried my best, as did Judy. But it was natural to want to be with each other, and we went out on dates a fair amount in the beginning.

I eventually won each of the boys over. I tried very hard to treat them like I would my own, and I think I was pretty successful at that. Although Casey naturally clung to his mother in the beginning, he eventually became like my own son. Because he was the youngest and had known his dad the least amount of time, he seemed to be able to bond with me more readily, once the initial period of apprehensiveness had passed. Casey went from being Momma's boy to being my boy in a relatively short period of time.

I think the boys were quick to realize that I truly did love their mother and that I was sincerely trying to develop a good relationship with each of them as well. Casey went from not leaving his mother's side to not leaving *my* side sometime in that first year. We would go to family functions (on my side of the family—Judy and Al were both from California and all of their relatives lived down there) and soon little Casey was sitting on my lap, not his mother's. From the time he was eight until he was about fourteen or so (when all teenagers eventually hit that It-ain't-cool-to-be-hanging-with-the-folks age), he was my constant little buddy. I couldn't go to the local Seven/Eleven or Fred Meyer without Casey jumping in the car (not that I wanted to—I thoroughly enjoyed his company).

Darin, too, would hang with me a lot in the first couple of years. But he was a teenager and had a lot of friends he spent time with. So did Michael. I loved them as best I could, and it wasn't long before they truly did feel like my own. Al got transferred to Los Angeles a few months after I met Judy and has been down there ever since. Consequently, contact with their dad was naturally much more limited than it was with me. (In later years they saw their dad a lot more and developed great relationships with him and also with their stepmother, Betty, who is a true sweetheart.)

Michael, being older than his brothers and more mature in some ways, was very friendly from our first meeting (of course, that was also Michael's way— he was just an extremely affable person, very sociable, very charming). Sadly, however, he was already into drugs and alcohol when we met, and much more than just on an experimental level. At least it seemed obvious to me that this was the case. He smoked a lot of pot and would get drunk fairly frequently. When I first moved in with Judy, we both did what we could to get him to at least stop drinking. When Michael drank, he got pretty wild. It was a difficult situation.

For me, personally, I felt somewhat hypocritical espousing to Michael the dangers of drugs and alcohol when I was a chronic user myself at the time. However, in spite of the stories I have related, after I moved in with Judy and the kids I toned down much of the craziness that had spotted my past. I was a so-called "functional addict" for the majority of my using days. I'm not excusing anything, especially some of my behavior, but I had a job and maintained a marriage throughout my chemical dependency, though I was dangerously close to losing both toward the end of my active addiction. Although we addicts are often proficient at leading a double life and fooling people, no one can do this forever.

We had a difficult (in fact, impossible) time keeping Michael from drinking. We would find empty hard liquor bottles in his room. He would come home drunk and loaded in the middle of the night, and there were a number of times over the ensuing years that we would get a call from one police station or another saying that Michael was in jail.

There is quite a bit of alcoholism in Judy's family, a factor that was definitely not in Michael's favor. She has had two brothers die from alcoholism. Ralph (who was a kind, but late-stage alcoholic when I met him) died of cirrhosis of the liver a few years after I met Judy. I remember being fairly shocked the first time I met Ralph. He looked the part of the classic alcoholic that everyone expects to see (there are far more alcoholics who don't look the part than do, I have since come to know). I recall dropping Ralph off under a bridge one night in Sacramento. (Judy is from Sacramento and her parents still lived there, as did her brothers Ralph and Randy and one of her two sisters, Linda.) All Ralph carried with him as I dropped him off was a loaf of bread and a six pack of Bohemian beer. He was very courteous as he said good-bye to me, and I remember feeling extremely sad for Ralph. No one wants to live like that.

Judy's oldest brother, Keith, shot himself while drunk one night. That happened fairly early on in our relationship, before I had met any of her extended family. I was with Judy when she got the call. (Sadly, it wouldn't be the last call of this nature we would get.) I remember Judy telling me that Keith had been her favorite brother (she had three brothers and two sisters). I never had the pleasure of meeting him.

So the odds were stacked against Michael once he had that first taste of alcohol. And although Michael experimented with a wide gamut of other drugs, it was always alcohol that got him into trouble. There are those alcoholics whose personalities don't change very much when drinking. (I was one of those, in spite of what some of the wildness of my youth might indicate. I have gotten other people's opinions on this subject, knowing full well my credibility on the matter is terribly suspect.) Michael was not one of those. Not that he would become violent or anything like that—he wouldn't. He just became different—not mean or angry, just not loveable Michael. And the real Michael was loveable. He had a very giving and loving personality. He was extremely gregarious and fun to be with when he was sober.

As Michael got older, he grew wilder and more out of control. Calls from police stations in the middle of the night would send our hearts racing. Usually the problem was drinking and driving, and eventually his license was suspended. Later traffic stops resulted in citations for driving with a suspended license. His disruptive lifestyle eventually became too much, and we had to ask him to move out—not just for our sakes, but for Casey and Darin's as well. He was nineteen when he left the first time. He would come back a few times over the next several years to live with us for stretches. He would rack up different legal charges, alcohol always being involved. When the charges against him in the state of Oregon became too much (nothing very serious, but he couldn't legally drive anymore and accumulated several outstanding warrants as time went by—he would fail to show up for court hearings), he would move down to Los Angeles to live with his dad for a while.

Eventually he would get into trouble down in California, and it wasn't long before he would wend his way back up to Oregon to live with us again. His stays with us never lasted long. It was only a short matter of time before we would get another call from the police in the middle of the night. It just always became too much. The same thing would happen in California and eventually his dad had to tell him that he wasn't welcome to live with them, either. We would each have to lay down rules when he wanted to stay with us and he just couldn't seem to abide by them. Consequently, more often than not he would stay with friends rather than with his dad or Judy and me. Eventually he would wear out his welcome with friends as well, because of his lifestyle. He ended up living in a park in Los Angeles, for the most part, during his mid-twenties.

Though trouble would continue to follow Michael, we never stopped loving him, of course. We wanted the best for him and hoped and prayed that someday he would change his lifestyle before it was too late. Although I was in the middle of my active using days, I never felt it was hypocritical to wish for Michael to stop drinking and using. Nor did I feel it was hypocritical to tell him he couldn't live with us anymore when his drinking became disruptive. For one thing, I was his parent, and in that sense felt a responsibility to try to steer him in the right direction, regardless of what I may or may not have been doing. And although my drinking and using hadn't abated since my twenties, my wild behavior had. Michael, being young, was still into sowing oats. But it wasn't this sowing of oats that worried me. It had more to do with the fact that his personality underwent a change when he drank. Something within me knew if he continued on his present path, he would eventually land in serious trouble. And sadly, he eventually did.

HONEYMOON

Judy and I were married on September 10, 1983. My brother Tim was my best man, and Judy's sister Pennie was the maid of honor. About 150 people attended the wedding. The reception was held in a downstairs banquet hall at Yaw's Restaurant in Northeast Portland.

Judy and I went back east for our honeymoon. Neither of us had ever been there before and it was one of the areas of the world we both wanted to see at some point in our lifetimes. My mother-in-law Maxine was kind enough to watch the kids for us so we could make the trip. We landed at La Guardia Airport in New York City at one o'clock in the morning, September 12. It was about 280 degrees outside with a humidity of around 7,000 percent when we arrived.

The cab ride to the hotel was interesting. Hearing stories about cabbies in New York doesn't quite do them justice. You really have to ride in one to get the full experience. We hadn't ridden but a few blocks when Judy and I began looking at each other wide-eyed, yet kind of smiling at the same time at the driver's style. He seemed to be in a monstrous hurry for some reason. As he rushed through the streets of Manhattan you got the impression that he would readily drive on the sidewalk if someone were to hold him up for more than a second or two. As he rounded one corner (at a rate of speed that would have made the Andrettis proud), Judy and I both let out audible gasps—not at his speed—but at the pedestrian who had just stepped off the curb in "normal time" and had to stop short due to the yellow blur that had suddenly flashed by her at warp seven.

"What—did she flip us off?" the cabbie shouted out after hearing our gasps. He began to apply the brakes. (What was he going to do, go back and beat the hell out of her?)

"Well, no—actually, you almost hit her." I responded.

"Ah!" he said dismissively with a wave of his hand.

The hotel was nice, though—if you were used to living in a cardboard village. The air conditioner in our room didn't work, the pop machines didn't work, and when we found a pair of men's underwear behind the dresser while looking to see if the air conditioner was plugged in, we decided we should change rooms.

The air conditioning in the next room wasn't a whole lot better, but at least there weren't any undergarments lying around. Still, it was muggier than hell, and all I wanted by this time was a rum and coke. I had a half gallon of rum in the suitcase, but no mix. The pop machine near our room didn't work, so I went to other floors in search of soda. It appeared that all the pop machines in the hotel were on strike. So off I went down the streets of Manhattan at one-thirty in the morning looking for a store.

A custodian at the hotel had told me there was a convenience store only a few blocks away. As I was making my way there, I suddenly recalled that I had six hundred dollars in cash in my front pocket and that I was in the mugging capital of the world. Too late (and too thirsty) to turn back, so I put on my best tough guy, ghetto walk (it's as good as Kevlar) and trudged onward.

Now, I am not prejudiced by nature, but when I arrived at the store and all seven people in it, including the cashier, were black, I must admit I was a little nervous. I wasn't sure about territorial issues in this neighborhood, having never been to New York before. But it was all good. I got my liter of Pepsi and made it back to the hotel unscathed. (Obviously, my ghetto look scared any would-be muggers away.)

The next day we did the obligatory tourist thing. We went to the Statue of Liberty, the Empire State Building, Times Square, etc. We spent three days in Manhattan and then rented a car to visit other areas back east.

We watched the sunrise at Beach Haven, New Jersey, one morning. We made the long, out-of-the-way trek to Niagara Falls. It was well worth it. Beautiful. Awe-inspiring. We went to Salem, Massachusetts, and saw a mock witch trial (I was hoping to see a real one, but I settled). In Boston, we saw The North Church and Paul Revere's home. We traversed the countryside in Pennsylvania. We spent three days in Washington, D.C. (talk about muggy). It was very interesting seeing the White House, the Lincoln and Jefferson Memorials, Ford's Theater, and the Smithsonian Institution.

I have now driven in Los Angeles, New York, and Boston. Without a doubt, Boston takes the cake for the worst place to drive. That is, if you're faint of heart. It's definitely not for the timid. At first I drove courteously, being the new guy in town. I had to test the waters. However, it became obvious rather quickly that if we were to *actually get anywhere* I was going to have to drive a little more aggressively. Now, given my driving history, I felt like I had finally arrived home. I had no fear when I was behind the wheel of a car (I figured if twenty-something collisions hadn't done me in, then it just wasn't meant to be).

We had arrived in downtown Boston at noon on a workday. I soon learned that using turn signals in this town was evidently for sissies. You could almost hear people snickering at you. Others kind of stared, trance-like, at your blinking signal light as if they had never seen one before. So, okay, gloves were off. I started driving like a Bostonian. I made some amazing cuts (if I do say so myself) into various lanes of traffic. Now, instead of getting snickers and puzzled looks, I was getting appreciative nods and thumbs up gestures, as if to say, "Nice move, buddy." We came upon one interesting driving venue—a huge circular patch of pavement about the diameter of a football field. There were no lane separation lines to be found anywhere and seven or eight streets emptied onto this vehicular arena. I've gotta say, I was even a little intimidated by the scene at first sight. (Some of the pressure was off now, though, due to the fact that my new bride was by this time huddled on the *floor* of the passenger side of the car, quietly sobbing because I was driving like "a maniac." As Mr. Spock would say: She "simply did not understand." It was us or them.) I maneuvered through the test maze successfully, was awarded honorary Boston citizenship, and made it to the North Church dent-free. Judy was able to get up off the floor of the car and continue on foot with the tourist routine. She's a trooper.

On the last day of our trip we drove back to New York and began looking for the airport. Although I'm fairly adept at driving in various kinds of inclement traffic conditions, there are times I can't find my way to the next intersection (but I get *somewhere* really fast). Although we had time to spare when we first embarked upon our search, we were soon racing against the clock. So, I drove *somewhere* faster. We came upon a bridge, and there was no way to avoid crossing it. As we approached the other side we were greeted with a big green sign that read: **WELCOME TO HARLEM.** Prejudice or no, I'm thinking, *This can't be good.* I was almost positive the airport wasn't in Harlem. Interesting place, however. The air conditioners in this area must not have worked very well, either, because most of the windows in the brick buildings that lined the streets were busted out. The only cars on the road at this time of the day (it was seven o'clock on a Sunday morning) weren't going to be moving anytime soon—they seemed to be missing some of the basic necessities for road travel—such as wheels and tires. Most of their windows were also busted out. (Was there no air conditioning anywhere in New York City?)

I guess we were fortunate it was so early in the morning. Any would-be muggers were probably passed out somewhere. I tried to hearten Judy with this insight, figuring this might encourage her to get up off the floor of the car again. Finally, when I told her that I was actually going to ask for directions, she reclaimed her seat. I asked a cab driver how to get to the airport. I was amazed once again that this method of locating a place actually worked. We found the airport and made it home safely.

In the more than twenty years that we've been married, Judy has never again sought refuge on the floor of any car I've driven. However, I have to believe that twice in one honeymoon has got to be some sort of record.

FAMILY LIFE

Life with Judy and the kids was good—although definitely different. One of the big changes for me was not seeing my friends as often. Judy was not as much into socializing as I had become accustomed to. This fact became a source of contention between us in the early years of our marriage. I came into our relationship with a host of friends and acquaintances. I had spent practically a decade hanging out with "the guys," and that lifestyle had become a part of my psyche. It was hard to think of changing that in any way. I wanted to have my cake and eat it, too.

Judy, on the other hand, brought just a few friends into the mix. A neighbor and a couple of coworkers perhaps, and she didn't seem to mind if she mingled with them or not. Her first husband had been a regional sales manager for Kinney Shoes, and he had gotten transferred a lot during their marriage. Sacramento, Los Angeles, Las Vegas, Fresno, Santa Rosa, Portland. Judy told me that every time she would get close to people, Al would end up getting transferred. Her favorite place had been Santa Rosa, where she and Al spent almost five years. It was after being uprooted from friends there that Judy began to shy away from getting too close to people. That's perfectly understandable, of course. It's just that our philosophies in this regard were rather opposite at the time we got married.

In the beginning of our relationship Judy went with the flow (*my* flow) and partied a lot with my friends and me. But it soon became clear that she would rather be at home. (A desire that would eventually become my preference more often than not as well.) Wish as I might, she simply didn't enjoy being with groups of people as much (or as often) as I did. It was like wishing the spots off a leopard. She was who she was. It took me many years to finally come to accept that Judy and I were actually very different people in a lot of ways. I have grown to respect that, learning through the years that accepting people for who they are is the only avenue to serenity. Attempting to change people is a very frustrating and fruitless endeavor. We may be able to influence people and perhaps effect positive change in their lives, but trying to remold them or force them to change is pointless (as well as aggravating). Once I came to accept this, I found that I really didn't want to change Judy or anyone else that I became close to, for that matter. Diversity is part of the beauty of this universe.

Judy and I did get together with certain groups of friends fairly often in those early years. The number of people that we saw, though, diminished with time. This was for a variety of reasons and not just due to Judy's proclivity toward solitariness. The fact of the matter is that many of my friends began to marry about the same time I did. And for better or worse, marriage often changes the dynamics of relationships that preexist the marriage. Other friends simply relocated to different areas of the country.

So for one reason or another, the number of people we socialized with gradually lessened. The only friends we saw with any lasting regularity became Mike and Debra Porter and Tom Work. And, of course, my brother Tim and his wife, Lisa. It was usually a case of people coming over to our house for board games or perhaps a basketball game on television. Back in those days the Trailblazers sold some of their home games on Blazer Cable, and I would usually buy the season package. I have been a Portland Trailblazer fan since the inception of the team (a fact which could alienate me from the greater populous of these United States). If it wasn't a ball game, we would play games like Trivial Pursuit and Pictionary when we got together. Those who played Trivial Pursuit with my wife were always amazed at Judy's vast wealth of knowledge, as well as her memory. She would not only know the answers to some of the most obscure questions imaginable, but sometimes would expound on the subject at hand (a habit of hers that did not always delight the more insecure, lesser informed of us).

Judy and I seemed to have merged on the issue of socializing with the passing of time. I am much more of a homebody now, and Judy is much more relaxed and open about going out to functions (perhaps even more so than I am at times). And she truly loves my family in Portland and likes being with them as much as I do.

Judy and the kids and I did a lot of fun things together over the years. My favorite sport is basketball, and it became Casey's favorite as well. Although Casey was never very tall, he became a great basketball player. We spent countless hours in the driveway playing hoops. Casey grew up to be one of the best shooters I've ever seen, and a great ball handler. I've often said that I would put him up against anyone (pros included) in a game of HORSE. Casey and I have watched a great many sporting events together. To this day, I love doing that with him. He's a very intelligent young man with a great sense of humor and a great love for animals. He has a lot to offer this world.

Our family did a fair amount of hiking as well. The Pacific Northwest is an awesome place for anything involving nature. It's beautiful here. Darin especially loved the outdoors. As he grew older, he and his friends did a lot of camping and hiking. He is really such a gentle soul, you can't help but love him. And he shares his brother Casey's (and his mother's and my) love for animals. When he moved back in with us for a time in his twenties, he and Judy would go on extended hikes together.

Over time we had a lot of family barbecues, inviting my parents over, as well as Tim and Lisa and their kids. We became (and still are) close to those kids. They love their Aunt Judy and Uncle Gary, and we love them. I've always said it's almost better to be an aunt or an uncle—you can have all the fun of being with kids without all the responsibility.

Tim is a great uncle to our kids as well. Being a karate expert, he was often showing self-defense moves to our boys. (I mentioned earlier that Tim is a fifth-degree black belt and Tai-kwon-do instructor. He has been taking and/ or teaching karate since his late teens. Three decades of learning how to defend himself and I'm a little disappointed that he's never even once beaten the hell out of anyone. Just kidding. I mean, no, he truly hasn't beaten the hell out of anyone. I'm kidding about being disappointed that he never has— because I'm not. My brother takes the spiritual philosophy behind the martial arts very seriously. He has always said, "It takes a bigger man to walk away." I admire that more than anything else he could say.) The boys all loved their new Uncle Tim. We did a lot of hiking with Tim and the kids—sometimes with the wives, sometimes without. But it was always a good time.

Judy and the kids and I traveled to Sacramento annually to visit Judy's parents. My first trip down there to meet the in-laws was in the summer of '81. Sacramento is nice in August if you're fond of 105 degrees. My in-laws, Buzz and Maxine, lived in an apartment complex with questionable air-conditioning. They did, however, have a swimming pool, and the kids and I found some relief there. (Only the kids and I would go in the pool—it seems the other adults found its hue unappetizing. The kids and I didn't care—it was wet and helped to cool us off.)

It was in Sacramento that I met Judy's brothers, Randy and Ralph, and her sisters, Linda and Pennie, as well as various other extended family members. Judy's mom passed away in 1986. She was a sweet and gentle lady. Judy still misses her a great deal. We continued to make the annual trek to Sacramento until Judy's dad passed away in 1989. After that, we stopped going down there, but we still meet up annually with Pennie and Jennifer somewhere.

It was Pennie's only child Jennifer that became the daughter I never had. When I first met her she was six years old. We just hit if off from the get-go. It's strange how the universe works sometimes (actually, it's strange all the time, when you stop to think about it). Jennifer's mom, Pennie (whom I love dearly), and her dad, Chuck, had been divorced for a couple of years when I met her and Jennifer. The year after I met them, tragedy struck. Jennifer's dad killed himself. He had been heavily into drugs. Jennifer was only seven.

So, here is this little girl without a father, and here I am, truly loving all three of my stepsons, but without the daughter I had always wanted. Although the situation was tragic, it was also magical. Little Jennifer and I became like father and daughter. We loved to make each other laugh (still do). She was the one I quoted very early on in this book who wrote to me once, "How can the funniest man I know also be the saddest man I know?" She was probably twelve when she wrote that. A very perceptive and compassionate young lady. Judy and I had Jennifer up to Oregon a couple of times for extended stays when she was younger. I have always been exceedingly grateful she came into my life.

Even though I hung out less with my friends after getting married, I still managed to continue drinking and using at a steady pace, with my use gradually accelerating as the years went by. Judy had rarely drunk at home with her first husband, Al. So Michael's penchant for drinking alcohol was not a reflection of Judy and Al. It was much like my own situation. As I mentioned, my dad never drank, and my mom rarely did, and yet I ended up being a fairly heavy consumer of alcohol in my adult life. My decisions to drink and to use had been my own, completely unrelated to parental influence. (This is why I questioned early on in these pages the true worth of examining one's childhood for clues to one's problems or mind sets in adult life. Children raised by the same parents oftentimes end up being totally different people, in spite of the vast similarities in their upbringings.)

It wasn't until I came along that Judy became a more frequent drinker, an influence of which I'm not proud. I don't remember at what point in our relationship that drinking on most nights became routine, I only know it was a gradual process over a period of years. (Judy ending up quitting on her own, several years before I did, and hasn't had a drink since.) What influence our drinking at home may have had on the three boys remains up to debate. Neither Darin nor Casey ever became big drinkers, and Michael, as I said, was already steeped in his addiction by the time I came into the picture.

There were certainly times that drugs and alcohol became a point of contention between Michael and us. On Christmas Eve of 1982 the boys and Judy and I went to my parents' house to exchange gifts. Michael was seventeen at the time. Against my better judgment, I told Mike he could have one drink. He had asked so politely, and at the time it didn't seem like that big of a deal. Well, Michael started going to the kitchen and sneaking more shots. By the time we noticed he was getting tipsy, it was too late. We told him he couldn't have any more. He seemed to be okay, but after we got home he asked us for the keys to his motorcycle. (We had told him there was no way he could have a motorcycle while he was living with us, but he had bought one anyway. We had explained to him that, for one thing, his license was suspended, and for another thing, it was insane to think that we were going to let a teenage boy who couldn't seem to stay away from booze, have a motorcycle. As soon as he brought it home, I had taken the keys from him.) Judy and I were emphatic in our refusal to let him have the keys.

Michael got pissed. It wasn't until that point that I realized just how drunk he had gotten. He started yelling at us, telling us that it was his motorcycle and we had no right to refuse him his keys. I tried to explain to him the reasons for our refusal, telling him that we loved him and we didn't want to see him get hurt. I also went through the whole scenario about him not having a valid license, the fact that he never had permission to buy the motorcycle in the first place, and that as long as he was living under our roof he had to abide by our rules, etc. Michael wasn't having any of it. He wouldn't let it go. We had tried to go to bed, but he kept coming into our room demanding his keys. At one point he went back to his room and began to play his guitar, wailing loudly as he did so. I got up and went to his room (which was just across the hall from us) and asked him to be quiet. The more rebellious he became, the louder I got. Soon we were yelling at each other, and Judy was crying, asking us to please stop. Michael was standing in the door to his room, and at one point I shoved him and told him to stay in his room and stop bothering us. That is the first and only time I had ever laid a hand on him. He reacted as if I had superhuman power and fell backwards across the entire width of his room and against the wall and then to the floor. It was the kind of over-dramatization I might have pulled at his age. I simply went back to my room. Within seconds Michael was out the door and Judy was yelling at me to not let him go. She was worried sick he would get into trouble. But I was unable to get him back; he was gone for the night. Fortunately he came back the next day unharmed.

Four months later, for my thirtieth birthday, Michael bought a pair of concert tickets for me and him. It was a very sweet gesture on his part, one that I shall always hold dear to my heart. He was trying to bond with me. He was two months shy of his eighteenth birthday at the time. So, off we went to see Angel City, a punk rock group from that era. Did I mention I wasn't into punk rock—at all? Michael was trying to show me the beauty of punk rock, I guess. So here I am, thirty years old, surrounded by an auditorium full of head-bopping teenagers, pretending, in the best manner I knew, to be having the time of my life. At one point Michael began asking strangers if they had any acid for sale. It was exactly the type of thing I was doing at his age (but not in front of my parents). In his own way, he was showing me he thought I was "cool," I suppose. But I had to ask him to please not try to score drugs while he was with me. Other than that, it was actually a fairly entertaining night, although I still didn't care much for the music.

It was about a year and a half later that we had to ask Michael to move out. Sadly, his lifestyle was just too much for the household. The next few years went by fairly uneventful. We moved to our present home in 1990. A couple of years later, not long after Casey finished high school, he moved out with some friends. Darin had already recently done so. Judy and I had been married nine years by this time.

Once the kids were gone, my drinking and using really began to take off. I had been drinking nightly for quite some time, but with the kids gone it was easier to toss down a couple more (or a few more) each night. It was in the nineties that my use of narcotic pain medication also began to skyrocket. These pills became the object of my most ardent pursuits.

STRIKES AND STRIPPERS

My job at National Steel ended with a strike. It didn't end for everyone—just some of the chosen ones. The strike lasted only two weeks, but it was one of the more memorable fortnights of my life. It was October of 1985.

We had the two separate plants by this time—the main plant and the old Gifford plant in the Willbridge area. Both had picket lines. You picketed at the plant you had been working in and on the same shift you had been working. Each employee picketed three or four days a week. We staggered days. I was slated to picket at Willbridge on swing shift. It was mid-October, and it was unseasonably cool. Downright cold at night. We had a fifty-five-gallon drum that we built a fire in every evening to keep us warm and to give us some light. And, of course, we had beer. It was like camping out with your friends.

Things were very slow from a traffic perspective at the Willbridge plant. It was out of the way of any regular flow of traffic. There was rarely anyone that would drive by and see our signs—only a few trucks here and there. The other plant, however, was situated on an extremely busy industrial street, so the guys picketing there had to be much more mainstream. We, on the other hand, stuck our signs in the dirt and played football or Frisbee in the late afternoon when we first arrived, and then cracked open the beer when we were done. Bret ended up sneaking over and spending more time on our picket line than on his own. It was just a much more entertaining place to be.

During our breaks we would head up to The Burnt Owl, the nude dancing tavern that the Willbridge crews frequented. (The *Blue* Owl had had a fire a couple of years prior, and when it reopened they had renamed it The *Burnt* Owl.) A few of us had struck up a friendship with a barmaid named Mindy, who worked there. She also danced once in a while—very versatile young lady. Actually she *was* a sharp gal with a great sense of humor. (People just shouldn't judge a book by it's cover—or lack thereof.)

One night Mindy showed up at our picket line with a full case of tall cans of Budweiser. She drank with us for a while, and then she noticed the security guard. He was parked a couple of hundred feet away and was sitting in his car on account of the cold. We suggested to Mindy that maybe the guy needed a little entertainment. He looked a bit lonely over there. Mindy, being the naturally shy girl that she was, strutted on over to about ten feet from the front of his car and started dancing. The next thing you know she was pulling up her top and exposing her upper-half to the guard. (Although it was damn cold out that night, it didn't seem to bother Mindy.) We were all whooping it up pretty good, but the security guard was just sitting in his car stone-faced. He took his four-dollar-an-hour job pretty damn seriously we were all thinking. His lack of reaction prompted Mindy to unbutton her jeans and push them down around her ankles and continued swaying to phantom music for the guy. The dedicated employee still didn't change his expression one iota. (They must have been paying these guys more than we thought.) However, he didn't exactly turn and look the other way, either.

Pretty rough duty, that picketing stuff. Of course, our Union, Teamster Local 206, only compensated us thirty-five bucks a week, so we hadn't felt the need to do much to earn our keep. While on strike I wrote a letter to the president of National Steel explaining our position. It was four typed pages. A fairly pleasant letter, really. I just told him how our major beef wasn't about money, but about contract language that threatened job security and seniority status. Ambiguous terms like "proper manning of the plant" and "work merits being equal" disturbed us because of the man in charge of interpreting those phrases. I didn't mention the plant manager's name in the letter, but it was implied and understood.

These were the first negotiations in the company's history where they had agreed to allow a couple of workers from the plant to sit in on the meetings. In the past it had just been the union reps, the company lawyers and management personnel of the company's choosing. This time we got to hear results of these negotiations first hand, from our peers. Our informants told us that when they introduced my letter, one of the company lawyers said, "So, Swoboda's writing letters again, heh?" (I *had* written a few "notes" to the-powers-that-be over the years, I suppose.)

Two weeks after the strike began the company had us another offer. It made the original offer look like gold, but the company lawyers had played this game before. They knew that most people with families couldn't afford to stay out on strike very long. The new proposal called for major pay cuts across the board; all the contract language initially proposed remained unchanged; and they could call us back to work in any order they chose, without regard to seniority.

Unfortunately, the union by-laws didn't call for a majority in order for the contract to be ratified. It was a real screwy deal. You needed two-thirds of the members voting to *turn it down* or it was an approved contract. What kind of a democracy is that? Anyway, the vote came back, and the contract was accepted. Less than fifty percent voted to accept the new offer, but because of the union rules the minority were able to ratify the agreement. We now had a new legal and binding contract.

Well, they called us back in any order they chose, all right. Passed me right up. One of the supervisors was a good friend of mine who had been a Teamster for thirteen years before going management and was a great guy. I called him several times to see what was up. Evidently my letter hadn't been too well-received by management, and they didn't want to call back a "rabble-rouser." So, they never did. (Funny, the guys in the shop seemed to like my letter.) They called almost everyone else back. They only skipped a few people who were considered undesirables. (I feel so dirty.) The thing that upset me more than losing my job, however, was losing my friends. I had a lot of comradery built up with these guys. I knew it would never be the same even if I tried to keep in touch. It just never is.

Within days, I got a job at a competitor down the street—Sanford Steel. I was hired five days after the strike ended. It was the first week in November, 1985.

BLACKOUT

I worked at Sanford Steel for just one month before being laid off due to lack of work. I proceeded to collect unemployment benefits for six months, which was the maximum. At that time you were allowed one six-week extension, which I applied for and received. Sanford Steel had indicated that they would call me back to work at some point, but I was beginning to sweat it. I had been married since September of 1983 and I was now responsible for more than just myself. I had a wife and three stepsons who were used to a certain standard of living, and I didn't want to let them down. The job offers I got during that six months were for far less than what I had been making. By this time, steel was what I knew, and I didn't know where else to turn. Besides, I was still hoping to get called back to Sanford because I was only a year away from vesting my Teamster pension.

I was three weeks into that six-week extension when the warehouse superintendent from Sanford Steel phoned me. He had apparently been impressed enough with my work in the month that I had been there that he was calling me back to be foreman of swing shift. There were two problems with that. The first was that I didn't want to be a boss. The second was that there were several people who worked in that warehouse who *did* want to be boss and who had been there a lot longer than I had—like ten or fifteen years compared to my lousy one month. In my mind, however, I had no choice. I had a family to feed. So I went back to work at Sanford as a working foreman. The foremen in many steel service centers do almost as much physical work as the rest of the labor force—but they're also in charge. They, of course, get paid more (not much more) for the "privilege" (a curse in my mind) of having to tell people what to do.

It turned out I was lucky enough on my first night to work side by side with one of the guys who had wanted the foreman position. This guy didn't talk to me for like three straight hours. I was beginning to feel like we were married, so at one point I simply stopped working and said to him, "Look—I know you wanted to be foreman. You've been here eleven years."

He just stared at me (not making it any easier).

I continued. "Hell, *I* think you should have been foreman. But I needed the damn job. I've got a family to feed. My unemployment insurance was about up. So you've got no call to be mad at me."

"I'm not mad at you," he conceded.

"Then why are you fucking acting like it? Look, I just want to do the fucking job and go home like every-fucking-body else." (Swearing a lot can sometimes be helpful when attempting to befriend a fellow Teamster.)

He seemed to lighten up after our conversation. I guess all he needed was for me to tell him that he should have been foreman. And no, it wasn't like the movies—we didn't become best friends after that. But from that day forward we did manage to get along quite well.

The workers in the shop all came to accept me in a fairly short amount of time. As I said before, getting along with people had never been a problem for me. Besides, I had several years experience dealing with a lot of different personalities in a steel warehouse. Also, I knew how to bad-talk management just enough to get on the good side of the guys in the shop, yet remain conscientious enough to get the job done. And, most importantly, I worked my butt off. It was crucial to show them that I was not some lazy "brown-noser" coming in there just to boss them around. Once they saw how hard I worked (and that I kind of knew what I was doing) they eased up pretty quickly.

A couple of my buddies from National Steel had gotten jobs at Sanford, as well. Fred Hogan had been at Sanford for a couple of years. He'd been let go at National Steel because of—hell, I don't recall the specifics. He'd been off with a back injury for longer than they cared for, I believe. When he came back they made sure they got him on every small infraction they could come up with so they could document enough to eventually get rid of him. Fred had been the pharmaceutical guru at National Steel. Now he was the pharmaceutical guru at Sanford Steel. He was a tall, slender fellow about my age, an intelligent man with a distinctively deep voice. He spoke with an air of confidence on a variety of subjects, including, as indicated, pharmaceuticals. His diversity of knowledge would become readily apparent to anyone who spent any time with him at all, and the self-assured (not arrogant in the least) manner with which he would calmly state his opinions compelled the listener to automatically accept his discourse as gospel. (I often thought that if Fred were to tell me the world was flat, I would be forced to at least balk momentarily at the more modern-day notion.)

Fred was fond of the medication that was provided to him as part of his back therapy. So was I. I had discovered several years earlier at National Steel that I liked what narcotic pain relievers did for me. I had hurt my back one day and the doctor had given me Percodan and I had fallen in love with the effect immediately. Never mind what it did for the pain. I instantly sensed the cessation of all underlying anxiety, and any thought of being depressed was instantaneously vanquished from my mind. Narcotic pain relievers not only (seemed to) work better than anything the psychiatric community had prescribed for me in my dark era, they also worked better than any street drug I had ever tried. And they were cheap (if you had a legitimate prescription for them).

What seemed strange to me was that a lot of people I met over the years didn't like painkillers. It was similar to how alcohol affects people differently. Or how some people can smoke a ton of pot and not be too wiped out or get paranoid (as I was prone to do). To me, and to a certain, relatively small percentage of people, pain pills were the crème de la crème. Fred (and a few other friends of mine) belonged to that percentage as well. We always found it baffling that listed in pill books under *potential adverse side effects* of painkillers is "feelings of euphoria." God, yes, we certainly want to avoid *that* at all costs, we would joke to each other.

Today, of course, I know the reason behind listing that reaction as an adverse side effect. Because, if you are one of the few unfortunates that experience this feeling of euphoria, and you are an addict of my nature, you will stop at almost nothing to get that feeling again. And again. And again. And again. The problem is, one's tolerance to those things builds up over time, and there comes a day when you just can't get enough, and the drug no longer does for you what it used to, regardless of how much you *do* get. But long before that happens, things get truly ugly. And the withdrawals—my God, the withdrawals. One of the most horrible things imaginable. Dependence upon narcotic pain medication is a very insidious form of addiction.

I had gotten painkillers several times during the eight and a half years I had worked at National Steel, usually for back pain (there are a fair number of back injuries in the steel business), once for a broken foot. In those days they prescribed Percodan much more readily than they did in subsequent years. But more often than not it was Vicodin or Tylenol 3 with codeine. Once in a while you would get Extra Strength Vicodin or Tylenol 4 with codeine.

Tylenol 4 seemed to be Fred's favorite, along with the Valium the doctor prescribed for him as a muscle relaxer. I wasn't that fond of Valium, but I liked the Tylenol 4s well enough. Tylenol 4s have sixty milligrams of codeine (the narcotic ingredient), Fred informed me. (Tylenol 3s are much more commonly prescribed and each contains thirty milligrams of codeine.) He received that combination of medication for a couple of years, at least. Fred would often give me a few when he got his dose. Sometimes more, sometimes less.

There was one particular day toward the end of my tenure at Sanford when Fred had just gotten his medication. I had moved to day shift by this time, and it was nearing the end of our shift. Fred handed me a couple of Tylenol 4s and a couple of Valium. I ate them. We decided to go to Red's after work. Things got a little out of control that night.

Linda at Red's was our absolute favorite barmaid in the world—indeed, the *best* barmaid in the world, in our minds. She was the friendliest lady imaginable and poured the meanest drinks in town. This night would prove to be no different. After a couple of drinks the pills were really starting to hit home, so naturally I asked Fred for more. He gave me a funny look. He had a much greater tolerance for the pills than I did (at least at that time in my addiction) and yet he wasn't ready for more. Nevertheless, he reached into his pocket. We each took another Valium (he had the 10 milligram "blues") and two more Tylenol 4s.

We took this particular dose of pills once more during the next hour. As we were sitting there bullshitting I mentioned to Fred that I didn't want to end up like Karen Ann Quinlan, the girl who had taken too many pills and drank too much booze and had ended up in a coma for years (a well-known case at the time). Fred tried to assuage my worries by reminding me that Karen had taken barbiturates, not painkillers, and that she had drunk a lot more booze than we were planning on drinking. (This comforted me somewhat, especially coming from the knower of all things pharmaceutical, but as the night progressed it became a topic of increasing concern with me.)

After a couple of more drinks and a couple of more pills, Linda did something she had never done to us before—she cut us off. She had served Fred and me hundreds of times over the years and had seen us get plenty hammered (more than a few times). But on this night she could see we were getting really, *really* wasted—and way too early in the evening to boot. It was only seven o'clock when she cut us off. She was very apologetic and wanted to call us a cab (she was truly concerned about us that night). But, of course, we refused the offer.

On that night I had a total blackout, an extremely rare occurrence for me. (I had nights when I forgot certain things, but only a couple when I remembered absolutely nothing.) It's a very scary feeling. I woke up the next morning and in a panic rushed to the window to see if my car was out front and what condition it was in. To my relief it was there and in one piece. Fred called me that morning to see if I had made it home okay, and I asked him what the hell had happened. I told him I remembered nothing. He replied that he wasn't surprised. Fred said that I had been a riot that night (at least from his rather inebriated perspective). He said I had become more entertaining as the evening progressed.

According to Fred, I got cut off at four different bars that night, including Red's. I had apparently walked into the first tavern after Red's, and the barmaid had simply taken one look at me and said, "No way!" That was it for that place. Next, we went to a topless bar in Northwest Portland called Frenchie's, and I ended up touching the dancer's backside when she was up on stage and they threw me out very quickly, Fred said.

The last place we had visited was The Refectory on Northeast 122nd and Halsey. The manager had been in the process of cutting me off when Fred walked up to hear me asking the guy why he wouldn't serve me anymore. The manager told me that I had been wandering around the bar for twenty minutes bothering everyone, asking them if they knew where my friend was (as if they knew who my friend was). He said the place just wasn't that big, and my friend shouldn't have been that hard to find.

Fred said we were out drinking until midnight. I don't know how many more Valiums or how many more Tylenol 4s we ate. Fred said I kept asking for more, and whenever he gave me a couple, he'd take a couple, too. He said I kept bringing up Karen Ann Quinlan every time we'd take a dose. Fred would tell me it was going to be all right—that we weren't going to slip into a coma or die or anything like that. But throughout the evening, in my increasingly drunken stupor, I apparently kept making Fred promise me that if I died he would have them engrave my tombstone with: *"See, Fred—I told you it was too many."*

Fred had gotten a big kick out of that. Fred's penchant for getting high often exceeded mine, but on that particular night I was definitely more intoxicated. I swore never to take Valium with alcohol again, and I never did. (I would continue to drink with painkillers for many years, but Valium is a benzodiazepine—a different class of drug entirely—and it affected me in a much more noticeably negative manner—hence the dictum on Valium.)

Fred was eventually laid off at Sanford Steel. A few days after he was let go, someone in the shop told me that Fred was out front and wanted to see me. I went outside and found Fred sitting in his red Camaro, smoking pot. I asked him what he was up to. He took a toke off his pipe and while holding in his breath, said, "I've got to take a drug test today." He'd apparently had a job interview a couple of days prior and they were considering hiring him.

Even for Fred, this was a little radical. "What in the hell are you doing, Fred? How are you going to pass a drug test?" I asked, my gaze directed at his pipe.

"That's what I'm here for," he responded as he let out the smoke. "Thought maybe you could pee in a bottle for me."

"What in the hell are you talking about, man?"

"You know. Go pee in a bottle and then bring it out to me," Fred explained, as if this was an ordinary, everyday kind of request.

"Fred, you're crazy. They'll be able to tell. It's gotta be warm for one thing."

"Let me worry about that, man. It'll be okay."

"What makes you think *I'd* pass?" I asked.

"You'd pass. You don't smoke pot. And you told me a few days ago that you haven't done any coke in a while. When was the last time?"

"It's been a couple of weeks." I wasn't using cocaine nearly as often at this point, and Fred knew it. (I was gradually going more and more in search of narcotic painkillers.)

"See, you'd pass. Coke only stays in your system a few days."

This wasn't something I was anxious to do. "What if I find out I have AIDS or something? Maybe I don't want to know."

Fred just laughed.

"What in the hell am I going to piss into?" I asked, my resistance weakening.

"Just use the orange juice container that you buy off the break wagon every day."

God, it was wonderful being that predictable. Morning break had just gotten over, and Fred knew that I bought the same thing off the gut truck every day—a can of chicken noodle soup (with four packages of crackers), a hard-boiled egg, and a small container of orange juice.

"Man, you're lucky I didn't just take a leak," I said, running out of excuses. I could simply have said no, but Fred was a good friend and he had given me many a Tylenol with codeine over the years when I was in "need." I just couldn't turn him down. Besides, the request was so off-the-wall I found it kind of intriguing.

I went to the break room, fished my empty OJ container from the top of the garbage can (George Costanza would have been proud), went into the bathroom, and peed into the plastic container. I then sheepishly brought it out to Fred. I gingerly handed it to him like it was a vial of lethal chemical warfare, but Fred grabbed it like it was an ordinary container of orange juice. *My* urine and Fred handled it easier than I did.

A few days later Fred dropped by to tell me that "I" had passed the drug test and that I evidently wasn't dying of any incurable disease. I was pleased. He thanked me and drove off.

Unfortunately, after all that, he still didn't get the job.

DAD

My father, Ambrose Joseph Swoboda, died of lung cancer on September 19, 1988. He had smoked all his life. Dad's death was hard on me. Really hard. We had been extremely close. It tore me up watching my dad slowly die. When he finally passed away I didn't think I'd ever stop crying.

My dad was a rare human being. Everyone who knew him loved him, and he loved people. (Both of my parents were well-loved by a host of human beings. My mom still is. My friends over the years always loved and appreciated my parents.) Dad had that wonderful sense of humor, and he was the least judgmental person I've ever known—ever will know.

The doctors operated on his cancer the first time and thought they had gotten it all. (It seems like they always say that.) When the cancer returned Dad was told he had just a few months left. I'll never forget the moment I found out. It was in June of 1988. I was typing when my wife came home. Her face bore the saddest look I had ever recalled seeing, and somehow I knew what that look meant. I knew my father had been to the doctor that day for tests. He had begun to experience pains in his chest again, and after procrastinating for a few weeks he had finally gone in to have it checked out.

"What's wrong?" I quickly asked my wife.

A lump immediately came to her throat and she couldn't talk. I begged her with my eyes to tell me.

"Your dad's cancer is back," she said, as the tears began to fill her eyes. She shouldered the added burden of having to tell me the news.

"Are they going to operate?" I asked, my mind now racing with dread.

She just shook her head and began to cry. "They can't do anything this time. It's spread too far."

"What—what do you mean?" I stammered. It was too sudden. I found myself not wanting the information that seconds ago I couldn't receive fast enough.

"They said he wouldn't make it through the summer."

And with that statement part of my world was forever shattered. I would never replace the piece of my soul that died that moment. It simply could not bear the shock. It could not exist in a world that had no Ambrose Swoboda. So it left. I don't know where it went.

My wife was wonderful, of course. Still seated in my office chair I buried my head in her chest and sobbed heavily. I didn't think it was possible to cry that hard. At that moment I was sure I would cry forever. I couldn't imagine any state beyond this unbearable sadness. It was all-consuming. She held me like a baby as she cried with me. There was never a man like him.

"I don't want him to die!" I remember wailing several times, as if somehow my desperate pleas could change my father's fate.

He never once complained. That's a fact we almost took for granted. I feel bad about that now. I know we told him that he was being brave. But we didn't tell him enough. At least I didn't. It was just so easy to see him being that way. It was the only way he knew how to be, so we more or less expected it of him, I guess. And that made it harder to be impressed. In retrospect, I go way beyond being impressed. There are no words for it. His courage was amazing, unbelievable. I know that I don't have half the courage and fortitude that Dad possessed. I know that if it had been me I would have been wallowing in self-pity somewhere along the line. I would have taken turns being angry and sad and scared. Mostly scared, I think, or mostly angry, maybe. I don't know. Certainly some unwelcome barrage of emotion should have captivated his waning days.

But I saw none of those things in my dad. Maybe he held them in for us. It would have been in character for him to suffer in silence. Certainly he withstood devastating physical pain and hardship with barely a moan. Coupled with the mental trauma that must have befallen him, it was unbelievable how he persevered. Though he lost his sight, and his voice became a barely audible whisper, and he hadn't the strength to stand up—he *never* complained. Even as the end grew very near, and he knew his time was up, he wouldn't feel sorry for himself. He never got mad. He never pounded his fist and said, "Why me?" He would only say, "Whatever the Old Man has in store for me," or words to that effect. Then he would smile.

That to me is amazing. My dad smiled more in the last few months than most people do in years. Of course, he always did. Humor was his heart and soul.

He lived with it, and he died with it. I remember him making people laugh right up to the end. As much humor as he had, he had even more love—a love for all people and all things. There'll never be another like him.

I think I know where that piece of my soul went. It never left, actually. It's tucked away deep inside somewhere. It would hurt too much to have it near the surface. But it's there when I need it—when I need to remember the pain. Sometimes it's good to remember the pain. It brings me closer to my father, and that can only be good. Then the pain turns to comfort, and to memories of a deeply kind and loving man. A wonderfully humorous man. A remarkable man.

After my dad was told he wouldn't make it through the summer, I wrote him a living eulogy. I wanted him to know how I felt *before* he died. Since he had lost his sight from the cancer, he couldn't read it. I had started reading it to him, but didn't make it past the first sentence. It was too hard. I broke down. I passed it to my mother, and she read it to him. A few minutes after she was done, and we had all stopped crying, he asked if I would try to get it published. So, I sent it to a few places. Two magazines and *The Oregonian* newspaper agreed to publish it. *The Oregonian* said they would publish it sometime in November of that year. I contacted the editor and explained to her that my father wouldn't make it to November. I told her that we really wanted it published before he passed away, so that he could have that experience. She was very gracious, and they ended up publishing it a few weeks before Dad died.

I received a lot of cards and letters from around the state thanking me for my article. Apparently it helped some people deal with the pain of their own losses, or impending losses. I actually got a call almost fifteen years later from an older gentleman who lived in Gresham, Oregon (where my wife and I live as well). The man asked if I was the "Gary Swoboda" who had written the article about my father in *The Oregonian* in 1988. I was rather taken aback, but I replied that I was. It seems that this man's sister had recently passed away. As he was going through her things he found my article in the night stand next to her bed. She had evidently kept it there all those years. We ended up talking for quite a while. It was a remarkable phone call that touched me deeply.

I wrote eulogies for my father when he passed away, and for my mother-in-law and my father-in-law when they passed away. I wrote how they were going to a better place, where they would be free of the pain and suffering of this world. In the past, this sentiment had been more of a hope than a belief. My faith had not been all that strong. But I had an experience during one of the operations that my dad endured that metamorphosed this hope into a belief.

A couple of months before my dad passed away, he had an unscheduled emergency operation in an attempt to stop some internal bleeding that wasn't being alleviated through medication. My mom and I were at the hospital in one of the waiting areas. While we were sitting there, I suddenly felt my dad's presence. (We learned later that there was a point during the operation when they thought they had lost my father.) At that moment I somehow *knew* my father had died. Yet, instead of experiencing overwhelming sadness (as I did a couple months later when he actually did pass away), I felt an all-encompassing peace and astounding joy. There was an overwhelming feeling of being surrounded, indeed immersed in or part of, a sea of totally unconditional love. It was the most peaceful moment imaginable. Truly, it was beyond imagination and way beyond words. A beautiful, indescribably wonderful feeling of complete and utter contentment. And underlying these feelings of intense peace and pure love was the *unquestionable* knowing that everything was all right. That nothing was wrong, that nothing had ever been wrong and that nothing could ever be wrong. It was totally unlike anything I had ever experienced, and like nothing I have experienced since. I knew in that moment that what I was somehow experiencing was our true reality, our True Nature, if you will. Why I was being granted this gift, I did not know, nor do I know now. What I believe is that I was somehow feeling my dad's soul, his presence, pass through me, and that he was sharing with me his glimpse of this True reality. What I know is that the experience remains as the single most real moment of my life—all else pales in comparison. I also know that whenever I recall this experience (in truth, I feel that "that" was reality and that "this" is an experience), it always puts things in perspective.

After having this wonderful touch of reality, which lasted maybe a single Earth moment, everything returned to normal. I reverted to feeling like I had always felt. I would continue to experience moments of suffering as well as moments of pleasure as my life progressed. But during that moment, no pain or suffering was possible—it was as if, in reality, those things didn't truly exist. Today I still believe this, although I am not always in touch with this belief. I also know that in our present human state we continue to experience the ups and downs of this life. I know that on this earth, my pain is real, as is the pain of others. Why we experience pain and suffering in this realm I do not know and in all likelihood I never will. There may be a few that come among us from time to time that learn to go beyond the veil of illusion that permeates this world. Perhaps this is our intended spiritual evolution. Maybe we are all here to attain this heaven on earth one day. I do not know. I only know what I experienced. I only know what is true in my heart. I have no physical proof of anything. But to expect to establish proof of a non-physical reality through physical means seems pointless, indeed absurd.

I simply know that I had a very real, albeit intangible, experience. I liken it to a near-death experience. I have heard men of science repudiate near-death experiences as something of a chemical nature, as possibly a reaction that occurs when the body and mind are breaking down. But I had this experience and *I* wasn't dying—my father was. And I hang onto that knowledge when I have doubts, and it comforts me.

TURNING FORTY

I turned 40 in 1993 and managed a bit of the obligatory middle-aged-crazy scenario. Nothing major, and I don't think the age thing really had that much to do with my growing disenchantment in life. The passing of time was a factor—definitely, but there wasn't a specific age that freaked me out. Nevertheless, I've got to admit, I did veer a bit when I turned forty.

Partly out of an effort to dispel any notions anyone might have about my being an alcoholic and partly to prove it to myself as well, I quit drinking for six months. Of course, I wasn't completely clean and sober during this time, as I continued to ingest narcotic pain relievers whenever I could. The whole concept of being clean and sober, the idea behind it, was beyond my grasp at the time. I didn't realize that for addicts such as me there was no dabbling with any drug. Partial abstinence simply didn't work. I ended up proving that to myself in the long run, and I've watched countless others prove it for me since I've been clean and sober.

Quitting drinking for a while is something every alcoholic worth his or her salt tries on occasion. We just put on a little show to prove that we can stop drinking whenever we want—thereby proving that we aren't alcoholic. It never occurred to me that non-alcoholics don't need to prove (to themselves or anyone else) that they can go without drinking. Or as a friend of mine puts it: "Non-alcoholics don't sit around wondering whether or not they're alcoholics."

To top off my turning forty stint on the wagon, I decided to become vegetarian. For me, the vegetarian thing has never had much to do with health issues. It's always been more of an ethical issue. I love animals, and can't imagine killing one for food, so I decided to put my mouth where my morals were. (A favorite customer from GOM Steel once called me a SNAG—Sensitive New Age Guy—due to my vegetarian and anti-war stances. I told him I prefer IJDLSSD: I Just Don't Like Seeing Shit Die.) For six months I ate no meat or fish. I wasn't a radical vegan or anything. I can't do the no-dairy-product thing. My parameters were pretty cut and dried: if something didn't die to make the food, it was okay to eat. But after those six months I went back to drinking alcohol and eating animal flesh (at an even greater consumptive rate than before—on both counts).

I ended up trying the vegetarian thing again seven years later, when I was about eighteen months clean and sober. At that point, I was trying to do it for the rest of my life, not just for a few months. When I went vegetarian it allowed me to be a little more vocal about my views on hunting. I had always felt it would be hypocritical to express my rather strong opinions on the subject too boisterously, because I had others kill my meat *for* me and then picked it up at Safeway.

At one point during this meat fast, I submerged into one of my depressions. I remember my mother throwing in her two cents worth on my mental state. One night while on the phone with her she snapped at me, "*You need some meat!*"

I replied, "Yeah, you're probably right. I'm sure if I rushed to the nearest pasture, butchered me a cow, and started gnawing on dead animal flesh, I would instantly be catapulted from depression." As she began to laugh, I added, "Never mind the fact that I've battled with depression for the past three decades, during which time I was Carnivore King. The meat I ate all those years didn't seem to induce any magical level of glee in me."

She backed off her stance and allowed me to be blue and "meat-less" for the moment.

After three hundred and sixty-three days of this second stab at vegetarianism, I cracked. Casey was over for dinner one night, and Judy had made homemade tacos for us. (Very good homemade tacos, just so you know, and it isn't the lettuce that makes them good.) I sat there looking at the two of them loading up their shells. As I stared down at my shell with nothing but cheese and lettuce in it, I unceremoniously said, "Pass me the goddamn meat." It was as quick and easy as that. (I'm reminded again of Burt Rice's statement to me those many years earlier: "You crack pretty easy, don't you, son?") I hadn't even been able to go another two lousy days for the full year. And once again, when I went back to eating animal flesh, I went into major carnivore mode. I swear, for the next year I ate more meat than I ever have. It's just so damn good. Pot roast, steak and bacon, for God's sake—does it get any better than that? I'm weak, what can I say? Well, at least I gave it my best shot.

So, hunt away—I don't have a self-righteous leg to stand on anymore.

But need you mount their frickin' heads? No, seriously. What the hell has *that* got to do with feeding ourselves? And what's with taking pictures of your "kill?" You don't see me down at Safeway with my Pentax snapping photos of my latest sirloin purchase. And I worked just as hard earning the money to be able to buy the steak as you did to shoot the damn deer.

Forgive me—I lost my head. (Maybe you could mount it on your wall.)

MOVING STEEL

Sanford Steel went bankrupt and shut its doors in the late eighties. Only two other warehouse employees besides me were retained to help liquidate the inventory. We spent three months loading up steel, tearing down racks and taking extended lunches at Red's. Some of Sanford's remaining inventory was bought by a man named Bruce Kellogg, the half-owner of R & S Steel in Vancouver, British Columbia. As it turned out, Bruce wanted to start up a company in the states, and he ended up purchasing two burning machines from Sanford Steel in addition to a fair amount of steel.

During the liquidation procedures I was introduced to Bruce Kellogg, and he eventually asked me to go to work for him. I agreed. Bruce leased a bay in an industrial park in Vancouver, Washington, (located just on the other side of the Columbia River from Portland). The burning machines and the steel Bruce had bought from Sanford were transferred over to the bay in Vancouver. Bruce flew me up to the office in British Columbia to familiarize me with their paperwork procedures.

Bruce was one of the best bosses I had had up to that point in my life. He hired several people from Sanford to work for him. But as much effort as we all put into making the place a success, Bruce eventually had to concede that, due to a variety of factors, we were not competitive enough to remain in business. After about a year and a half, Bruce sold the burning machines and remaining inventory to Art Shatner and Chad Lewis. They were the co-owners of Unity Steel, a company that was leasing a couple of bays directly across from the bay we were leasing. It was the spring of 1991.

Art and Chad hired me, as well as a few others, to work the burning department (the process of burning steel had not been a part of Unity Steel's business up to that point). I was the foreman of the bay, and a salesman from Sanford was hired to bring in as much burning business as he could. (Art and Chad would end up selling their business to GOM Steel about four years later.)

After about six months of working for Art and Chad, I was gradually moved into the office to program shapes for the burning machines on a Cad system. Within a year or two, I would be integrated into sales as well, since there wasn't always enough programming to keep me busy full-time.

While at Unity Steel, my using and drinking continued unabated. Although my cocaine-using days had come to an end (I had parted ways with anyone that was friendly with that particular substance as an aid to my departure from it), I was now beginning to maximize efforts at acquiring various forms of narcotic pain medication. Though I had used and abused painkillers off and on since my mid-twenties, my use had primarily been limited to chance opportunity and availability. It wasn't like I didn't pursue painkillers when I could. It's just that my efforts at the time paled in comparison to the lengths I would go to in later years.

THE DARK SIDE

THE OTHER EDGE OF THE SWORD

I had nursed a multitude of debilitating hangovers over the years. I had also lain in bed on countless nights staring at the inner lining of fluttering eyelids as my heart thumped wildly inside my chest, its steady rhythm echoing madly in my ears (a victim of cocaine abuse once again). In spite of these toxic undertakings, my life seemed to be maintaining the status quo. As the nineties loomed on the horizon I stood now a couple of decades removed from my "dark period."

But where had I arrived? And what had I gained for my travels? My slowly progressing disease of addiction was strategically playing its well-rehearsed game. It was allowing me to pretend to live a normal life, allowing me to persist in the illusion of being a so-called functional addict. Yet, all this time it had been pulling me deeper within its narrowing and confining walls. After getting married and acquiring a ready-made family, it was true that the relative brazenness of my escapades had diminished in nature. (I was no longer crashing through airport parking gates or drive-in theater fences.) Yet the incidence of my intake of intoxicants had not slowed, nor had the escalation in the consumptive quantity of my drugs of choice (namely alcohol, cocaine, and painkillers) abated in any fashion whatsoever. Though in December of 1989 I had taken my last dose of cocaine, and never returned to that particular substance, my subsequent abuse of pain medication began its accelerated rise at this point in time. I had merely traded one type of addiction for another—not lessening the severity of my addiction in any way, shape, or form. And although my personality did not appear to significantly alter in any appreciable way when I was loaded (at least a vast majority of the time I toed a pretty straight line in that regard, particularly in front of the kids), that fact could do nothing to detract from what was transpiring within me. Relentless havoc was being wreaked upon my soul due to my continued substance abuse. Darkness was once again beginning to envelop me.

The fact was that I was becoming more and more disenfranchised from reality, feeling less and less confident that I could hold my life together much longer. My depressions had not yet driven me to the depths I had experienced prior to my voluntary induction into the hall of horrors at Holladay Park Hospital a score ago (and subsequent shock treatments). However, they were nonetheless increasing in frequency and severity. This increasing frequency and severity seemed to coincide with the kids' growing older and beginning to leave the roost. It was as if the boys had allowed me to maintain a higher degree of focus in life—or perhaps disallowed me to focus on the negativity in my head quite so much.

And although my marriage to my beautiful wife, Judy, had initially (and for quite some time) shut the door on the loneliness that I had felt in my single days, it could not be expected to fill the "God hole" I spoke of earlier. As the years went by, this hole became more evident to me, more pronounced. The more the void revealed itself to my psyche, the more I tried to fill it in the only manner I had come to know—through further substance abuse.

Although suicidal thoughts had always been an integral part of my psychic repertoire, they, too, became increasingly frequent and severe in nature over the ensuing years. ("Suicidal ideation" the psychiatric community calls it now, as if establishing a new moniker somehow indicates a better grasp of it all.)

As I moved into the nineties, the thought of ending my existence on this sphere became an ironic measure of occasional relief to my perpetual psychic pain. I sometimes reveal to fellow recovering addicts (and I insist on the factual nature of this revelation) that the very first thought that came into my head whenever I closed my eyes—*whenever* I closed my eyes—was that of putting a gun in my mouth. This went on for years, whether I was having a good day or a bad day or a medium day. And I've never even owned a gun in my life (fortunately). That's nuts, isn't it?

No, that's not nuts—it's just suicidal ideation.

THE NARCOTIC NINETIES

One of the salesman at Unity Steel went through a period of time when he was getting painkillers on a regular basis (legitimately) and he would share them with me. They were almost always Tylenol 3s (my least favorite, *but far preferable to nothing*, was my feeling at the time). At one point I remember suggesting to him that he try to get something "better" the next time he went to the doctor. I told him to just tell the doctor that the codeine wasn't setting well with his stomach.

After his next visit to the doctor, this salesman called me at work and without saying hello, asked, "Do we like Darvocet?" I told him that "we," indeed, did. (I remember Luke never cared much for Darvocet (active ingredient, Propoxyphene), but then Luke preferred codeine over Vicodin, which was opposite of my preferences. Peoples' reactions to different medications varies, just as with alcohol. Everyone's body chemistry is different. The point was, *I* liked them. And being a good addict, that, of course, was all that really mattered to me.

The more accustomed to taking pain meds I became, the more I began to seek them out. And this seeking out caused me to eventually veer down a very different path from the one I had been on in the past. This path divergence accelerated with my association with Luke. Luke had maintained a relationship with both my brother Tim and me over the years. He had become close to my brother's kids as they came along. However, as I mentioned earlier, due to Luke's drug abuse Tim would eventually have to tell Luke that he was no longer welcome at their home. Conversely, Luke's drug abuse was precisely why my contact with Luke became increasingly *frequent* over the years. This became particularly true in the nineties, as my addict nature began substituting pain meds for cocaine.

Although I had been drinking alcohol on an almost nightly basis for a number of years, only in the very beginning did it seem to be enough for me. Early on,

I had felt the need to combine other drugs with alcohol to augment my high. For years these other drugs were cocaine and/or painkillers. When I stopped using cocaine it became strictly painkillers, which were far more difficult to consistently obtain than were street drugs. I knew that narcotic pain meds were merely synthetic opiates, and that heroin would be an easier opiate to procure on a consistent basis, but I had always drawn the line at "the big H." Also, I had always heard that heroin was the most addictive drug there was, and I didn't want to go there. Little did I know that pharmaceutical painkillers could become as addicting as heroin and could produce withdrawal symptoms equal to those associated with heroin. (These are facts that remain generally unspoken to the public at large. Could there be monetary reasons behind this glaring silence?)

Though I had, by this point in my life, tried and usually abused virtually every type of drug I could think of (I had also done meth a couple of times at Sanford Steel, but had not cared for it—a blessing, to be sure), I had always told myself that I would never do heroin. My reason was obvious: I always knew what kind of addict I was (whether I called myself an addict or not didn't matter) and I knew what I would do if I liked heroin. I knew I would abuse it and become addicted to it, which, of course, I eventually did.

Yet it never occurred to me, even as I became more and more dependent on painkillers, that I was not much better off than a heroin addict, if at all. I had some opiate kicks from pain meds that were every bit as insufferable as withdrawal from heroin proved to be. (I had nurses in rehab, and many a recovering addict since, attest to this reality as well.) As my abuse of narcotic pain relievers skyrocketed over the next eight or nine years, so did the frequency with which I had to come off of them (when the current supply ran out—which it always eventually did). However, when my initial withdrawal from painkillers occurred, I had no idea why I was so sick. In my relative naiveté, I was unaware that "mere pills" (and legal ones to boot) could induce this level of addiction and withdrawal.

Luke began to call more often with offers of pain meds. Initially, he would come over for a Blazer game or maybe just to shoot the breeze. He would end up turning me on to a few pills (usually Tylenol 3s—the pills he was getting from a couple of different doctors). As time went by, I began to seek out his company more and more. And as my desire for larger quantities grew, I began to give him cash for the pills. (I do not in any way wish to imply that Luke was responsible for getting me hooked. I made my bed. I was the one seeking the narcotics. And Luke was destitute, living in the immobile bus I spoke of early on, always in need of cash. We supplied each other with what we felt the other needed at the time, and there was no right or wrong to it. It just was.)

Luke and I would soon begin to supplement his regular prescription doses with visits to ERs. As the nineties wore on, this method of narcotic procurement became increasingly frequent and increasingly insane.

EARLY WINNER, LATE LOSER

As my drug addiction was progressing, so was my problem with gambling—although I never acknowledged it as a problem until after I got clean. And that was only with a little help from my wife. When I came home from rehab in April of '99, one of the first things Judy said to me was, "You quit gambling, too, you know."

That statement took me aback. Initially I thought, *Oh, really?* However, being freshly aware of the pain I had caused my wife, I had bitten my tongue and slowly said, "All right." In my mind I told myself, *Well, I'll quit for a few months until the 'heat' wears off and then I can start back up again.* Little did I know that those next few months would provide me with the time to reflect on not only the depth and severity of both my drug *and* gambling addiction, but also would reveal to me, bit by bit, the depth and severity of the pain I had caused my wife, particularly over the last few years of my active addiction.

Thankfully, at least for aspiring gambling addicts, Oregon has in place several avenues of approach available on a daily basis. Video poker is probably the most enticing of these gambling venues. There is also Megabucks, Lotto, Keno, scratch tickets, and Sports Action. And we mustn't forget Horse Racing and Dog Racing. Add to that list the two casinos within a hundred miles of Portland that the state eventually sanctioned, and Oregon has become a gambler's paradise. Of these available options, only Horse Racing managed to escape my investment portfolio.

The dog track was only minutes from our house, *and* they served booze, so it was a fairly attractive setting for me. I didn't go there as often as one might think, but I got on binges where I would feel lucky (the bane of every gambling addict), and spend a few nights in succession throwing good money after bad. I pretty much had my way with each of the other attractions as well. Everything but video poker was available in practically every convenience store in the state, and I was a long-time convenience-store junkie. Lotto and Megabucks were automatic twice-a-week affairs (that's how often they draw numbers for these multi-million dollar games). Keno and the scratch tickets were daily affairs. I couldn't buy a can of beer or a can of soda (or a can of tuna, for that matter) without buying at least one scratch ticket (and usually more, of course). And I almost always felt lucky when it came to Keno—I just knew my numbers were coming up on the next game (I was due, damn it).

And Sports Action—forget about it! They saw me coming a mile away. Yet, the fools weren't aware that I was about to develop a system. (I'm the first gambler in history to come up with a system. I know—how lucky is *that?)* You see, I figured the problem with most investors in Sports Action was that they were just too damn greedy—always going for the bigger payoffs. They couldn't see the forest for the trees. I, on the other hand, began to see the loophole, the inherent flaw in their game. The format of Sports Action allows a bettor to pick anywhere from three to fourteen games a week. Of course, you have to beat the spread. (The odds makers are uncannily good at picking the spreads, wouldn't you know?) If you play a three spot, you have to get all three games correct to win anything. If you bet the minimum two dollar ticket and hit all three games, it pays ten dollars. It occurred to me, after losing countless six-thru-fourteen-spot tickets, that I had been going about this the wrong way. I needed to bet on lesser numbers of games (where the odds were much better) and simply bet *more money.* After all, how hard can it be to pick three winners every week? Sheer frickin' genius. So, I immediately set in to check out my system. Being nobody's fool, I bought only ten tickets the first week, at two dollars each. I chose five or six games that I thought were the easiest to win and bought various "three game" combinations. All I needed to do to break even was hit two out of ten tickets. Everything after that was money in the bank. Like I said, sheer frickin' genius.

The first week I hit six tickets out of ten and cleared forty dollars on my twenty-dollar investment. This was just way too damn easy. I almost felt guilty. It was like taking candy from a baby. The poor fools.

So, having completed my scientifically-proven, extremely thorough, flawlessly controlled experiment, I knew what to do next. The following week I bought *240 dollars' worth* of twenty-dollar tickets—all three spots. (I had computed how much I would need to "invest" weekly to make about fifty thousand dollars a year through Sports Action. It would require me to buy at least twelve hundred dollars' worth of action per week. However, being the incredibly controlled person that I was, I was starting out slowly.) I only needed to hit three of the twelve tickets to come out sixty dollars ahead. Everything after that was gravy. Now all I had to do was sit back and wait for the money to start rolling in.

I hit zero out of twelve tickets. That's nada, zilch, negative on the profit, positive on the loss. One-hundred-percent loss. Well, that had to be a fluke. How could I possibly lose every single one of them? As any good gambling addict will tell you, there's only one way to compensate for that type of bad luck. I bet *three hundred dollars* the next week.

Once again, I hit zero tickets. That's nada, zilch, etc. I was wearing a big, flashing "L" on my forehead. Of course, as Judy watched me poring over this rather large wad of tickets, she asked me how much I had lost. (She always just assumed I lost—what was up with that?) I lied and told her "about sixty bucks." (I felt horribly guilty about lying and was literally nauseated from the remorse and shame my insane two-week venture had elicited. Guilt is a huge part of a gambling addict's curse.) So much for my systematic foray into Sports Action. After that, I gave up on my system and went back to "normal gambling."

Video poker was my most frequent state-sponsored gambling hook. To me, nirvana was a belly full of painkillers and a steady supply of rum while sitting on a bar stool playing video poker. I would hit winning streaks but invariably I would put it all back in and then some. Video poker became my biggest gambling nemesis. In the last few years of my active addiction I was constantly leaving the house to go play a few quick games ("few" or "quick" never happened). Or I would hit a bar on the way home from work in order to have a drink and play video poker (or on the way home from an ER hit, or on the way home from *anywhere*).

Then, of course, there were the countless treks to Spirit Mountain Casino, about eighty miles east of Portland, or to Chinook Winds Casino in Lincoln City at the coast (about twenty miles further). Blackjack had always been my game. I had become pretty serious about it at one time in my twenties and began reading up on ways to beat the odds. I even read a book that revealed a simplified counting system that actually can increase (slightly) your odds of winning. However, there are a couple of inherent flaws within any system. First of all, to properly take advantage of counting cards you need a one-or two-deck table. Most of the tables in Oregon (and Nevada and Atlantic City) now have five-or six-deck shoes. Secondly, even if you are successful at counting cards, your odds are still always less than those of the house. Besides, it gets kind of boring concentrating so much and having to limit your bets until a more favorable betting scenario arises. True gambling addicts can't tolerate boredom. One of the things that attracts us is the action, the excitement. And counting cards, though I managed to become fairly proficient at it, was not exciting. That, combined with the booze, would always eventually entice me to wander from the discipline needed to stay engaged in counting cards and in betting according to the count.

All in all, my gambling losses compounded the guilt and depression that were becoming an ever-present part of my psyche, sometimes pronounced, sometimes just lingering in the back of my subconscious. But always there.

As much money as I lost over time in these various gambling arenas, it paled in comparison to the swiftness with which I lost money in the investment world of the stock market. It wasn't until I worked at Unity Steel that I started delving into stocks. (I'm not blaming Unity Steel. I'm not blaming anyone or anything, anymore, for anything.) A few people at work dabbled in the market, and I began to grow curious about it. My first purchase was only a couple hundred dollars' worth. But as I became more interested, my addict brain began working overtime. I recognized that there was a much greater degree of probability of "winning" in the stock market than there was of winning at gambling ventures. (I was already approaching it from a gambling perspective.) Of course, to "win" any substantial amounts required fairly substantial investments. Thanks to my spending habits (on drugs and booze, but also on pretty much anything else I felt like buying—cars, stereos, whatever—it's called "retail therapy" in recovery circles), Judy and I hadn't had a savings account in years.

Since we had virtually no savings, the only way to get extra money was to borrow it. Fortunately (or unfortunately in this regard), we had always had good credit. We had a couple of decent credit lines, and I ended up borrowing five thousand dollars to make my first substantial stock purchase. (Who borrows money to invest in the stock market?) To make matters worse, not only did I not buy blue chip stocks, I didn't even have the discipline to buy medium-risk stocks. No, being a true addict, I felt the need to buy high-risk Canadian mining stocks.

But the real problem began when that first investment actually paid off—

and paid off handsomely. Within a year and a half's time, that first Canadian mining stock, Centurion Mines, went from about seventy-five cents a share to over four dollars a share. I cashed out for over twenty-five thousand dollars. I ended up clearing twenty thousand dollars on a five thousand dollar (borrowed money) investment. That really got the gambling juices going. *The problem,* my gambling mind began to tell me, *was that most people don't have the balls to invest enough money to make decent profits or the brains to see the trends that certain stocks are taking.* More frickin' genius thinking on my part.

So, as I was wont to do, I began calculating how much money and how long it would take for me to parlay this twenty-five thousand dollars into retirement city. *Not long,* I figured. Since I had quadrupled my first real investment, I felt I could at least double the next several. From there, the computations were child's play: *Fifty thousand, one hundred thousand, two hundred, four hundred, eight hundred, one point six million, three point two—and good-bye to working for a living!*

Over the next three years or so, not only did I lose the twenty-five thousand dollars I had pulled out from Centurion Mines, I lost an additional thirty thousand dollars. And it was all money borrowed from the bank, of course. My salary wasn't a whole lot more than thirty thousand dollars a year at the time. It was a significant chunk of change for us—for "us"—Judy had absolutely nothing to do with my insane investments. And insane they were. The more I borrowed, the deeper in debt I put us. However, after my initial success with Centurion Mines, I just couldn't stay away from penny Canadian mining stocks. And that's what all of the stocks I purchased over the next three years were eventually worth—mere pennies. (I guess God *wasn't* sending me stock symbol tips through stranger's license plates after all. Go figure.) Again—sheer frickin' genius.

I experienced horrible guilt and remorse over my stock losses, of course, the same as I had with other significant gambling losses over the years. Even before I had met Judy and gotten married I would feel that way about losing money gambling. Granted, the feelings were much more pronounced after I got married, because now I was losing *our* money, not just my money. But it had never felt good to lose money. My losses were slowly eating away at my soul, just like the drugs were.

Not everything that I did with money was negative, however. We did manage to purchase a home in January of 1990 (prior to the birth of my stock-market period), thanks in large part to my ex sister-in-law, Lisa. She's a mortgage loan officer and was very instrumental in helping us obtain our loan. She also discovered an affordable lot in Gresham, and we were able to have the home built. My parents were good enough to donate three thousand dollars to help us with the down payment. (My parents had struggled to make ends meet most of their lives, but they came through for my brothers and me when we most needed assistance.)

Judy and I always kept our bills paid and up to date, which is why we were extended a few decent-sized credit lines over the years. By the time I eventually got clean and sober I had tapped out our ten-thousand-dollar credit line and was halfway into our eighteen-thousand-dollar credit line—the vast majority of it going to gambling and drugs.

As the nineties trudged on, and as my addictions deepened in severity, so did my dissatisfaction with life. And the more disenchanted I became with the way things were going, the more desperately I sought a quick fix. Being a properly conditioned child of American society, I came to see money as my way out of despair. More and more I would get drunk (and drugged) and gamble in hopes that I could buy my way out of my station in life. The irony was that the more I used and gambled the more depressed I got about what I was doing to myself and my loved ones. But I had passed the turning-back point by this juncture in my life. My disease would have to play itself out now. On my own, I was completely powerless over it.

PROCURING NARCOTICS

For many years something inside me yearned to escape. For a period of time, painkillers seemed to provide me with that escape. They charged my batteries. They seemed to put some fire back in my soul, though I know now they were merely sedating it, numbing it.

The main objects of my narcotic pursuits were: Percocet (oxycodone being the main active ingredient); Vicodin (hydrocodone), and to a lesser degree Tylenol 3 (codeine) or Tylenol 4 (codeine). Each of these also contains either aspirin or acetaminophen for additional pain relief. These were my temporary saviors, the fruits in my garden of Eden.

I would almost always combine the painkillers with alcohol, as I have said. None of these drugs are particularly good for your liver. Combining them with alcohol makes it worse, of course. And although it doesn't come up for your average over-the-counter medication consumer, there is a daily toxicity level for acetaminophen. That level is 4,000 milligrams. Toward the end of my active addiction I would on several occasions take in that amount in a single dose (I mentioned earlier that I would eat up to eight Lorcet 10s, each of which contains 10 milligrams of hydrocodone and 500 milligrams of acetaminophen) and immediately follow that with a dose of heroin. The kicker was, as I have also mentioned, I was no longer feeling any euphoria whatsoever. There were no pleasurable sensations involved at all—just an extremely sedated feeling. Loaded out of my mind, but getting no true high from it.

The state of drug-induced euphoria had ended for me well before I had resorted to using heroin. Yet I continued to abuse drugs every chance I could. I was powerless, on my own, to stop my downhill spiral. In fact, I pursued and created further opportunities for drugs with all the strength and conviction I could summon.

You see, when you first discover that something as simple as swallowing a few pills can (seem to) erase all of your psychic pain (as well as any physical pain), and at the same time induce an unbelievably pleasurable state of euphoria—where is the decision? What is the dilemma? How could you refuse it? Why would you refuse it?

And, of course, I hadn't. I didn't. To this day, I can't understand the mind of a non-addict (a so-called "normy")—just as a lot of non-addicts simply can't understand addiction. They wonder why don't we just stop if it has become a problem? They especially wonder this if it's a non-physically addictive drug like cocaine (although there are some withdrawal symptoms from cocaine, it doesn't enslave the body the way opiates do). Or they ask why we started in the first place? But for me, the opposite is just as puzzling. I know non-addicts who will have a drink or two once in a while and call it good. I ask them, "Why do you take a drink in the first place?" Their response is invariably, "Well, it relaxes me" or "It makes me feel good." Precisely. So, why do you stop? Why don't you want to do it more often? If something relaxes you and makes you feel good, why wouldn't you pursue more of it and pursue it more often? In fact, why wouldn't you want to feel that way all the time?

Perhaps it's because they know what the inevitable outcome of addiction is. Perhaps they can simply rationalize in this manner and call it good. And they're right, of course. Because once the drugs begin to turn on you, once they begin to show the other side of that double-edged sword, it's too late to go back. They will eventually bring you to your knees. Or they will land you in prison or in an institution or kill you. It has been the experience of a great many drug addicts (I include alcoholics in this term, because alcohol *is* a drug) that once you get to that point of no return, no earthly power can stop the downhill cycle. The addict is powerless on his own to stop the insanity. (Else he would have done so long ago, don't you think?)

I had reached that point of no return years before. There was no turning back for me now. Hitting the ERs. Making a run. Procuring medication. That became my life for a number of years. It absolutely consumed me—my time, my money, and my soul. Without a doubt, the biggest problem someone who is bent on ingesting pharmaceutical narcotics has is the ability to maintain a steady supply. They are not easy to procure, and if one does find a source outside of legal means, they are quite expensive. And, as I have said, coming off those mothers is a bear. I had some extremely brutal "dope sick" days. Not a pretty way to live. Withdrawals from narcotics made hangovers seem entertaining. (A really bad hangover is admittedly horrible, but it still doesn't compare to being dope sick. Besides, if I had painkillers when I was hung over, I could take them for the hangover and they would ease the pain immensely. The opposite wasn't true for me—I couldn't drink through my dope sickness. The thought of booze gagged me during withdrawals from opiates.)

So, if the biggest problem (from my addict perspective), was maintaining a steady supply of pills, what was the solution? Well, when you "need" something, you begin to develop connections. So that is what I did, year after year.

By the time the early nineties rolled around, Luke was getting hundreds of pills a month from a couple of different doctors. (He hadn't as yet acquired his third "steady-supply doctor." That would come a few years later, after I had joined his narcotic-procuration endeavors full time.) Luke, as I mentioned, had begun to sell me some of his supply. But it became impossible to sate us both on what he was getting. Luke began asking me to take him to ERs, where he could try to get us some more. For quite a while, I balked. In my mind, I knew where this would lead. Eventually, however, I caved in. I wanted those meds too badly to resist for long any opportunity to get them, no matter what the cost—financial, physical, or spiritual. The euphoria I experienced from pain pills in the first few years was too intense to resist further pursuit of them. Hell, just the internal relief that I received in those first few years of increased use was too great to ignore. Even on days when I wasn't experiencing any overt anxiety or depression, I could sense a relief from any such underlying feelings. Indeed, the pills were like magic to me for quite a while.

So, at some point, Luke and I ventured forth to an ER at a local hospital. I couldn't begin to tell you at which hospital we made our first "hit." We made so many runs over the next seven or eight years that the earliest runs soon became a distant and foggy memory. But it was like anything else—once I tried it, I was hooked. Garnering as many pills as I could became my main focus in life. That pursuit became the center of my universe. For a while, it was a matter of juggling my time to squeeze in another ER run. Eventually, it became a matter of squeezing my life in around ER runs.

The premise was that Luke would go into the ERs and try to score. My role was banker. He scored the meds—I paid for them. He didn't have much money—I always had access to it (no savings, like I said—but I had those credit lines along with a decent income). I also bought Luke a lot of booze, cigarettes, and various food items during the years that we were doing the ER thing. We split the meds right down the middle. That was the deal. Nice and simple.

There were times as the years went by that Luke would pester *me* to go into an ER and score. He said my chances of scoring were better because I looked straight. But I didn't have the same nerve Luke had. It made me anxious just thinking about going in and lying about having pain from some fictitious injury. (Nine times out of ten, back pain would be Luke's "problem" when he went into an ER or clinic. It was usually at least partly true.) "Besides," I would tell Luke, "if I go in, what do I need you for? I *have* money."

As the years went by, however, I found myself doing just that—going to ERs or clinics on my own to supplement my growing addiction. I almost always used back pain as my reason for being there, since it was the hardest thing to detect. (Ironically, I found that my back actually did start to hurt on a fairly regular basis as the nineties wore on. Although I had some legitimate back pain over the years, it didn't become chronic until I started hitting ERs. The mind is a funny thing. Today I have occasional back pain. I take ibuprofen for it.)

An average ER wait was about two hours. The least amount of time we ever spent waiting was about forty minutes. However, short runs like that were extremely rare. Many, many times we would wait two and a half to three hours—sometimes longer. Of course, we only hit the ERs when we were out of medication via other means. I had become like a magnet for painkillers by this time. If anyone within my sphere of influence had narcotic pain medication, I would learn of it. I would always beseech them to part with a few. Sometimes they were reticent, but more often than not they were more than compliant. As I said, the majority of the population doesn't seem to like the effects painkillers produce.

However, my sources were relatively few, and there were long stretches of time in between any connections I could produce. Most of my medication came from Luke—either via his doctors or our ER runs. It wasn't very long after that first ER visit before we were hitting hospitals at least one or two days a week. It took maybe three months for us to get to that stage. I couldn't say what the time frame was for sure. All I do know for sure is that we eventually were hitting ERs way more than I had ever wanted or intended.

Our "score" ratio was sporadic. We had good streaks and bad streaks, just like in gambling. There were periods where we would procure narcotics five or six times in a row from ERs. Then there were times we couldn't reap a single pill to save our lives. At other times we would wait for almost three hours and get a prescription for only six or eight pills. But even then, getting something was always better than striking out.

As time went on, it became more difficult to score locally. Luke had been to every ER in town many, many times. Although he never paid for any of these visits, he almost always gave his real name. (Emergency rooms can't refuse medical treatment based on lack of insurance coverage.) We eventually started coming up with aliases, but it wasn't to avoid any monetary situation. It was just that Luke's name could throw up a red flag because he had been to all the ERs so many times. Often it didn't seem to be a factor, but there were times when Luke could tell that the treating physician either recognized him or had checked the records and was none too pleased about his attendance record.

There came a time when Luke began to bug me about introducing a third party into our ER runs. He said we were striking out too much. We needed to increase our odds of scoring. Luke told me there was a guy he had been friends with since his teen years that was extremely proficient at procuring meds from ERs. He was about our age. His name was Mitch Hampton.

At first I said absolutely no way. As much as I wanted more pills, I didn't feel at all comfortable bringing in a stranger, or even someone I knew, for that matter. I was already feeling terribly guilty and embarrassed that my "need" had brought me this far. I couldn't imagine stepping my addict-related behavior up another notch. But Luke continued talking up this Mitch Hampton guy big time. He even went so far as to say that Mitch was "The Number-Two Man on the West Coast for procuring narcotics from ERs." He would continue to repeat this bizarre statistic as he badgered me more often to comply with his request. It was at the point when he recited this statistic that I would usually question Luke's sanity. I mean, I hadn't just fallen off the turnip truck. *Who the hell keeps statistics on the percentage of success of procuring narcotic painkillers from ERs?* But Luke kept insisting on his data as if it were scientifically unimpeachable. You know how if you hear something enough times it begins to sound true, or at least feasible? Well, it was at least beginning to pique my curiosity.

Finally, after months (or was it weeks?) of continual pestering from Luke to meet this Mitch guy, I acquiesced. We agreed that I would pick Luke up on the following Saturday morning, and Mitch would accompany us to enhance our odds at procuring our pleasure.

"THE NUMBER-TWO MAN ON THE WEST COAST"

Mitch had a lot to live up to, what with being heralded as "The Number-Two Man on the West Coast for narcotic procuration from ERs." But after a few weeks of hanging with him I was thinking *maybe this guy **is** the Number-Two Man on the West Coast.* I had to admit he was good. His success ratio was quite high, at least in the beginning of our relationship. However, as time went by, his margin of success came back down to earthly levels. Perhaps he had been more pumped up in those early weeks, more focused on trying to show me (the new guy) what scoring painkillers from ERs was all about.

There was also the fact that Mitch enjoyed drinking his booze and his inability to control his intake detrimentally affected his prowess in ERs. Like Luke, he had almost no money (they both got minor monthly stipends from the state—Luke for his disability, and Mitch was a veteran with a bad back). After Mitch and I were done making ER runs for the day, I would always buy him a bottle of booze—usually a pint or a fifth of Hood River vodka. I bought him his booze whether he scored pain meds or not. I would sometimes be paying him for his efforts, even though I was getting nothing out of it. (Even back in those days I was at least *somewhat* honorable. Though not scoring would usually send me into a deeper depressed state, I always took care of my drug runner's basic "needs.")

The problem of scoring less frequently began to compound as Mitch started drinking more often before we would head out on an ER run. Aside from the fact that doctors are leery about prescribing narcotics to people who come in with alcohol on their breath, the booze also effected his "talent," his ability to communicate convincingly with these medical people.

Also, the stark reality of the situation was that both Luke and Mitch had been doing this off and on for years in Portland. And not just Portland, either. They had been to the main Salem hospital (about fifty miles south of Portland)

and to some of the hospitals on the Oregon coast numerous times as well. They had been to Eastern Oregon and as far east as Idaho before, on med runs. Between the two of them, the medical bills they had racked up over the years had long ago passed the six figure mark. Consequently, their names and their faces became pretty well known in some of these places.

We tried our best to stagger our hits at the various hospitals. Most of the time we stayed in the Portland area, and we concentrated on spreading out our visits. I even kept a chart on it for a while: *who* had been *where* on *what date*. But after a short period of time I gave that up. We were hitting ERs so often we could no longer wait the three or four weeks (in between specific hospital visits) that we initially thought better increased our odds of scoring narcotics. There are, after all, a limited number of hospitals in the area: Providence, Providence Milwaukie, Mt. Hood Medical Center, Portland Adventist, Oregon City, Kaiser, Hillsboro, Forest Grove, Emanuel, Eastmoreland General, St. Vincent, Woodland Park, and Good Samaritan were the main ones in and around Portland.

Vancouver, Washington, also had two hospitals right across the river, but they were bad news as far as scoring meds. Those two hospitals were very particular about who they passed narcotics out to. I remember when working in the shop at Unity Steel I tweaked my back badly. I was in legitimate and obvious agony for three hours at St. Joseph's Medical Center in Vancouver before a doctor saw me. And when he was done examining me, he didn't prescribe narcotic painkillers. When I requested them, he said, "This is a *hospital*. We don't dispense narcotics here." I'm still having a hard time understanding that one. I know I didn't look like the stereotypical drug addict, and I was truly in legitimate pain. Could this guy somehow see into my soul? He wrote me for an anti-inflammatory (Mitch and Luke called that getting "flim-*flam*'d"). I ended up going to a local clinic in Gresham the next morning where the doctor could see immediately that I had a bona fide injury and wrote me for twenty T-3s (Tylenol 3s).

You would think that more than a dozen hospitals split among only two people would last awhile. But at the rate we were hitting them, they didn't. We would often go from sunrise to sunset on a Saturday hitting ERs. If we didn't score well, we would try again on Sunday. Of these dozen or so hospitals, there were a few we didn't hit very often simply because the odds of scoring at them weren't very good. In fact, we *never* went to Eastmoreland General. Luke had been there so many times that the staff had told Luke not to come back unless he was dying. Mitch got similar treatment there. On occasion, and more frequently as the years went by, they would be asked to leave at other hospitals as well. Luke or Mitch would come out to the car and tell me they had gotten GOMERed (**Get Out of My ER**).

As the hit ratio fell, we had to widen our horizons. We started making more frequent runs to the coast, but our success there began to dry out, too. For a while we started hitting clinics, but this was too costly, because many of them would make us pay cash up front for their services. Then if they didn't prescribe for us, it was even more painful.

Mitch did make some amazing scores over the years, though. He had legitimate back pain a lot of the time. He had had back surgery in the past, and often doctors at ERs would recognize that he had very real problems with his back. One such doctor at Providence Medical Center referred him to a specialist. The specialist took Mitch in (Mitch had recently gotten insurance through the Oregon Health Plan) and began to prescribe Percocet for him on a fairly frequent basis. The doctor told Mitch that he needed another surgery (which he eventually did have, but not through this physician).

After a couple of months of visits to this specialist, Mitch went in for an appointment, and the doctor was waiting to have a talk with him. He had a file laid out on the table and he told Mitch that one of the nurses had recognized him. She used to work in the ER at Providence, and it suddenly dawned on her that that was where she had seen him before. The doctor had gotten the hospital records and confronted Mitch about them.

He started out by saying, "You've been to this particular ER more than anyone—*ever*—we believe." The doctor continued, sounding more amazed than anything else, Mitch related, as he revealed what he had discovered. "You received narcotic pain medication on most of these visits. There were several doctors that wrote in their reports that you had alcohol on your breath, or even that you were visibly intoxicated, and yet they still dispensed prescriptions for narcotics to you."

Mitch said the doctor then stared at him with a look caught somewhere between curiosity and wonder and simply asked, "How do you do it?"

Mitch replied, "I don't know, doc. I guess I'm fairly persuasive."

The doctor shook his head at Mitch's understatement. Then, as he was telling Mitch he couldn't come back anymore, *he began writing him for another prescription of Percocet.* He *must be* the Number-Two Man on the West Coast.

Yes, alcohol on his breath was becoming a more frequent occurrence with Mitch as we progressed in our pharmaceutical endeavors. He could drink like no one I had ever seen. Mitch was about my size, five foot nine, and maybe ten pounds heavier. He could appear much more normal-looking than Luke (when he didn't have too much to drink). He was a decent-looking guy in his mid-thirties, with light-brown curly hair and a great smile. And like Luke, although he didn't have much of a life on the surface, his frequently positive attitude was nothing short of amazing to me. All in all, Mitch was a very likeable guy. However, when he got to a certain point in his drinking, you wanted to steer clear of him. Not that he would get violent or anything—Mitch was *never* violent. In fact, in the years that I hung with him, I rarely saw him even get angry. Luke and I got angry a lot, for one reason or another—and often at each other—but Mitch seemed to always remain even-keeled. However, there was a point in his drinking when he would become a "crawl across the floor, pee-in-his-pants" type drunk. Of course, if most anyone else drank the amount of hard liquor he would on occasion ingest, chances are great that they wouldn't even make it to the crawling stage. They would be in a coma.

I had been out drinking with Mitch in bars after an ER score before, but the first time I saw him drink when he had possession of more than just a cocktail glass in his hand—I was literally blown away. It was just the two of us that day (here I was just a couple of months prior not even wanting to meet Mitch, and now the two of us were making runs together). I don't remember what the med score was, but I remember being pretty excited when I saw Mitch's expression as he approached the car, prescription in hand. (Although once in a while Mitch or Luke would mess with me and pretend like they hadn't scored when they had, most of the time their demeanor gave them away. They were as pleased as I was to make a good hit.)

Whatever the score was that day, I ended up buying Mitch a pint of Hood River vodka (it was the cheapest, and Mitch didn't care what brand he received). Then we went to Seven Eleven at Mitch's request, where he picked up some sort of fruit drink in one of those Big Gulp cups they have. When he got to the car, he dumped half of the fruit drink onto the parking lot and then proceeded to pour the entire pint of Vodka into the cup. That's not the part that amazed me. What did amaze me was that less than five minutes later, Mitch was tossing the empty Big Gulp cup on the floor of the car. I could no more drink a pint of booze in four minutes than I could fly to the moon. But Mitch did it with ease. He had tipped that cup back just a couple of times and chugged until it was gone. The hell of it was, he didn't appear to be even slightly inebriated. I learned at a later date that he could drink an entire fifth in less than twenty minutes and hardly show the effects of it at all, either. It was when he got about halfway through a second bottle (if he had one) that you wanted to get away from him. As I said, he never got violent or anything, but he would become an extremely sloppy drunk at this point.

Although I always mixed alcohol with any pain meds we scored, my intake of booze paled in comparison to Mitch's. If we had a good score, we would sometimes go to a bar and drink and play video poker. In the bar, I had at least some control over how much Mitch drank, since I had the money (although he was very persuasive in that arena, as well). But he was fun to hang with when we could keep his consumption down to a fifth or less. Of course, he would also bug me for money to play video poker with, and I would spot him a few bucks on occasion to appease him. (This was especially true if we had scored well, and I was feeling good and grateful.)

As much as narcotics led to my ultimate surrender, it was alcohol that was Mitch's biggest downfall. I lost count of how many times Luke and I (or Meg) had to take Mitch into detox because he had become unmanageable on the booze. He would become totally dysfunctional after he had binged for a while, and the only way to dry him out was to get him into a hospital or clinic. Otherwise, he would always find a way to get another bottle. We figured he must have been to detox units at least twenty times in just the five years that I knew him.

As far as painkillers went, Luke's tolerance well exceeded mine in the early years. Mitch's tolerance lay somewhere in between us. (Although both Luke and Mitch had used heroin on a number of occasions, and I hadn't as yet, they never had the funds to become too reliant on that particular drug. They weren't into crime to support their habits, either, thank God.) However, as the second half of the nineties progressed, so did my tolerance for pain meds. I remember marveling one time when Luke and I scored twenty Vicodin, and he decided to take all ten of his at once. If he didn't have any muscle relaxers to go with his pain meds, six or seven was usually a good number for him. But on that day he didn't want to do two "fives" as he felt he wouldn't get high enough on either intake. So, he simply took all ten at once.

The hell of it was, Luke with those ten painkillers in him was similar to Mitch on a pint of booze. You absolutely couldn't tell he was loaded. He was feeling very good, but he wasn't showing any effects whatsoever. I remember he met our family (Mom, Tim and his kids, and Judy and me) in the park later that day to watch us blow off some fireworks for the Fourth of July. I expected him to either not show up or to at least arrive staggering or bleary-eyed. I was expecting to see *something* to indicate that he had recently absorbed a rather large quantity of synthetic opiates. But he was as sober-appearing as a judge. I remember thinking to myself that day: *If my addiction ever progresses to the point where I eat ten pills at once, I'm in trouble.* It wouldn't be too much longer before that occurred. I would end up far surpassing any level of pill intake that I had known Luke or Mitch to ingest. And I would be combining heroin with those large doses of painkillers.

Over the next few years, Mitch and Luke and I would share many a bottle of pills together. Addiction is a very powerful entity—I had been so adamantly resistant to meeting Mitch and yet I ended up spending as much time with him as I did with Luke. Indeed, I spent more waking hours with the two of them than I did my own wife.

THE NUT TRICK

As our scoring frequency began to fall, our willingness to try more desperate acts to gain narcotics rose. Due to the great number of visits Mitch and Luke had made to area hospitals, as well as the increasing severity of Mitch's alcohol intake, our percentage of successful hits was dropping rapidly. We definitely were being threatened with a demotion to the minor leagues.

As a sidebar, some might wonder (well, some addicts might wonder) why I didn't pursue narcotic painkillers over the Internet. Without getting too specific on the subject (I do not wish to encourage anyone to do this), the simple truth is I was unaware of any potential for such procuration avenues (access simply wasn't that easy to begin with and also was quite expensive). Ironically, I was about a year and a half clean when I first tried this method. Early recovery is hard for everyone, and mine was no exception. For me, recovery was very up and down for the first three and a half years or so. In those first years I was intermittently insane, suicidal, homicidal—you name it. If it was emotionally unpleasant, I experienced it, it seemed. I simply hadn't yet learned how to deal with the feelings that I had covered up with drugs and alcohol for the prior three decades (feelings that had now resurfaced in all their bare, raw, glory).

Subsequently, at various points in my early recovery, I was extremely tempted to drink or use. The psychological pain would get so bad that the only logical solutions (in my tortured mind) became either suicide or getting loaded. Around sixteen months clean, I had such an episode. It was on the Fourth of July in the year 2000. I had been in a severe depression for days and was becoming increasingly suicidal. I didn't think I could take the psychic pain anymore. My mind (my "disease," if you will) told me a drink or a drug would straighten me out—or would at least bring me some relief from the major anxiety I was experiencing. Since liquor stores weren't open on the holiday, the thought struck me to try to get some narcotics through the Internet.

I got on the Internet and typed the word "Vicodin." When I hit on one of the sites listed, I became astounded by what I saw. I scrolled rapidly, seemingly forever, witnessing an endless list of people looking for relief for their back pain, headaches or whatever. The disease became readily apparent to me. Addiction itself was staring me in the face, it seemed. I felt sickened by the literally thousands of people who appeared to be in denial, or were pretending to have legitimate physical problems. It didn't matter which—they amounted to the same thing. And it made me sad (sadder).

Nevertheless, I double-clicked on one person's name. At that point I wasn't sure what I was going to type. My mind was screaming *Ask him for drugs.* But as I began to put words on the screen, I was surprised by what I saw. Instead of asking this person for narcotics, my very first sentence was: "You don't have to live like this anymore."

Recovery was working. Some unseen force beyond my limited human self was overriding my desire to use. Some power I did not understand, but for which I am eternally grateful, saved my life that day. My desire to get high left me in that instant. I was still feeling down, but no longer suicidal. I went to a Twelve Step meeting and shared, and the support I received was once again overwhelming—and therapeutic. The foundation of recovery I had built in those first sixteen months (with a lot of people's help) was holding me up on that day.

During the time that Mitch, Luke, and I were hitting the ERs, I had no such foundation (none of us had any legitimate defense against the desire to use in our respective stages of addiction). Consequently, as our hit ratio began to weaken, we succumbed even further to our respective diseases. We listened to the devil on our shoulders more readily, so to speak.

We began to experiment with various ways to increase our odds of scoring narcotic painkillers. The first method beyond the norm that I recall was when Luke and Mitch began discussing a blow to Mitch's back. They had used this successfully in the past (before I had started taking them on runs). The idea was for someone to slug Mitch in the lower back as hard as one could, hopefully creating a bruise, or at least leaving a mark of some kind. I couldn't believe they were even talking about this, yet part of me was secretly relishing the idea. *Anything to increase our odds of scoring*, was my thinking at the time. I was truly addicted to my medicine, and my self-centered obsession reminded me that it wasn't my back that was getting punched. Besides, Mitch seemed more than willing to take one for the Gipper. I was not about to stop him.

212

But then the focus came *my way*. Luke suggested that it should be *me* that delivered a blow to Mitch' back. I had been willing to let someone else do the dirty work, but I wanted no part of intentionally trying to hurt someone. (I didn't even kill spiders and flies in the house, for God's sake—I set them free outside.) Yet Luke was being his stubborn self on this one. I kept suggesting that he do it, but he wouldn't let go of his idea. Finally, after much badgering, this "fly-saver" agreed to get out of the car and punch Mitch in the back.

My first delivery was understandably soft. I didn't want to hurt Mitch, after all. I had actually grown quite fond of the guy over the months we had been hanging out. He and I got along quite well, which was more than I could say about Luke and I at times, especially in the later stages of our relationship. However, after Mitch literally laughed at my weak attempt at inducing injury to his back, I gathered a little more courage. I punched him harder. He laughed again. The man's back was solid iron, I tell you. I damn near broke my hand. I tried a third time, and he and Luke were now both scoffing at me (and my hand was throbbing—I was hurt far more than Mitch).

So Luke got out of the car. As he set himself to smack Mitch in the back, you could readily see that this was something they had done before. Mitch braced himself while Luke set his stance. Luke asked Mitch if he was ready. Mitch said, "Go." Luke did. I was impressed by the power of his punch. He actually rocked Mitch, where my blows hadn't budged him one iota.

Luke immediately asked Mitch if he was all right, genuine concern coating his voice. Mitch grunted, and said, "Yeah." Then after a couple of seconds he added, "That was a nice one, Luke. Good job."

Moments later, as we pulled into the hospital parking lot, we checked Mitch's back. Sure enough, a mark was definitely beginning to show. There was a redness in the area where Luke had hit him.

A couple of hours later we were divvying up medication. When both Luke and Mitch came along on a run, we would split it up a little differently. If they were each going to make a run, then we would distribute the drugs evenly, three ways—even if one of them scored and the other didn't. They were both trying, and we rewarded effort. But there were times when Luke already had medication but didn't have enough left to share with us. In those instances he was just along for the ride, and since he wasn't going to contribute anything to the cause, then he didn't get any of our score. On occasion, if Mitch and I were having a good day, or made a particularly impressive hit, we would cough up a few pills apiece for Luke. Usually, we would get pills that were different from what Luke had, and he would crave some of our pills, just to have something different. A large percentage of Luke's scheduled meds were T 3s, and Mitch and I preferred Vicodin or Percocet over codeine. Those were the meds that Mitch went after in the ERs. It's not like they bring you out a menu or anything, but Mitch had ways of telling the doctors what "worked" for him (or what didn't) without sounding like a seasoned addict. (When I later started hitting clinics on my own, I became fairly proficient at this, myself.)

Over the next few years Mitch would occasionally resort to self-mutilation, as Luke termed it, in an effort to score meds. That was one area Luke completely shied away from—inflicting pain upon himself, that is—and I didn't blame him. (However, he didn't seem to have any problem punching Mitch in the back. Of course, after brief resistance, neither had I.)

Mitch hurt his thumb one time, I remember. I don't recall how he did it, only that it wasn't on purpose. He may have hit it with a hammer, I'm not sure. But he let that thumb of his stay bad for several weeks. He scored quite a bit during that time. He would actually bang on his thumb with an unopened pocket knife to make it swell before going into an ER. It was painful to watch, although it seemed to hurt me more than it hurt him.

There was one particular run toward the end of Mitch's "thumb days" that I will never forget. It turned out to be the worst day in my ER life. We hit three ERs one Saturday and spent a total of eleven hours waiting and scored *nothing*. The third hospital had been the VA Hospital "on the hill" in Northwest Portland. Mitch, being a vet, could utilize their services, but they were notoriously slow, so it was always a last resort. That wait alone was a grueling *six hours*. Eleven hours total that day, for nothing. It was sheer hell. All those long hours, mostly sitting in my car, trying to read or sleep and being able to do neither. If it was early on in a run I could usually relax enough to do a crossword puzzle or maybe read a bit. But as time dragged on I would become increasingly agitated and impatient. I would be unable to concentrate enough to do anything other than stare in the rear view mirror every five frickin' seconds hoping to see Mitch walking my way. And there was no way I could relax enough to sleep. It was a really fucked up way to spend a weekend, all the while feeling guilty for having left my wife at home alone. (If she was at work I always felt less pressure.) That eleven hour day was the pits, to put it mildly.

The hell of it is, the VA Hospital kept Mitch overnight. They were actually discussing amputating his damn thumb! He had let it go for so long that it had become badly infected. The other ERs had prescribed antibiotics and anti-inflammatories for him (which, of course, we hadn't filled). The VA Hospital thought it was much more serious. Yet Mitch walked out of there the next morning. (He did stop messing with his thumb after that, and it eventually healed.) But it was another example of how desperate addicts can become.

There were a few occasions when either Luke or I would take Mitch into an ER in a wheelchair. His claim to the hospital staff would be that his back pain was so severe he couldn't even walk. We seemed to have a fairly high success rate with this approach, yet anytime you deviated from the less obtrusive type of visits, you were spotlighting yourself. We couldn't pull off these more desperate measures with too much frequency, lest we be discovered pulling the same stunt twice at the same hospital. As I said, we hit so many ERs over the years, that it became impossible to keep track of *where* and *when* we had done *what*. So, it was necessary to limit these approaches that strayed from the norm.

There was one night that Mitch and I were on a run, just the two of us. We had gone to a couple of hospitals and had been shut down on both visits during the afternoon. We had spent probably close to five hours by this time trying to procure meds. As a last effort for the day we were going to try Good Sam's (Good Samaritan Hospital) in Northwest Portland, but we wanted to come up with something to increase our odds of scoring. We had been thinking about it for several minutes when Mitch came up with an idea.

"You can run over my foot!" He suddenly blurted out (with far too much exuberance, I must say, considering what he was suggesting).

I remarked that surely he was kidding. He assured me that he wasn't.

"I'm not going to run over your foot, Mitch!" There was no way I was going to run over the man's foot, for God's sake.

But Mitch began to turn on his persuasive powers. He told me he had done it before and that it didn't hurt, and it didn't cause any real damage. I asked him why the hell he wanted to do it then. He said it would leave a mark and he could actually tell them that someone had run over his foot.

I reiterated my refusal to perform this act of insanity (with slightly less resistance this time, however). Mitch in kind, reiterated his conviction that it wouldn't hurt him. Then he got out of the car. He walked to the front of my Nissan Sentra, put his foot under the tire and told me to "just do it, man!"

I was feeling extremely uncomfortable with this maneuver, but I wanted some goddamn pills. I gingerly stepped on the gas and felt the tire meet the resistance of Mitch's foot. I backed off in a panic. "I can't do this, Mitch!" I yelled out to him.

"Yes, you can!" He yelled back. *"Just do it!"* He shouted, making the famous Nike slogan from that point forward take on new meaning in my life.

So I did. I ran over Mitch's damn foot. At that moment, I felt about as low as I had felt in a long, long time—perhaps ever. I had become willing to inflict pain on another human being in order to maybe get drugs for myself. This was getting way out of hand.

Mitch yelled out to me that it wasn't good enough—that "it didn't do anything." He said we had to do it again. He wanted me to take a bigger run at it. So I ran over his foot again, this time from a little further back. It didn't hurt him, thank God. It didn't leave much in the way of a mark, either, but he scored, nonetheless—which, of course, was all that had mattered to us.

And then there was "The Nut Trick," as Luke and Mitch had coined it. This particular form of self-mutilation epitomizes to me the depths to which addicts will sink to procure their drug of choice. (This is another segment of my life that I hesitate to include because of its humiliating nature. But I recall my wife's earlier challenge: "If you're going to sugar coat your story, why tell it?" Her words supply me with the courage and the humility to continue.)

When Luke and Mitch first suggested trying The Nut Trick as a means with which to heighten our chances of scoring, I steadfastly refused to be a party to it. Luke had told me about The Nut Trick before I had even met Mitch. It seems that they had used this ploy on occasion in the past. Mitch, once again, was the one being mutilated.

The Nut Trick is not something one can use very often due to the rarity of the injury being portrayed. Talk about throwing up red flags. It had to be used very sparingly. Besides, it was not for the faint of heart, and this particular means of self-mutilation is not something even the most desperate, hard-core users would wish to engage in with any regularity. Mitch was the only one we knew of who was crazy enough to do something like this in the first place— and as crazy as Mitch was, even he had limits as to how often he would mutilate himself, particularly in this manner.

It seems, according to "Doctor" Mitch, that the area of skin encasing the male testicles is not very sensitive, due to a minimal number of nerve endings.

(He learned this little tidbit by accident I had always assumed. I'm fairly certain it never came up on Jeopardy: "I'll take *Genital Sensitivity* for two hundred, Alex.") Personally, I found it to be a rather ludicrous claim, but I wasn't about to perform The Nut Trick on myself to disprove his theory. Regardless, the deal was that Mitch would chafe a section of his testicular sac with whatever crude instrument he had at his disposal. And the theory was that no doctor in the world would refuse pain medication to a man who had just *slammed his nuts down so hard on a bicycle bar that it made them bleed.* Mitch also knew that a physician most likely wouldn't have a clue as to what level of pain such an injury would actually instill, having no personal frame of reference from which to garner their assessment. It certainly *looks* painful (one would think—I truly never bothered to look at Mitch's nuts before *or* after he would chafe them).

It seems that the good doctor (whomever he or she was) would often want a urine sample when Mitch would go into an ER with this particular injury. As time went by, Mitch became more sophisticated with his technique (if one can employ the word "sophisticated" in any context when speaking of The Nut Trick). He would drop some of the blood from his wound into the urine sample in hopes that they would think his urethral tube had been partially crushed or some damn thing. Who wouldn't prescribe narcotics to a man with *bleeding balls and a crushed urethral tube?*

It took several different attempts on the part of Mitch and Luke to get me to agree to allowing The Nut Trick to be performed in my car. I simply had not wanted to be a part of anything that disgusting, gross, repulsive, conspicuously wrong, etc. It made me ill to think that any of us could stoop that low. But I had my addiction to feed, and my demons to expel, and after going scoreless one Saturday morning, I finally acquiesced.

"Just don't get any blood on the goddamn seat, Mitch!" I chided him before he had even begun the dirty deed.

"I'm not going to get any blood on your precious seat, man!" Mitch retorted.

"Man, this is sick," I muttered, mostly to myself, as my virgin trip into first-hand exposure to The Nut Trick commenced.

"But you'll gladly partake in the reward it brings, won't you?" Luke contributed from the front passenger seat.

"Yeah," I not so enthusiastically admitted. And then as the thought of the reward took hold in my addict brain, my enthusiasm also took root. "Yeah, I suppose I will, Luke." Then, returning my attention to Mitch, I added, "Just hurry on up with it, Mitch!" I looked around to see if anyone was paying attention to us. "This makes me awfully damn nervous."

"I don't know why the hell it should make you nervous—I'm the one scraping skin off my balls with a fucking screwdriver, for Christ's sake," Mitch replied.

Yes, The Nut Trick is a sick and twisted, bloody mess. But it usually did the trick. Scored pain pills for us, that is. Yet, as hard as it is to believe that any doctor would *not* prescribe pain medication for a man who had just *slammed his balls down so hard on a bicycle bar that they made them bleed and possibly crushed his urethral tube,* Mitch did get shut down once in a while. Although the percentage of getting GOMERed was absurdly low when employing this method, it was still not something you did every week. No, this particular form of self-mutilation was saved for the most desperate of times. Just being party to The Nut Trick showed how desperate I was to seek relief from my psychic pain and to experience one more high. I don't mean to justify the overtly insane measures that I went to (or allowed others to go to) to procure narcotics. I simply was doing what I felt I had to do to retain my fleeting grip on sanity.

As my tolerance skyrocketed (in those last couple of years in particular) and I began to take larger and larger doses, I needed more and more pills to maintain my addiction. Due to these increasing needs, I would run out of pills more frequently, regardless of our additional efforts to increase our narcotic acquisitions. This also meant that I was experiencing more frequent withdrawals. It meant I was jonesin' for pills much more often. And when you're dope sick from narcotic withdrawal, you will do almost anything to "get well." This would include, of course, being party to The Nut Trick.

But there was a lot that led up to this point. A lot. I didn't just go from taking a couple of Tylenol with codeine for back pain to witnessing—hell, eventually actually encouraging—self-mutilation of a fellow human being in one fell swoop. Nor did I just decide on a whim to risk a good job, a good marriage, and a stable family life by later illegally altering or forging prescriptions to satisfy my craving and to treat my ever-growing levels of anxiety and depression with ever-increasing doses of pain medication. This level of desperation didn't occur overnight. Nor was it just a spur-of-the-moment decision that would soon make me take the ultimate plunge of trying heroin.

And though I was experiencing growing guilt over the time and money I was spending on procuring narcotics, I was only doing what I thought I needed to do to alleviate my psychological and emotional pain. In retrospect, much of my suffering was self-created and self-perpetuated, but I had no tools with which to combat my pain at that time. In my sick and diseased mind, getting and using drugs was the only thing I knew to do, short of ending my existence on this sphere.

ALTERING REALITY

Another practice we began engaging in to increase our supply of pharmaceutical narcotics was forging or altering prescriptions. Changing prescriptions for regular-strength Vicodin into extra-strength tablets was by far the easiest form of doing this. That is, if the doctor had unwittingly left enough room to add an "ES" (Extra Strength) at the end of the word "Vicodin." Sometimes the prescribing physician would put the quantity too close, as in "Vicodin 14," and in those instances it thwarted any attempt at adding the "ES." On those occasions we would look at the possibility of altering the quantity instead. Sometimes you could make a "10" an "18," or a "14" a "24," for example. But when the doctor wrote out the *word* for the quantity after the numerical designation, as in "12 (twelve)," that would nullify any quantitative adjustments we could make as well. Also, we couldn't add the "ES" on prescriptions that had the hydrocodone milligram count on them, as in "Vicodin 5 mg." Regular strength Vicodin contain 5 mgs each and Extra Strength have 7.5 mgs, so when we were able to add an "ES" it gave us quite a boost of additional narcotics. (Of course, our favorites were the Lorcet 10s I referred to earlier, equivalent to two regular-strength Vicodin, each containing 10 mgs of hydrocodone.)

It was a couple of years into abusing the medical system before we got bold enough to start altering "scripts." It was a felonious offense, so we were naturally a little apprehensive about it (I know several people who were busted for that very thing). But once we started doing it and saw how easily we could get away with it, it became a more frequent event.

As time went by we began to familiarize ourselves with prescription language, much of which was in Latin. There were quite a few times that a physician would prescribe an anti-inflammatory or a muscle relaxer and not prescribe a narcotic pain reliever. On many of these prescriptions there would be enough room at the bottom to add another medication. We would use that empty space to prescribe for ourselves a narcotic painkiller. Then you just hoped and prayed that the pharmacist didn't call in the prescription for verification.

I was the one who was doing the actual script-altering. Mitch and Luke just didn't have the handwriting for it. Part of the problem was their hands were often shaking too much—Luke from abuse of muscle relaxers and Mitch because he was a serious alcoholic. But I was able to copy a doctor's style in pretty good form after practicing on scratch paper for a few minutes. I even began carrying in my car an assortment of different colored pens with various levels of thickness—fine point, medium point, etc. I wanted to match the original prescription as closely as possible. Mitch and Luke would, without fail, pester me incessantly to hurry up as I was practicing my forgery. I would always retaliate by asking them if they wanted pain meds or did they want to get busted? My extra caution paid off in the long run. We only got shut down once on an altered script, and it wasn't necessarily due to my forgery. The pharmacist said they had to call it in for authorization, which they did on occasion. I knew once he said that, we were screwed. So, we left without the meds. No way they were going to authorize an altered script, of course.

Our biggest claim to infamy was adding forty Lorcet 10s to a prescription one late summer afternoon. Mitch had gotten a prescription for forty ulcer pills. They had left enough room on the bottom to add the couple of lines of wording that it took to prescribe a medication. So, after practicing my Latin forgery (with extra diligence on this specific occasion—forty Lorcet 10s was a lot to try to abscond with), my anal retentiveness once again paid off for us. We got away with it. The only problem was that in order to not look suspicious, I paid for the ulcer pills, too—and they cost eighty dollars. The pain meds had cost around forty dollars, and by the time I bought pizza and beer for all of us in celebration of our coup, the cash outlay for the night came to over one hundred fifty dollars. Of course, I felt guilty about spending that much in one evening, but at the same time I was elated over our score.

My financial outlay was growing in direct proportion to my habit. Although the one-hundred-fifty-dollar night was an exception, there were plenty of days and nights I was spending fifty to a hundred dollars to maintain our disease. In order to minimize potential detection of these expenditures from Judy, I began to transfer money from one of our credit lines to our checking account over the phone. Then I would withdraw that amount from an ATM, writing down neither transaction in our checkbook. This would keep the checkbook straight, but our credit line debt and subsequent monthly payment would increase each time I did this.

My attempts to hide my excessive spending became an increasingly impossible venture. And Judy was certainly no fool. There were several times in those last few years that she would come to me with a bank statement in her hands and tears in her eyes wondering where all the money was going. It breaks my heart when I think of those moments. She had done nothing to deserve the type of manipulation and deceit I was perpetrating upon her. But because I was immersed in my addiction, I would make bogus excuses about my expenses, knowing I wasn't fooling her, but too afraid to come clean. I couldn't risk losing my connections to the drugs I craved. She knew I was making ER runs—this much I would tell her. I couldn't be gone all those hours without some explanation. I justified these ER visits with typical addict excuses: "If anyone else had to put up with the mental anguish I've had to endure and they found something that helped them when psychiatrists had been unable to, they would pursue those ends, too." What I was saying I firmly believed, at the time. In fact, I believe it to this day—that anyone else experiencing the level of angst that I was experiencing during those years would go to the same lengths (or depths) if they could find no other means of relief. There is no doubt in my mind that this is true. (In fact, I believe that most people would have blown their brains out if they had spent more than about thirty minutes in this head of mine back when it was doing it's thing. Hell, they'd be crazy if they hadn't.)

Although Judy disapproved wholeheartedly with what I was doing, of course, she knew I wouldn't listen to any dissuasion on her part. It was easier to go with the flow than to try to combat the iron will and stubbornness of an addict. Besides, as she told me after I had gotten clean (when I was making amends to her for my past transgressions), she had been glad to be rid of me when I would leave the house to go on an ER run. She said I had become a "geek" in my addiction, if I recall her loving description of me accurately, and she had been happy to see me leave.

I would invariably lie to Judy about how much these runs were costing me, although she obviously knew the truth. The guilt I experienced from the pain my deception was causing my wife only served to heighten the anguish I was attempting to alleviate through drugs.

MICHAEL

In the middle of all of this insane running to ERs and pursuing narcotics, tragedy struck in our home. In 1993 my oldest stepson Michael had been busted for a burglary charge in California. Because of his previous record and outstanding warrants the judge sentenced him to two years, which he served in a federal prison. During those two years we exchanged letters with Michael fairly often. Judy sent him care packages religiously. We would talk to Mike on the phone, and he would express to us his desire to straighten his life out. In the last couple of years before he went to prison Judy had hated talking to him when he called because he was usually drunk, and he just wasn't Michael. However, in prison he was off of the alcohol and she had meaningful conversations with him. So did I. We were also encouraged by the upbeat nature of his letters from prison. We knew Michael would often say the right things, but he seemed sincere this time about wanting to turn things around.

Unfortunately, on Michael's first day out of prison, he did something that's not recommended for addicts—he went back to old playmates, playgrounds, and playthings. During much of the last couple of years before going to prison, Michael had resorted to living in a park in Los Angeles—Reseda Park—and this is where he ended up on his first day of freedom. It was a place where he knew people. (We had known Michael was getting out soon, but he never let us know the exact date. Consequently, we weren't even aware he had been released.) He got drunk and loaded that first day out in the real world. As we later found out, he was arguing with a guy named Dave off and on all day long. When there was no more alcohol, Michael asked to borrow this Dave guy's bicycle to go to the liquor store. Dave said no. Mike just wanted to use it to get another bottle of booze—he would have brought it right back, and the guy knew it. So Mike hopped on the bike anyway, but before he could get away, the man pulled out a knife and stabbed Michael once through the heart. He died within minutes, before the paramedics arrived. That was September 13, 1995. Michael was thirty years old.

I was the one who got the phone call from Al, Michael's biological father. Actually, Casey was at our house when Al called, and he had picked up the phone. But Al didn't want to break the news to Casey over the phone, so he had asked for me. Casey could tell something was terribly wrong and I was troubled by the look in his eyes as he handed me the phone. He said to me, "It's my dad. Something about Mike."

"Hi, Al," I said into the phone. There was no easy way for Al to tell me. "It's Michael. He was found stabbed to death in a park," he said, the pain obvious in his voice. My mind raced with a combination of disbelief and heartache when Al told me the news. I could barely speak. I was in shock. I would have to tell Casey. I would have to tell Judy—she was at work for another hour or so. Jesus. It was awful. I had never felt so sick in all my life. I asked Al a couple of questions, but he didn't know much at that point. He and Betty had been called in to identify the body. Horrible. Unbelievably horrible.

I got off the phone and told Casey. Casey and I were crying when moments later Darin showed up at the door, and I had to break the news to him. He went running out the door. None of us had seen Michael since before he had been to prison, and now we never would.

I didn't know how I could tell Judy. The thought of it was more than I could bear. Her first-born son, dead. I debated whether to call her at work. I called my mother to tell her. I called my brother as well. I didn't know what to do. Both of them, and Casey, too, told me not to break the news to Judy over the phone. They were right, of course. She was the only one working at a small retail store in Gresham. She would be home in an hour.

It was without a doubt one of the most excruciating hours of my life. I kept envisioning the pain that Judy was going to have to endure. I couldn't think of how to tell her that her first-born son had been killed. She came through the door that long hour later, smiling as she saw me, unaware that her world would soon be senselessly and irrevocably shattered. She and Michael, though separated by distance, had held a very deep bond, a bond only known by a mother and her child. Although their relationship wasn't perfect, I know of no mother and son who loved each other more deeply, and who wished happiness for the other more profoundly.

I firmly grasped my wife by the shoulders. She immediately knew by my expression that something was terribly wrong. Knowing that there was no way to soften the blow, and not wanting to leave her hanging, I simply uttered the words, words that haunt me to this day, "It's Mike—it's bad—he's dead." My voice cracked as I spoke, and the tears welled up in my eyes—her ensuing pain haunts me deeper than anything I have ever known. I thought she was going to die in my arms. An indescribable moan as she began to sob—only a mother's loss could exude such total anguish. The look on her face would have heartbroken the hardest of hearts. We wept in each others arms, Judy sounding more like a wounded animal than anything human. Moments later she cried out between sobs, "He had a good heart."

Casey and Judy and I all lay down together and cried. Hours later, in the middle of the night as Judy and I lay in bed, she suddenly sat up and yelled out, "I can't stand it!" and began weeping again uncontrollably. I'll never forget her pain.

Judy and her sister Pennie and I traveled to L.A. and went to the park where Michael had died to lay down flowers. We talked to a man who had been there when it happened. He had administered CPR to Michael that night. He told us as much about what had happened that day as he could and we thanked him and told him we were very grateful to him for trying to save Michael's life. We then laid the flowers down on the spot where he had shown us Michael had died.

The man who had given Michael CPR would be called a transient by most. That's how the LA newspaper identified Michael when they reported the killing. I wrote the paper a letter letting them know that although I understood their usage of the word "transient" I felt that a more sensitive approach in the future might be "male" or "thirty-year-old male." Michael was a thoughtful, kind, caring human being with a generous spirit, not simply a "transient."

And "he had a good heart."

Because it had been a homicide, Michael's body was held for a few extra days while the investigation was underway. He ended up being "coincidentally" buried on September 19, the same day my father had died seven years earlier. I wrote Michael's eulogy as well.

Alcohol and drugs robbed Michael of the ability to pursue a normal lifestyle. They stole his grasp on life, never let him get a firm grip. I can relate to his pain. I can relate to his escapism. Michael had a very outgoing, charming, and dynamic personality—without drugs or alcohol. If only he could have recognized that fact more fully. Sadly, I recall he once told us that life was boring without drugs or alcohol. I only wish that Michael could have lived and learned to see the total falsehood of that statement for himself, as I came to see when I eventually entered recovery. If only we could've helped him somehow. But we all did the best we could. Al and Betty and Judy and I took turns over the years trying to provide him with a stable environment. It just never worked out. It became a tragic story with a very tragic ending.

Judy had quit drinking on January first of the same year in which Michael was killed. Her resolution had sprung from several motivating factors. For one thing, she had decided on her own that it was simply the healthy thing to do. There was also the fact that she came from an extremely alcoholic family—having lost two brothers to the disease (and now a son), as well as having a couple of other siblings who were deeply immersed in their disease. Judy was a functional drinker, not a sloppy drunk at all, and certainly not a mean drunk. Neither Judy nor I underwent radical personality alterations when we drank, as I've noted. However, both of us drank almost nightly, and she knew it wasn't leading anywhere fruitful. But perhaps her largest motivation was derived from her thinking that maybe if *she* quit her intake of intoxicants, that perhaps Michael and I would follow suit. I know now she had been growing more and more disgusted with my increasing pursuit of drugs—she had desperately wanted to see me quit. Unfortunately, it would be another four years before I would enter rehab. Maybe if Judy and I could have both gotten sober sooner, we would have had more knowledge about helping people stay sober—knowledge that we could have passed onto Michael. I don't know. One thing I have learned is that I can't control another person's intake, I can't stop them from using or drinking, and I can't keep them from drinking or using in the future. I can only tell them what I have done to get sober and to stay sober and hope that someday something will click within them. Tragically, it is too late for Michael, but it's not too late for those who are still among us.

Dave, the man who had killed Michael, was caught before a couple of hours had passed after he had stabbed him. He was eventually sentenced to three years in prison, after copping a plea bargain. Not a lot of time for ending someone's life, even if they *were* borrowing your bicycle without your blessing. Al and Betty and Judy and I were sent notices of his sentence hearing and were told we were welcome to come and say whatever we wanted at that time. Frankly, we were all pretty much of the same mind set. I've never understood it when people get up at those things and start spewing hateful barbs at the offending party. Neither Judy nor I have ever once felt hatred toward the man. It just seems rather pointless. Nothing will ever bring Michael back, certainly not hatred. Certainly not revenge. Surely we felt some anger toward this David person in the beginning. I know Darin and Casey did—the man killed their brother, after all. But I never felt like I wanted the man to die because of what he had done. What would that accomplish? *What would that make us?* has always been my thinking.

Regardless, Judy and the boys wanted me to write something to be read to Mike's killer at the sentencing. So I did. I wrote a three-page letter, which Michael's stepmother Betty was brave enough to read for us in court. (The sentencing was in Los Angeles, where Betty and Al live.) There was nothing hateful, nothing spiteful, nothing vengeful in that letter. I only asked this person to take a hard look at what he had done and to try to imagine the grief he had caused Michael's family and friends. I described to him how Michael's mother had reacted when she had learned of her oldest son's death. I told him that we only hoped he would learn a valuable lesson from this great tragedy and seek to improve his life. We hoped that he would take this horrible event and make something good come of it. I asked that he make the most of the three years he would serve behind bars and take that time to reflect and to search within himself for the willingness to commit to a better way of life.

I have no idea what became of Michael's killer. I only know that Michael will never get the opportunity to experience life as it was meant to be experienced.

Just a few months after I had first met Michael, back in the summer of 1981, there was a day when his mother and I picked him up from work, as we often did. On the way home, the song, "Free Bird," by Lynyrd Skynyrd began playing. Michael, like most sixteen-year-olds, loved music. But I sincerely believe he loved it even more than most. Music was truly part of his soul. "Free Bird" was my favorite song, and I wanted to share it with Michael that day. I blasted the car radio as loud as the speakers would take. It's a very long song with a beautifully melodic first half and a very up-tempo second half.

When it was over, Michael exuberantly exclaimed, "That was awesome! Those guys rock!"

He genuinely loved it and I was glad we were able to share that moment.

Since Michael's death, I have always thought of "Free Bird" as "our song." And although it was my favorite song, for a long time after Michael's death I couldn't listen to it without breaking down. Occasionally it still conjures up some powerful emotions. And that's okay. The song never fails to remind me of Michael, and I consider that a blessing.

On the day celebrating my first year clean and sober, I chaired a Twelve Step meeting. I announced at the beginning of the meeting that I was dedicating my first year anniversary to my deceased stepson, Michael. After the meeting, as I was driving out of the parking lot, I decided to turn on the radio. I literally hadn't listened to the radio in weeks. I had been listening to various audio tapes and CD's. But the *instant* I turned on the radio that night, "Free Bird" began to play. Chills traveled up and down my spine. A "God shot," as some might call it. A mere coincidence, others might say (I personally no longer believe in those). Whatever anyone else might want to call it, it was a deeply moving experience for me, and something I'll never forget.

A couple of other "coincidences" occurred regarding Michael after I got clean and sober, one tragic, one touching.

The first occurred in the late summer of 1999, six months after I had gotten clean. One early morning Judy was reading the newspaper when I heard her suddenly gasp and then start to cry. I asked her what the matter was, and in between sobs she told me that Michael Turner, son of my good friend, Bret, from National Steel days, was in the obituary column that day. He had been Bret and Susan's oldest son, just as Michael had been our oldest. He'd been born in 1965, the same year our Michael had been born. Michael Turner died at the age of thirty-four on September 13, four years *to the day* that our Michael had been killed. Tragically, Michael Turner had died of a heroin overdose.

Same first name, both eldest sons born in the same year, both died of drug related causes on the same date, September 13. And our families were linked—Bret and I had been best friends during my days at National Steel. A tragic coincidence? A tragedy, most definitely—horribly sad, devastating. But coincidence? Like I said—I don't believe in them.

I hadn't talked to Bret in almost a dozen years, but I called him that day and offered him and Susan our condolences. As our conversation progressed, I told him I had gotten clean and sober earlier that year. He was shocked to learn that I had become addicted to heroin, but was glad I had gotten off of it before I ended up like his son. I asked if it would be okay if Judy and I came to Michael's funeral. He replied, "Of course."

I have now watched two grieving mothers bury their oldest sons because of drugs and alcohol. It is the saddest sight imaginable. We are not supposed to outlive our children. But drugs and alcohol don't follow any rules, they don't adhere to any guidelines of decency, they harbor no conscience, they suffer no guilt, they extend no mercy.

On a much more uplifting note there is my good friend, Shelley Slayton. I met Shelley at a Twelve Step meeting four years after I had gotten clean and sober. We came to discover that she and Michael had been the best of friends in their mid-teens. My memory over the years is very spotty at times, and I didn't remember her from back then. But Casey saw her at one point and recognized her. Judy and Darin remembered her as well. We have since become close friends with Shelley. Judy and I have been to Shelley's for dinner and she has been to our place. We have reminisced about Michael at times, but more often than not we talk about recovery from addiction. Shelley has gone with me to Portland Adventist Medical Center to share our "experience, strength, and hope" with the addicts and alcoholics in rehab there (a monthly commitment I have done since I had my first year clean and sober). She is a beautiful person, inside and out, and I know that our meeting was no coincidence.

In just a few short years my wife Judy had lost her mother, her father, two brothers, a father-in-law whom she dearly loved, and her oldest son. That is more pain than anyone should have to bear. Although I can't explain the reasons behind this suffering, I have to believe that it ultimately serves a higher purpose, as I've stated before. I know that my poor mother has been through a tremendous amount of pain in her life as well (and has withstood it heroically, remarkably). And although I can't explain the reasons for this, either, what I do know is that these are two of the strongest and most loving people in the world. Through their pain, and their dealing with this pain, others have gained the strength to endure their own suffering.

I remember telling a counselor in my early months of sobriety about all of the losses my wife had to experience in a relatively short period of time. He looked at me and said, "That's a lot of pain for someone to go through."

I replied, "Yeah. I don't know how she does it."

He had responded, "Yes, but I was referring to *you*. You were there, too, weren't you?"

What I know today is that no one need suffer alone. We are all given opportunities to help each other through this life. That, I believe beyond a shadow of a doubt, is one of our main purposes here.

We love you and miss you, Michael.

THE DISEASE PROGRESSES

In spite of the tragedy of Michael's death, and in spite of the fact that his death was directly linked to drugs and alcohol and the lifestyle that went with it, my personal drinking and using slowed down not one iota. I have seen people hit incredible bottoms and not stop their use of intoxicants. People can go to insane places and witness loved ones die because of drugs and alcohol and yet remain steeped in their own addictions. I know. I was one of them. I have come to know that people will stop if and when they are ready, and there is no earthly force that can change that. That's not to say that others can't be inspirational to us along the way. Surely, the paths of others who have successfully trod before us can plant the seeds that may eventually aid us in our own efforts at sobriety. Conversely, the sad demise of others can also be compelling factors in urging us to stop. But unfortunately for many of us, until that certain something clicks within us, until we arrive at that abysmal point of total despair and desperation, those seeds that have been planted by others will have little chance to sprout and grow.

In compliance with that notion, I hung hard and fast to my path of self-destruction in spite of the tragedy that had befallen us. Michael's death had changed something in me. That much I could sense. But the severity of his tragic example had done nothing to alleviate my psychic pain. The grief at that point only served to exacerbate that pain, and I responsively looked for ways to free myself from it.

Along with all of this, of course, was a deepening sense of guilt and shame for my inability to stop this caving in to my self-indulgent ways. Aware of the tremendous pain that Judy was in because of Michael's death, I was further sickened by my own behavior, knowing it must have only added to that pain. She had quit using partly in hopes that I might quit as well—though she never once threw that fact in my face. She stoically, silently, bore her suffering. Sadly, it wasn't until after I got clean and sober that I would become fully aware of the depth of the suffering my actions had caused her. That realization would come to me slowly over time, little shots of awareness that simultaneously stabbed the pit of my stomach with a sickening force the instant they registered in my psyche.

But for now, in spite of whatever bits of awareness I may have had regarding my wife's pain, I was powerless at this point to stop the progression of my disease. My pain, and the attempted alleviation thereof, took precedence in my self-centered brain. I knew of no other way. I wanted to stop this insane ride, but I seemed to have no access to the controls. All of this compounded my frustration, which in turn, only served to heighten my desire to numb it all out. In proportion to this desire, my self-destructive path would become more desperate and more deviant as the days and months wore on.

I wasn't alone in my powerlessness. Mitch and Luke would continue to join me in the quest for drugs, each of us undeterred by whatever impediments appeared before us. But in spite of the fact that all three of us were part of a joint venture, in my mind I still held onto the grand delusion that I was somehow above my wayward friends. After all, I had a job, a wife, a house, two cars— the whole MaryAnn. I even had an IRA (one culturally accepted mark of maturity and functionality)—and there was actually money in it. I hadn't reached the depths of homeless-half-the-time Mitch and bus-ridden Luke, I would tell myself. Ah, it was all part of the great American illusion. Status quo on the outside, major dysfunction on the inside.

I remember being put in my place by a street junkie one Saturday afternoon. Luke and I had gone downtown to see what we could score. Luke was looking for heroin on this particular occasion, but I, not having taken that final step as yet, was hoping to find narcotic painkillers. Luke and I hung out on 3rd and Burnside for a while (Portland's skid-row area), waiting for the right-looking person to ask about scoring dope. Luke got a few negative responses before asking this very gaunt and frail-looking lady who looked like she had lived on the streets for quite some time. She said she could get us some heroin, but I interjected from the front seat of my car that I didn't want any heroin, I wanted some pain pills.

She scoffed as she looked at me sitting in my new Nissan and said, "Don't be looking down your nose at us—you're after the same thing we're after."

I told her that I wasn't looking down on her (but, of course, I had been). She was right on both counts. I was no better than she was, and I basically *was* after the same thing she and Luke were after.

A couple of years before I got clean, Luke and Mitch and I were together on a dreary Saturday morning in Northeast Portland. All three of us were dope-sick that day, and we were trying to decide which hospital we had worn out our welcome at the least, so we could find something to help us get well. In spite of the gloomy weather and in spite of us all jonesin' for drugs, Luke made us laugh that morning.

As we were overanalyzing our hospital options, Luke mentioned that he needed to go to the bathroom. He was feeling sick. We happened to be in an area on Northeast Airport Way that contained a veritable sea of fast-food restaurants. I spotted a Wendy's up ahead and told Luke I would pull in there so he could use the facilities.

Luke rebuked my suggestion, saying, "Could you go down to the Burger King instead?"

"What the hell difference does it make what bathroom you go to, Luke?" I asked him. The man lived in a bus, for Christ's sake. "Wendy's, Burger King—what's it matter?"

"Burger King has the ultra-soft double ply," came Luke's earnest response.

Mitch and I about died. The hell of it was, we knew Luke was deadly serious about his preference for Burger King latrines. Leave it to someone who didn't even have his own bathroom to be a connoisseur of bath tissue at various public restrooms.

It was just a few weeks later that Mitch went into Oregon Health Sciences University in Southwest Portland for a back operation. As mentioned, on some of the ER hits that we had made over the last few years, Mitch would be told by examining physicians that he was going to need another surgery on his back someday. It finally started bothering him enough that he made the decision to go in and have the procedure done. Brain cell fatalities prevent me from remembering exactly what it was they were doing, but Mitch had the surgery, and it was ruled a success.

The pain medication that accompanied Mitch's post-operative period was substantial. We were now "shitting in high cotton" (whatever the hell that means). After spending several days in the hospital, Mitch was transferred to a recovery center in Northeast Portland to convalesce. There he received morphine pills in addition to having a patch placed on his arm that dispensed narcotics into his system (much like a nicotine patch dispenses nicotine).

Every morning on my way to work I would pick Mitch up at this facility. I would then take him to McDonald's for coffee and an Egg McMuffin (if he wanted one). Mitch, in return, would give me a 60 milligram, twelve-hour time-released tablet of morphine. He was being given two of these pills a day, and he would save one for me, holding it under his tongue and pretending to swallow it when they brought it to him. He said the patches they were giving him kept him on an even keel, and between that and the one morphine pill he was more than fine. He had always been far more generous with his meds than Luke or I had ever been. And all he wanted in return was a lousy cup of coffee and an occasional Egg McMuffin.

This went on for several weeks, and during this time I was getting other medication with Luke as well. But Mitch eventually got caught holding morphine for me. The nurses in charge at the rehab center had evidently noticed me picking him up every morning and had become suspicious. They booted him out of there immediately.

Mitch subsequently went to stay in Luke's bus while continuing to see a doctor affiliated with OHSU for his back pain. This doctor prescribed oxycontin for Mitch, in addition to 30mg. tablets of morphine. Oxycontin contains oxycodone (the same active ingredient in Percodan or Percocet) in a time-released form. The doctor wrote Mitch a prescription for one hundred of these potent painkillers. We were really "shitting in high cotton" now.

I got quite hooked during this period, as did Mitch. I had been taking sixty milligrams of morphine daily for several weeks. Mitch had managed to get fentanyl (a potent narcotic) patches for Luke and me shortly before he got kicked out of the convalescence home. I had waited a couple of days before I began wearing a patch on each arm (their effect lasted three or four days, and I wasn't sure what they would do to me. But I functioned fine with them, and, of course, liked what they did for me). Mitch, Luke, and I ran through Mitch's first batch of one hundred oxycontin in a couple of days. (We were eating five or six at a time every few hours, in addition to the morphine.) Mitch waited a while, of course, and then the doctor wrote him for another script of one hundred before cutting "us" off—cold turkey. Between the fentanyl patches, the oxycontin, and the morphine I had been taking for weeks, that was one very mean kick for me. Mitch and Luke drank booze through their withdrawals, which was something I could never do. I was one hurting addict for several days.

Mitch had suffered from a combination of physical discomfort and emotional unrest over the years. I was never privy to the source of his psychic pain—he never seemed to want to talk about it (or his physical pain much, for that matter). The bulk of our relationship centered on the pursuit of pain relief, not discussions about the source of pain—at least not the source of *his* pain. However, Mitch was a sensitive and caring individual who often seemed eager to discuss *my* emotional and mental troubles, while paying little attention to his own.

Mitch: The Number-Two Man on the West Coast. I had always wanted to meet the Number-One Man. As it turned out, not surprisingly upon learning it, the Number-One Man on the West Coast was Mitch's older brother, an ambulance driver by trade, of all things, a brother who had taught Mitch everything he knew about scoring drugs, a brother who would die of a heroin overdose during the days that I was running with Mitch and Luke.

TRADING BUSES

Luke acquired a third doctor a couple of years before he died. We had to travel to Kelso, Washington (about thirty miles north of Portland) to see this doctor, but he made it worth "our" while. Those visits increased our regularly scheduled monthly intake by about twenty-five percent. The doctor would write Luke for sixty Lorcet 10s and ninety Somas once a month. (In addition to Luke's back pain from his various prostheses over the years, he also had intermittent pain from stump soreness. Consequently, some doctors would be extremely generous to Luke with their prescription pens. I had tried a couple of these doctors on my own: one of them flat refused to prescribe narcotics to me; the other one wrote me for about a quarter of the amount he was prescribing to Luke on a monthly basis.)

Mitch eventually visited this same doctor in Kelso, and although he didn't do quite as well as Luke, he fared far better than I had. During one of the many times Mitch was in rehab, a visit to this particular doctor ended up getting him kicked out of the treatment facility. Usually Mitch would go into detox for a few days just to dry out, but on occasion he would attempt further rehabilitation. One of these attempts was through a veteran's program in Vancouver, Washington. It just so happened that I was working in Vancouver at the time, and Mitch called me shortly before lunch one morning to ask if I wanted to run him up to Kelso to "see the good doctor." I quickly questioned his sanity, reminding him that he was in rehab, but Mitch talked me into it (as if it took much persuasion to get me to go on a drug run).

On that particular visit Mitch got forty Lorcet 10s and sixty Somas. I hated the Somas—they only made me tired, but Mitch would eat them if they were available. Mitch split the pain meds with me as usual and kept the Soma. As I was dropping him back at rehab, I offered to hold most of the Soma for him. I just knew he would screw up and take too many. Mitch, Luke and I could all eat relatively large doses of painkillers and function normally for the most part,

236

but the Soma were a different story. These are fairly potent muscle relaxers and, of course, Luke and Mitch wouldn't take them as prescribed. But Mitch said he could keep the pills with him and be fine. He promised me he wouldn't mess up. Neither one of us wanted to see him get kicked out of this rehab facility, because he didn't have a place to live without it. It was an extended-six-month treatment program that was providing him room and board.

Predictably, later that afternoon I got a call from Mitch. He had eaten too many Soma and had become quite visibly intoxicated at the rehab center. They had sent him packing immediately. Treatment programs don't tolerate relapses. I picked him up after work and took him over to Luke's. He ended up staying in Luke's bus again for a couple of months.

It was somewhere around this time that Luke was told he had to move his bus off of the property he had been living on for seventeen years. The property had a small ranch-style home on it that had been used as a residential-care facility for elderly people. Meg (the Meg who was with Luke when he later died of a heroin overdose) was the caretaker of the facility, and Luke had been allowed to move his bus onto the property in the late seventies in exchange for doing some maintenance work and chores around the place.

The people who had owned the home and the property all these years were finally selling it. The last of the elderly patrons had recently passed away (they had stopped taking in new patients quite some time before, knowing they were going to be shutting it down). Luke had the bus towed (since it was incapable of self-propelled mobilization) to a private property in Beavercreek, a rural area about fifteen miles south of Portland. He agreed to pay the property owners monthly rent. But his stay there lasted less than six months. He was evicted for failure to keep up with his payments.

Luke ended up putting his bus in storage at a parking lot in Northeast Portland, where he paid a nominal monthly fee for the space. He had contacted an old friend of his, "Doc" (a nicknamed derived from the man's fondness for the world of chemistry, not because of any medical credentials), who had agreed to let Luke live on his premises for a while. Doc was in his early seventies at the time. He was very slight of build and had long white hair, always in a ponytail. Doc owned an old, run-down, two-story warehouse on Martin Luther King Jr. Boulevard. He had resided in the sizable building for at least twenty years. This place was a trip. There is no way one could adequately describe the contents of the interior of this warehouse. I often wished I had taken a video of the place. Unbelievable. Doc had been a chemist of some kind (more like a mad scientist, I think) in his earlier life. There were literally thousands of dust-caked beakers littering the endless shelves that bordered the walls of certain sections of the warehouse. There were hordes of boxes and barrels containing God knows what, interspersed among countless items of junk scrapped from some bygone era, covering almost every square foot of space in the mammoth building.

Doc slept in a room upstairs. I had gone up to Doc's room once when Luke had first known him many years ago, and I only recall feeling eerily uncomfortable in that place. Luke had delved quite deeply into astrology over the years, and I knew Doc was into that stuff as well. But I had a strong feeling that astrology was only the tip of the iceberg when it came to what Doc was "into." As it turned out, my intuition proved to be correct.

I always thought Doc's warehouse would have made a great opening scene to a movie depicting someone with an extremely bizarre lifestyle. I say "would have," because in the fall of 1988 the warehouse was quarantined by the EPA and a mass of environmental scientists in "spacesuits" took several months going through the mountain of stuff in that decrepit place. Shortly before this occurred police had responded to a reported disturbance at Doc's warehouse. They had subsequently spotted some of the chemicals in the building and found the situation there unsettling enough to contact the EPA.

Lest I be accused of hyperbole, I have saved one of the articles from The Oregonian that described Doc's warehouse at the time. The headline states: "N.E. Portland toxic waste site worse than feared." The first sentence reads: "A dilapidated warehouse in Northeast Portland is proving to be one of the most toxic sites ever uncovered in Oregon." Other snippets: "The situation is much more serious and complex than first thought." And: "The cost of cleanup is up to about $1.5 million…. This is the most complex and time-consuming cleanup we have ever worked on," cited Rodin, EPA project director. "Current levels of toxins could require gutting the entire building. Preliminary results have found unsafe levels of lead, mercury, cyanide, cadmium, and other heavy metals."

"EPA investigators also have discovered significant amounts of lead-contaminated dust in old clothing, books, furniture, shelves—even on the walls."

"The owner had extensive chemicals stored there, including those used to make methamphetamine." And another favorite: "EPA officials suspect that the owner used chemicals and a large kiln in the building to extract gold and precious metals from processed alloys and ore." (Speaking of bizarre things that Doc was into.)

They had also found a dozen "transients" living in the warehouse in various rooms. These people had since scattered, but the EPA was now concerned about the health issues and wanted "to check the transients for illnesses that could result from inhaling the dangerous fumes and dust." I was *so* glad upon reading this article that I had visited Luke many times at that warehouse.

Luke himself had moved out just a couple of weeks before the EPA had "moved in." While he'd been at Doc's he had lived in a broken-down bus (Luke was a bus guy, I guess) in a small graveled lot on the south side of the building. As it turned out, in addition to the dozen transients they had found living in the warehouse, there was a pregnant fourteen-year-old girl living in the same bus Luke had lived in (after Luke had moved out, I must make clear). Nice place.

I had visited Luke at Doc's (drug visits of one kind or another, of course) on quite a few occasions. You had to walk through the warehouse to get to the lot out back where Luke lived. I remember one particular lunch hour that I had rushed to his place to get some pills. As Luke was counting the pills out for me I spotted two huge rats scurrying about in the small, weed-infested lot that surrounded the bus.

"Jesus Christ, Luke—there's fucking rats out there!" Something about seeing large rats milling about in broad daylight was very creepy (not that seeing them at night wouldn't have been creepy—it's just that they seemed so bold right out there in the sun like that. I was quite certain at the time that they were direct descendants of Willard).

Luke had a wildly different reaction. His take was one of excitement, bordering on glee, as if the existence of creatures in his lonely parking lot was a welcome notion, rats or otherwise. "Where?" Luke jumped up excitedly— I hadn't seen him move that fast in thirty years.

"Right there!" I exclaimed, pointing out the brazen bastards mingling among the gravel and the weeds.

"Cool!" Luke remarked, as if he now had friendly "roomies" to talk to.

And I have no doubt that he did talk to them after I left.

ICE CREAM AND KNIVES

During one of my many visits to that dilapidated warehouse, Luke asked me to drive him and a friend of his to get some heroin in Northeast Portland. This was a few months before I had started using heroin and I had no desire to take Luke and his friend, John, to score dope for themselves. I had dropped by that day after work (there was no phone at Doc's place) in hopes that Luke might have some meds. He didn't. So I really hadn't felt like taking two other dope fiends to score while I went without. But Luke said it would only take a few minutes—that the place was just a little ways from the warehouse. And I didn't want to feel like I was using Luke just for his meds (I felt that way a lot over the years and constantly faced internal battles regarding the low-life feelings this perspective would conjure up within me), so I agreed to take them to get their dope.

As it turned out, it was more than "just a little ways from the warehouse." It wasn't all that far in actual miles, but it was quite a bit deeper into the Northeast section of town than I cared to go—the area with the densest black population in Portland. Now, I may not be prejudiced, but I *am* white. And right or wrong, us white boys just don't feel all that invited to such racially segregated areas. But Luke's friend, John, "happened to be black," so I felt *slightly* better about it. That was until we kept wending our way deeper and deeper into an area you could say was "predominantly black" if you left out the "predominantly," and people began giving Luke and me the once-over as we wove slowly through the residential streets.

At one point a large man in a white tank top, sporting bulging biceps, walked in front of our car and stopped, blocking the road. He glared at Luke and me without moving—until he spotted John in the back seat. Then he kind of shrugged and slowly moved out of the way. (I had wanted John to get in the front seat in the first place, just because I knew it would look better, but Luke had hopped in his usual spot in the passenger seat. Luke, incidentally, was completely color blind when it came to race. Truly. And that was certainly very

240

cool and everything, but because of his total lack of prejudice and idealistic nature, he would sometimes place himself in situations that weren't too cool, as will be seen.)

When we arrived at our destination John got out of the car and walked to a house a couple of doors down from my car and went in. No sooner had John gone out of sight when two women approached us and without hesitation draped themselves on either side of my car, one leaning up against my door and the other doing the same on Luke's side.

"Whatchu boys doing here?" The lady on my side welcomed me with.

"Just waitin' on a friend," I replied.

"You a long ways from your neighborhood, ain't you?" she asked.

"Yeah," I said. (I had a way with words at times.)

Luke, however, had no problem striking up a conversation with the lady on his side of the car. For someone who hadn't had a job for twenty years and had lived in broken-down buses the entire time, his self-esteem seemed relatively unaffected, at least when it came to dealing with human beings. He didn't seem to be intimidated by people from *any* spectrum of society—rich, poor, black, white, young, old, whatever.

While Luke was making chit-chat and I was stammering, an ice cream truck pulled up. And I do mean "truck." Not like the cute little ice cream wagons I was accustomed to seeing in my neck of the woods. This looked more like an armored tank, complete with camouflage coloring. So what does "un-intimidated" Luke do? He tells the ladies he's going to buy "the kids" some ice cream and hops out of the car.

There were about a half dozen kids playing in the street and Luke shouted out to them, "Hey kids, you want some ice cream?"

This was the type of person Luke was. He rarely had a dime to spare, and often didn't have a dime to begin with, but here he was willing to cough up ten or twelve bucks to buy ice cream bars for some kids he had never seen before.

The children came running, of course, not yet as tainted by skin color as most adults become to one degree or another. Luke flagged down the armored tank, lined the kids up, and started buying ice cream for them.

Now, I, being somewhat "tainted" by the world view that had been presented to me by society, was quite nervous about this whole scenario. *This just can't be good*, I was thinking, regardless of how nice it was of Luke to be doing it.

241

It turned out that my tainted world view was, sadly, more accurate than Luke's idealistic version. When Luke got back to the car, one of the ladies that had been conversing with us stood in front of the passenger door, blocking his entrance. "Whatchu doing, sucka'?" She was clearly upset about something.

"What're you talking about?" Luke said, his defensive posture immediately aroused by her attitude.

"You don't come into *my* neighborhood and buy *our* kids ice cream!" she spurted angrily.

Oh, this is good, I was thinking.

She wasn't done, naturally. "Now you gots to buy me one, sucka'!" Her tone was quite menacing.

"I'm not buying you anything, lady." Luke never allowed anyone to brow beat him.

"You spent two dollars on the kids, now you gonna spend two dollars on *me*, sucka!"

This is going well, I thought.

About this time John arrived at the car and got into the back seat without saying a word.

"I'm not buying you any ice cream," Luke steadfastly refused to budge.

Then, out came the knife. "You're going to at least give me two dollars or I'm going to stick you, sucka'!"

This is perfect, my mental dialogue continued. *Now we're actually going to die over two dollars.*

And apparently, Luke was willing to. "No way in hell am I giving you two dollars, lady." Luke could be unreasonably stubborn at times. *We're talking about two dollars, here, Luke.*

It was time for me to get into the act. "Just give the lady two dollars, Luke, and let's get the hell out of here!"

Luke wasn't budging. "No way," he told me. Right about then a man came out of nearby house and started heading toward my car, looking a lot like he might be her back-up.

"Luke, get in the fucking car!" I had resorted to shouting.

"He gets in the car, and I'm on his lap, sucka!" she snapped at me. (Apparently I was a "sucka," too. I really needed to get out more.) "He's not going nowhere until I gets my two dollars!"

"Luke, give her the fucking money, and get in the goddamn car!"

"*You* give her the two dollars," came Luke's stubborn rebuttal.

John now gets into the act, not even having a clue as to what this was all about, but said with earnest, "Luke, give the lady two dollars so we can leave."

Luke turned toward me and said, "Will you pay me back if I give her the money?"

"Yes, I'll pay you back! Just give it to her, and get in the fucking car!"

At last, Luke handed the lady two dollars and we were out of there.

On our way back to the warehouse John and I berated Luke for his idiocy. "You going to get stabbed over two dollars, Luke?" John chided him. "What the hell were you thinking, man?"

I reiterated John's comment, shaking my head with disbelief.

When we arrived back at the warehouse, Luke asked me for the two dollars.

"I don't have a dime on me, Luke." Which was absolutely true. It was extremely rare when I didn't at least have a couple of bucks on me, but on that day I truly hadn't. (If I had, I would have handed the lady the two bucks in the first place.) "And if I did have two dollars on me, I wouldn't give it to you, you dumb shit." I was half-mad, half-kidding. Mostly just plain relieved to be out of that situation. "I saved your frickin' ass by making you pay her, you fool."

That was the "two-dollar ice cream event." I left Luke and John standing outside the warehouse, never so glad to be leaving Doc's place as I was that day—even if I didn't have any dope for my troubles.

CONCEALED OPEN CONTAINER

About six months before I got clean and sober I received the only alcohol-related citation of my life. Luke and I were heading back to his bus at Doc's place one rainy evening, having just made a run to Luke's doctor in Kelso, Washington. I had instantly eaten four of the painkillers that we had scored and stashed the rest of my cut in Luke's Lorcet 10 prescription bottle and shoved it in my coat pocket. Luke put his portion of the Lorcet 10s in with the Soma he had been prescribed. I had gotten a coke at McDonald's and had been mixing it with rum from the perpetual half gallon I kept stored behind the front seat.

And then I got pulled over by the police.

If one is driving around with a significant quantity of narcotic painkillers in a prescription bottle bearing someone else's name, and drinking rum from a half gallon that has been carelessly tossed on the floor of the back seat, it is a fairly good idea to have current license tags on your vehicle. Mine were not even close to current.

A female State Patrol officer pulled me over in Vancouver, Washington. Somehow I instinctively knew I wasn't going to fare very well on this occasion. In the past, I had gotten pulled over many times and had always skated by without a D.U.I., but I somehow sensed on this night that my luck had run out. Luke was barely conscious at this point, having swallowed his usual insane quantities of Soma and painkillers. My breath, and probably the entire inside of the vehicle smelled like a rum factory. And, as luck would have it, this particular officer was not the friendliest human being on the planet.

She asked me for my license, registration and proof of insurance, of course. I could tell immediately, by her expression, that she smelled the alcohol. As she was telling me that my tags were expired, she spotted the McDonald's cup in my drink carrier and asked me what was in it. I knew there was no way I was going to bullshit my way out of this one. There was no point in lying about it, yet something within me just couldn't come right out and tell her that I had alcohol in the cup. So I opted to simply stare straight ahead and say nothing. She asked me to give her the cup. Well, she didn't actually ask, and she didn't say please, either. In spite of her lack of manners, I handed her the cup.

One sniff from the officer's nose, followed by those dreaded words, "You wanna' get out of the car, please?"

Again, more of a demand than a request, but at least she had said please. I got out of the car. She began quizzing me about how much I had been drinking, where I had been, where I was going and all that stuff. I told her I'd only had a little bit to drink, and that I was taking my friend, Luke, home. After this brief conversation she told me to empty my pockets. I began putting the contents of my jean pockets onto the hood of her squad car: Lifesavers, change, handkerchief, etc. Then I moved onto my outside coat pockets (all the while trying to figure out how I was going to avoid extracting the large bottle of painkillers from my inside coat pocket). I was heavy into my sugar addiction by this point and almost always had a coat pocket full of candy, usually either a large bag of Peanut M&Ms or a wad of loose Candy Corn. Tonight was a Candy Corn night. I wasn't sure where to put them, so as I pulled them out I just showed them to her. She seemed to indicate she wanted me to release them from my grasp. She had her hand extended with her palm up, so being at least as smart as a trained chimp, I assumed that's where she wanted me to deposit them. So, I did. As the loose Candy Corn cascaded into her palm, a look of disgust immediately blanketed her face and she scolded me for my obvious faux pas. She callously tossed them onto the hood of her car.

I acted as if I were done emptying pockets. The officer, however, was evidently well beyond the trained-chimp stage and asked me what I had in my inside coat pockets. There was nothing left to do at this point. I sheepishly handed her this obscenely large bottle of Lorcet 10s (the prescription had been for the usual sixty, and Lorcet 10s are fairly good-sized pills). Not just some rookie fresh out of the academy, she actually read the patient name on the bottle and cleverly deduced that it didn't match the name on my license.

"These aren't your pills," she said haughtily, as if uncovering the crime of the century.

"No, they're Luke's," I said, nodding back toward my car. "He had a couple too many, and I was holding them for him."

This had always been the story Luke and I were going to use if we ever found ourselves in such a situation. The officer gave me a dubious look and said, "I'm going to go ask *him*," nodding toward Luke, "and he better say the same thing." (I didn't think there was any call for threatening tones.)

When she got to Luke's window she turned to me and said, "You stand over there and don't say a word!" Like I was going to try to tip Luke off as to our story. As soon as she looked back toward Luke I began to try to tip Luke off as to our story. I started mouthing words to Luke, who, by the way, couldn't have read mouthed words at this point if the fate of the entire universe were riding upon it. He was completely wasted, and there was absolutely no visible evidence to the contrary. With severely droopy eyes and an even droopier manner of speech, Luke told the cop that I was holding the pills for him. I was impressed.

But now came the third degree. "Do you have any more drugs on you?" She had turned back toward me.

I told her I did not (which was the truth).

"If I were to search the car, would I find any drugs?"

"No," I told her. "I don't do *drugs*," I said with disgust, as if it were an insult to even suggest such a thing.

But she wasn't taking "no" for an answer. She repeated the question verbatim: "If I were to search the car, would I find any drugs?"

This irritated me. "I said *no*."

"You seem irritated," the officer retorted. "Why is that?"

"Because you keep asking me the same question," I replied.

Then came my first walking-the-line sobriety test. Twenty-six years of drinking and driving and being pulled over on countless occasions, and I had never been asked to walk a straight line. The officer told me to walk nine steps toe-to-toe and then walk back to her the same way. There was a steady mist in the cold, night air as I began my short trip. I wavered ever-so-slightly on my second or third step, but completed the remainder of my tour with relative grace, I felt. When I finished walking back to her I asked if I could do "the front nine" over again. (A little golf humor—I was trying to lighten her up a bit— she seemed very tense.)

Not a crack in that armored face of hers. She then pulled out the little breathalyzer doohickey and asked me to blow into it. (This was also my virgin exposure to breathalyzers.) I blew into it, but not hard enough, apparently. She had to have me blow into it three times before it finally registered, and then she didn't tell me what the reading was.

So I asked her, "Did I pass?"

With a look of major disappointment etched on her furrowed brow she replied in a subdued tone, "Yes."

I was pleasantly surprised, to say the least. But I wasn't about to tell her I thought her little machine might be off.

Then out came the citations. The first one was for failure to wear a seat belt (yes, I had all my bases expertly covered that evening). The second was for the expired tags, which, by the way, is double the fine if they've been expired beyond ninety days, which mine had. Last, but not least, came the citation for "concealed open container," which, by the way, is also double the fine compared to your mere "open container" citation. I found this to be rather odd and still do, frankly. I sometimes joke to people (again, not that drinking and driving is funny, because it's most certainly not—but these citation variations kind of are) that if you're going to insist on drinking while driving, it's a lot cheaper to just wave the bottle of booze around than it is to pour it into a McDonald's cup.

The irony of the whole situation to me was the fact that there was a partially full half gallon of rum lying in plain sight on the floor of the back seat. I guess since it was an *un*-concealed open container it wasn't worth wasting paper on. (In truth, I was very grateful she hadn't spotted it. Three citations were plenty for one evening.)

Everything considered, I felt extremely fortunate not to be going to jail and to still have a driver's license. I dropped Luke off at the warehouse and called it a night, feeling horribly guilty about the further expenses I had incurred for our household.

Just a few days after this incident, Luke made his final move in life. He went from the bus at Doc's warehouse to that motel room in Kalama, Washington. It was in this same flea-bag motel room, after years of inner turmoil and decades of resistance to "the mother of all drugs" that, on a cold Christmas Eve in 1998, I evidently decided to become a heroin addict. And it was in that same sad room that Luke would die of a heroin overdose on March 26, 1999, a few months later—and just hours prior to my entry into rehab.

CHIEVA

In the late afternoon of Christmas Eve, 1998, having no prescription narcotics to indulge in, Luke offered me some heroin. As I said, Luke would occasionally suggest I try some, and I had continually rejected his offers. At one point, I had followed my refusal with the question, "What kind of a friend are you, anyway? I told you before I don't want to get into that shit."

To which Luke had replied, "You can't become addicted to something you don't have access to." A statement which went way beyond bordering on the ludicrous, in my mind.

"Where the hell do you think I have gotten drugs all my life, Luke? Through the *Easy Access to Drugs* catalog? Man, what are you thinking?" I berated him. "And I know what kind of addict I am. If I try it and like it, I'm fucked. And I have to assume I would like it."

But that night, something was different. I was tired of the chase for drugs. I was tired of no longer feeling the euphoria that I had experienced with my use in the past. And I was tired of living the way I had been living—the drugs, the time, the money. It was all making me feel lower and more depraved each day that passed by. The irony was that the only way my skewed brain could think of to deal with feeling low about my life of drugs was to do more drugs. The thought of spending the holidays without something besides alcohol to deaden these feelings of despair and worthlessness made me feel even more forlorn. So, standing there in Luke's tiny motel room in Kalama, I looked at him and simply said, "Give me some of that shit." That's all, just a split-second decision, with no forethought, no pre-meditation, just a spur of the moment, "Give me some of that shit" statement. That's what it came down to after thirty years of rejecting the thought of doing heroin—a single instant of weakness.

And I was off. I snorted it that afternoon (it's not easy to snort tar heroin, but where there's a will there's a way—and I found an efficient way). I bought a small quantity from Luke and snorted more that night and Christmas Day.

I picked Luke up the day after Christmas and went with him to his connection and bought more. That day I fired it intravenously for the first time. But after a couple of times of doing this, I switched to shooting it intra-muscularly (into my upper arm or my butt), telling myself I would be less likely to become a full-fledged junkie that way. In the ensuing months I would go back to snorting it most of the time.

At first, I didn't personally meet Luke's connection. But after driving him there a couple of times over a few days, I met Rodney. Now that I had established a face-to-face relationship with a heroin connection, I no longer needed Luke. As cold as it may have been, I pretty much cut Luke out of the situation. (I had needed Luke to scam for pills at ERs, but heroin I could buy for myself, once I'd found a dealer. That was the cold, hard truth of the matter—and of my selfish-addict mentality.) No way was I going to drive all the way to Kalama to pick up Luke every time I needed a fix. Rodney lived in Gresham, just a couple of miles from where Judy and I lived. I had access to money, and now I had access to the heroin. And I would continue to access this drug religiously over the next few months.

I talked to Luke a couple of weeks later, and when he found out I was still doing heroin, and on a daily basis to boot, he was upset. And surprisingly, not because I was scoring without him, but because he was genuinely concerned about me. Somehow he had deluded himself into actually believing I wouldn't pursue the drug without him, and since he himself only bought heroin on a fairly infrequent basis, he assumed that's how it would go with me. He asked me what the hell I was doing.

"I told you this is what would happen," I answered.

I remember Luke coming back with, "If your mother found out, she'd kill me." (As I mentioned, Luke had a great relationship with my parents in earlier years.) Luke pleaded with me to stop while I still could, but as any true addict knows, that's not going to happen until the person is ready. And apparently I wasn't ready. (I heard someone say recently that trying to keep an unwilling addict from using is like trying to teach your dog to read. It's just not going to happen. "When the student is ready, the teacher will come.")

A few weeks into my "relationship" with Rodney, I called him to score, and he told me he was out of dope. He said he was going into rehab. I immediately panicked. I had been using daily since that first night, five or six times a day by this point, and my individual dosage amounts were rapidly escalating as well.

And I was not ready to stop. Although I was scared to death of becoming severely addicted, I kept putting off terminating my use—one day at a time. It was as if I felt I could quit "tomorrow" and still not have too bad of withdrawals. However, the longer I continued, the more I doubted my withdrawals would be easy.

Rodney told me not to panic. He gave me the phone number of his connection, Alejandro. He said he had told the guy I would be calling.

A note on Rodney: he had been a heroin addict for more than fourteen years. He had no possessions to speak of. During the time I knew him he was living with his sister. He had no money and no access to money. Luke and I (and now mostly just "I") had been his last connection to a source of heroin. Rodney would call this Alejandro guy and score the dope for us and we would give him a cut—ten or twenty dollars' worth depending on how much we had bought. In spite of my being basically his only viable means of scoring heroin, after a couple of weeks of calling him on a daily, or semi-daily basis, he had taken it upon himself to let me know what he thought of my pursuits. He told me to "get out of this shit" while I still could. He told me that I didn't need to become like him. And then he had literally screamed at me a couple of times in succession: "THIS IS NOT A FUCKING GAME! THIS IS NOT A FUCKING GAME!"

That had taken great compassion on Rodney's part—to, in essence, attempt to cut off his last link to dope in an effort to save my butt (part of him may have been trying to save himself as well, I realize—but it took courage and compassion nonetheless). So, I don't relate at all to people in sobriety who claim that they "didn't have any decent friends out there when they were running and gunning." I don't relate to that sentiment because the people I knew were decent people—Luke, Mitch, Rodney, etc. They were merely caught in the throes of their disease, just as I was—just like every addict is. None of us are any better or any worse than the next person. We can't afford to rate ourselves like that (a commitment that takes continual vigilance). Our egos and our judgmental attitudes will get us loaded.

In any event, I called Alejandro, and he agreed to meet me just south of the intersection of 122nd and Foster Road. Alejandro was the Mexican dealer that I mentioned much earlier, the one whom I could barely understand, his accent was so thick. I eventually deciphered his words and went to meet him at the designated spot. A few minutes after I arrived, Alejandro and another man pulled up in a nondescript older car—mid-to-late-eighties model Chevrolet. They parked behind me. The passenger got out, walked up to my car and got in.

"You Alejandro?" I asked.

He simply nodded and said, "Drive."

I put it in gear and drove for a couple of minutes, with Alejandro's amigo following behind us. When he became convinced that no one was tailing us and that everything was cool, he told me to pull over. I took out forty dollars and he proceeded to reach under his tongue and pull out a few small, round balls of heroin wrapped in balloon material.

This is nice, I was thinking. But I gave him the forty dollars and when he handed me one of these saliva soaked balls of heroin I grabbed it without hesitation. (For a moment I thought *maybe that's why he's so hard to understand—he's got those fucking balloons in his mouth.* However, I was pretty sure he didn't walk around like that all day long.) I thanked him, and without saying a word, Alejandro got out of my car, went back to his friend and drove off.

I immediately did a dose, of course. I went to great lengths over the next few months to hide my use as best I could. In the beginning I was so paranoid my wife would find out that I went to the trouble of hiding my syringes in the woods on a trail near our home. Eventually I found a safe spot in our 1991 Nissan Sentra to hide my drugs and paraphernalia. (Judy was now driving the newer Nissan we had bought, and I was exclusively driving the older car.) The front driver's seat cushion had become dislodged (although it wasn't visibly noticeable) and I could pull back the cushion and hide the junk in there.

I met Alejandro and his various accomplices many times over the ensuing months. As I pointed out earlier, they were quite punctual. It was such a welcome relief from the countless hours wasted in ER parking lots, not knowing whether or not we were even going to score. That was part of the reason I stuck with the heroin, simple ease of access. (I would often find myself scoffing at Luke's words from Christmas Eve: "You can't become addicted to something you don't have access to.")

About ten days after I had started buying heroin directly from Alejandro, I received a message from Rodney on my cell phone. He wanted me to call him. The last thing in the world I wanted to do was talk to Rodney, so I put off calling him back. Over the next twenty-four hours I received messages from

Rodney that became increasingly threatening. He was saying things like, "Did you think that phone number I gave you was free? I paid a lot of money for that phone number." Then he began making more ominous threats, saying he figured my wife wouldn't want to find out that I was using heroin. The last message made a direct threat to my family. Although Rodney had no idea where I lived, he had seen my car on numerous occasions, and could have gotten my license and traced my residence, for all I knew.

Threatening my family was off limits. I called Rodney and told him he could say whatever he wanted about me, but told him not to ever threaten my family. I told him that I had just done what he had told me to do—I had called Alejandro for dope. Then I asked him what the hell he wanted.

Rodney's demeanor was very different from the messages he had left me. He was very subdued and apologetic, saying he had just needed some dope. He told me it hadn't worked out at the rehab place, and that he could really use a fix. I asked him what he meant about paying a lot of money for Alejandro's number and he told me he had paid a hundred dollars for that number. I didn't believe him, but I also knew I didn't want to get more threatening phone calls in the future, so I was determined to square things between us.

That day I bought a gram and a quarter of heroin (for a hundred dollars) from Alejandro and brought a forty dollar bag of it to Rodney. He went into shock when I showed up. He couldn't believe that I was actually giving him heroin (guess he forgot about me paying for that phone number). Over the next week or so I brought Rodney another twenty dollars' worth and then another forty dollars' worth of dope. Before I gave him the last amount, I held it back from him and said, "This makes us even, right?" He was not about to say "No" with forty dollars' worth of heroin on the line.

"Yeah, man. We're even. Hell, we were even before this. Thank you—I really appreciate it, man."

Rodney wasn't a bad man—just a dope fiend hooked on drugs—just like I was—just like many others have been and are in this world. I never called Rodney again, and he never bothered me again. There is some honor among addicts.

It was about halfway through this heroin run of ninety-four straight days that I tried to kick my habit. As I stated earlier, I made it forty-two hours, freezing and sweating and dry-heaving, before I couldn't stand the suffering anymore. A mad dash to my car for the dope and a phone call to Alejandro, and I was well. Then, it was off to the races again.

After that kick attempt and after talking with Mitch on the phone a couple of times (who was miraculously now clean and kept repeating to me that I needed help to quit), I made a decision that I was going to check into rehab. However, making the decision and actually carrying it out are not necessarily the same thing. I kept putting if off. First of all, I had no idea who to call or how to go about this thing. I was also scared to death of facing withdrawals again.

A couple of weeks after I had made the decision to check into rehab, I was informed at work that I had won a sales award. GOM Steel has a large sales meeting every year, which usually takes place in one of the western U.S. cities where they have steel service centers. About a hundred and twenty people in suits and other formal business attire attend these annual weekend functions where they talk about sales a lot and hand out various awards. Evidently, I had qualified for such an award. Although the volume of my sales didn't even begin to approach the average (they increased substantially in following years, but in the beginning of my tenure with GOM Steel I only handled sales in the burning end of the business, which significantly suppressed my numbers), I apparently had a high profit margin on the sales I did have. In a virtual panic, I expressed my disbelief, but was assured that I had indeed won such an award and that I would be getting up on stage in front of all those people and giving my acceptance speech.

Now I was really panicking. As I have made extensive reference to previously, I had developed a huge fear of speaking in groups—and this was quite a group. A hundred and twenty men and women in formal business attire staring at me while I fumbled for appropriate words of gratitude. *If you really want to show your gratitude for whatever it was I accomplished, don't make me get up there on that stage!*

As soon as I understood that they were truly serious, my first thought was: *Well, I can't go into rehab yet—I have to accept this damn award. And to have any ray of hope of getting up on that stage without completely wilting in a state of panic, I will have to stay loaded for the next few weeks.* To this day I don't know why I felt I needed to accept that award—I honestly couldn't have cared less about it at the time. I guess I just figured if I went into rehab and missed the sales meeting that "they" would be really pissed off. These meetings are very important to the-powers-that-be, and they make that quite clear when you become a member of GOM Steel. (The thought of losing my job while addicted to heroin was extremely frightening to me. In retrospect it's evident to me that I wouldn't have lost my job over the situation, but as a heavily using addict I was fairly delusional at the time.)

So, stoned I stayed, for the next three weeks. On the day of the sales meeting, which just happened to be in Portland that year, I continued my abuse of heroin (and pain pills—I was still getting my regular loads from Luke). That day I was doing doses every couple of hours (as had become the norm for me), but I was minimizing the dosage amounts to the best of my ability so I wouldn't get too messed up for the big sales meeting.

Finally, the magic hour arrived, and I found a table with seven of my male cohorts from our Portland branch. The first thing I did upon sitting down was to check out the itinerary of this illustrious event, trying to estimate when I would be appearing on stage. My best calculations put it at about an hour and half into the meeting. (These meetings typically lasted three and a half to four hours—and that's after having attended a two-hour motivational seminar prior to the sales meeting.)

I had done a dose of heroin and taken a few pills just prior to entering the building. Over the next hour and a half I would go to the bathroom three times to do another dose of each, minimizing the amounts as best I could, but not quite feeling at any point like I had attained enough of a relaxation level to stop the doses altogether. On my last visit to the restroom, I did about ten dollars' worth of heroin and took four Lorcet 10s (as I have described, the equivalent of eight regular strength Vicodin). This was twenty minutes before I was called up to the stage.

When they called my name, I "courageously" went up and accepted my award (the award was a decent-looking ring, I must say, though I'm not much into rings—and I most certainly didn't give a damn about rings at that point in my life). After the vice president of sales at GOM presented me the award, I turned to the microphone and said—well, I don't remember what the hell I said, actually, shocking though that may be. I'm sure I gave a typical acceptance speech, not unlike the Academy Awards, and yet nothing like the Academy Awards: *Thank you very much for this award. I know I couldn't have gotten this without the help of everyone at GOM Steel. This is an honor and a privilege that I share with all of my co-workers. Thank you.* It wouldn't have been much longer than that—a few sentences or so. A very short speech to get as worked up about as I had. (It remains a comforting thought to know that quite a few other recipients often comment about how much they hate getting up there and how nervous or scared to death they are.)

I returned from the stage to a round of congratulatory handshakes and "Good job's" from everyone at my table. No one had a clue that I was loaded—that's where my tolerance had taken me. After the meeting some of us went into the bar, where I proceeded to add six or seven rum and cokes and several more trips to the restroom to my insatiable appetite for drugs.

Although, as I said, I'm not much into rings, I still wear my award ring on occasion. It's not because I'm proud of my sales achievement or because of the looks of the ring. I wear it because it reminds me of my addiction. It reminds me to never forget where my addiction took me, and that I don't ever want to go back.

It was a couple of weeks after that sales meeting that Judy called me on my cell phone as I was weaving my way home from work, after she had found some heroin on the floor of our bathroom. Three days later I checked into the chemical dependency unit on the fourth floor of Portland Adventist Medical Center.

I didn't tell anyone at work that I was going into rehab until Friday, the day before I checked in. I was a complete wreck by this time, emotionally as well as physically and psychologically. I knew I couldn't tell my bosses what was going on without breaking down. So, I had written a short letter explaining that I was addicted to narcotic painkillers (I saw no reason to tell them about the heroin—too much stigma attached to "chieva").

Toward the end of that day (the same day I had delivered the heroin at lunchtime to Meg, the heroin that would kill Luke a few hours later) I handed the letter to my good friend and co-worker, Rory Heaton. Rory was in his early sixties. He and I shared an office apart from the rest of the sales staff (who occupied a single, larger room around the corner from us). I had been able to hide my opiate use from most of the so-called "normies" of the world, save at least, from two people. One was my wife, of course. The other was Rory. Aside from Judy, Rory saw me more hours during the week than anyone on the planet. He had the "advantage" of viewing me for more than a few minutes at a time. I had, in my drug-induced stupor, been unaware that Rory had suspected anything. However, his actions upon reading my letter that day proved to me that he had been quite aware. I'll never, *ever* forget how he reacted. It was the first (outside of my immediate family) of many such touches of compassion that I would be blessed with in my recovery.

Rory walked slowly up to me, as I stood there with tears streaming down my cheeks. He put one of his hands, palm first, gently against my chest, and placed his other hand softly upon the middle of my back, and in as compassionate a tone of voice as I had ever heard, approvingly said, "This is the smartest thing you've done in a long, long time."

I was almost sobbing now. Another co-worker, Coby Bernard, came into the room at this point and saw me crying. Coby also was as compassionate that day as a human being could possibly be. He asked what was wrong, and being unable to talk, Rory answered for me. Coby firmly put his hands on my shoulders and said, "None of this matters." (He was looking around the room indicating "work.") As I started to try to explain something to him about one of my customers, Coby interjected, "Don't worry about any of this. We'll take care of it. You just take care of you."

My boss, Chad, was equally compassionate when he read the letter. Surprised, but compassionate. With genuine shock in his voice as he was reading the letter he uttered the one-word-rhetorical question, "Painkillers?" But he, too, told me not to worry about anything. He said that they would do whatever was necessary to help make me better.

I owe a debt of gratitude to those people and to the hundreds that have followed in their footsteps. Their reactions, along with the compassion showed by countless others in ensuing years, have allowed me to amass, in my opinion, what constitutes a mountain of indisputable testimony as to the True Nature of humankind.

SURRENDER

The young boy said to the teacher: "Pretend you were surrounded by a thousand, hungry tigers. What would you do?"

The teacher thought for a while, and unable to come up with a solution, finally answered, "Well, I don't know. What would *you* do?"

The young boy replied, "I'd stop pretending."

—Catherine Ingram

REHAB

Checking into rehab on March 27, 1999, was one of the more surreal experiences of my life. It was also undoubtedly the most life-altering (aside from, perhaps, my initial decision to begin doing drugs in the first place). My mother, who has never failed to be supportive of any of her children or grandchildren, and my brother Tim, who has always been there for me as well, picked me up that morning to take me to the hospital. Judy was working that day, and I convinced her it wasn't necessary for her to take the day off. She could come up and see me later. (She had been through far too much already).

When my mom and brother arrived to pick me up I told them that I had to go *do something* before we left. I had been loaded 24/7 for a long time, and I was not about to make the frightening move of going to rehab be my first sober act. That's what I was going there for in the first place, I felt—to learn how to do stuff clean and sober. *If I could've gotten clean for rehab—well, then I wouldn't have needed rehab*, was my thinking. The whole idea scared the bloody hell out of me. I needed as much false courage as I could to go through with this thing. I remember my mother just rolled her eyes and said, "Well, hurry it up." At any other time she would have been reading me the riot act, but she was so glad that I was going in for treatment, she had bitten her tongue on this particular occasion. I went into my room, swallowed four Lorcet 10s and did the last dose of heroin I would ever do. (It is both sad and haunting for me to note that at that moment I didn't know Luke's lifeless body was lying in a morgue somewhere, having died some fifteen hours earlier from the same batch of dope that I had just partaken of.)

When I checked into the chemical dependency unit on the fourth floor of Portland Adventist that morning, I had no idea what to expect. What I hadn't expected was that I would be getting a room without a television. It wasn't that I had been anticipating a stay at the Ritz, but I had more or less assumed that the normal amenities found in a hospital room would be available to me. Having never resided in a detox unit or rehab center, I was clueless as to how things worked. I simply couldn't imagine coming off of heroin without a television to help distract me from the suffering. (Although on previous opiate kicks, I had rarely turned on the television in my bedroom. There was really nothing that could successfully take my mind off of the ugliness of withdrawal. Yet it was a psychological imperative to at least have one available.) I was ready to exit upon hearing this bit of news. My mom and brother could see that I was starting to lose it. And when the nursing staff began going through my suitcase (they search all incoming baggage for drugs) and confiscated my lemon drops, I began to cry (literally). I didn't understand why in the world they would take my lemon drops. I needed those things to help with the unbearable taste that was ever-present in my mouth during withdrawals. But the chemical dependency unit at this hospital allowed no sugar or caffeine.

It was when the candy confiscation brought me to tears that one of the nurses asked me how much heroin I had been using daily (evidently finding something abnormal about a forty-six-year-old man weeping over the loss of lemon drops). With my mother standing there I hadn't wanted to tell the truth about the extent of my heroin use (as if she would have derived any meaning from whatever quantity I revealed—my seventy-four-year-old mother was not a big heroin user). So, I lied. I told the nurse that I had been using about a quarter of a gram a day. After I had hedged on a few more answers, the intuitive lady asked my mom and brother if they would step outside the room for a few minutes.

When they were gone, the nurse looked at me and said, "Okay—now how much heroin have you really been doing?"

So I told her the truth. I had consumed more opiates in the last three months then I ever had in my life. I was using at least a gram of heroin a day, along with toxic quantities of pain pills. I was one messed-up Jose. Physically, psychologically, mentally, emotionally—I was at the end of my rope. And I was spiritually bankrupt, with only the slightest sliver of hope left in my psyche for any sort of salvation. This was, as they say, the last house on the block for me. I desperately wanted their help, but I was also scared to death of going through this particular withdrawal. I was terrified, but I was also broken. Broken to the max. I was at a point of willingness I had never before reached. Without knowing the first thing about any Twelve Step program, I knew two things with total certainty: *I was absolutely powerless over my addiction, and my life had become completely unmanageable.* (These are the two admissions in the first step of a Twelve Step program.) I was, in essence, throwing up my hands and saying, "Please help me—I am completely and utterly lost." I was at the mercy of what I was hoping were good, caring and knowledgeable people. And I was willing to do whatever they asked of me.

Yet, in spite of my state of willingness, something as relatively benign as confiscating my lemon drops had apparently been the straw that broke the camel's back. (Once more, Burt Rice's words come to mind, "You crack pretty easy, don't you, son?") At the time, in my drug-hazed head, weeping over lemon drops hadn't seem at all bizarre to me. Compounded with the news of no television, it seemed as if they were torturing me (not intentionally, but torture nonetheless). Ridiculously absurd in retrospect, but ever so real at the moment. Although almost every part of my being wanted to immediately jet from that place, there evidently remained a shred of self that was desperately clinging to hope. Somehow I sensed it was then or never. I didn't want to live in my addiction anymore. So I stayed.

It was on my second day in detox that they discovered I had pneumonia, which they said was induced by my opiate use (from the extremely shallow breathing that accompanies opiate abuse and perhaps the snorting of the heroin, some of the fluid filtering into my lungs). That, coupled with a dangerous drop in my blood pressure upon giving me Librium and Clonidine (Clonidine is a high-blood-pressure medication that is sometimes used to aid with heroin withdrawal), forced them to transfer me down to the medical ward on the third floor. The chemical-dependency unit wasn't equipped to handle medical complications of this nature.

It was in the medical ward that my friend, Tom Work, first came to see me. I will never forget his visit. I was too weak and shaky to get a utensil to my mouth, so Tom spoon-fed me, or at least attempted to. It soon became obvious that my body wasn't interested in food, and the doctors put me on an IV for almost five days. But Tom's caring gesture was something I'll never forget. That mark of compassion will always remain especially dear to my heart.

The withdrawals were horrible, of course. I remember thinking, in my naiveté, that the medical world was somehow going to alleviate all of my symptoms, or at least drastically reduce their impact. On that first day in rehab I had asked the nurses about that. I had expressed my belief to them that they were going to make my withdrawals easy, hoping to hear a resounding chorus of, "Of course we are, sweetie." Instead my already tortured mind was met with, "Heroin withdrawal is never easy. All we can do is take some of the edge off, and medically supervise you."

Not at all what I had in mind. I had next suggested that perhaps my withdrawal wouldn't be as severe because I had only been snorting it rather than shooting it the last couple of months. It was then that I had been met with, "Heroin is heroin, honey." (This was before the advent of Buprenorphrine— a drug that actually does make opiate withdrawal easier. Maybe too easy, in this addict's opinion.)

Ironically, during those five days that I spent in the medical ward, I had a television set in my room. I remember a sense of relief upon spotting it when I had first been taken to my new surroundings. The kicker was, they said I never turned it on—not even once. (But it was there if I needed it, damn it— that psychological edge had meant a lot to me.)

My wife and my mother came to visit me on my second day at the hospital, shortly after I had been transferred to the medical ward. I remember Judy telling me weeks later that both she and my mother had been shocked when they had first seen me that day. Upon entering my room they had spotted me from behind, and by the way I was moving they didn't think it was me. They thought they had the wrong room. The figure before them couldn't have been me—it was a much older man, they were certain.

I recall a week or so later, a couple of days after I had been taken back up to the chemical dependency unit, commenting to another patient on how bad this particular lady looked. She had just come in the morning before, and when she first arrived she had looked pretty well put together. She hadn't started detoxing yet. What a difference a day makes. As I watched her literally shuffle to the food cart that next morning, I was shocked at the drastic change in her looks, just as my wife and mother had been with me. She appeared to be a completely different person. She was a mess. Aside from the no makeup and her overall disheveled appearance, she looked like a veritable zombie, complete with glazed eyes, parted lips, and shuffling gait. I remember expressing these opinions to this other patient. He gave me a bit of a surprised look and said, "Dude, you looked worse than that a week ago." I guess it's all relative.

Toward the end of my fourth day at Portland Adventist, while I was still in the medical ward, I decided to cough up the four Lorcet 10s I had snuck into rehab in my sock. (They had rifled through my suitcase, but had never searched me personally.) I mentioned much earlier that one of the reasons I had traded Luke some heroin for some pills the day before I checked into detox was in case I couldn't handle the pain of withdrawal. But nearing the end of that fourth day I knew that the worst part of the withdrawals were over. I felt I could now make it without them. So, when Judy came to visit me that day I proudly handed the pills to her.

Perspective is a funny thing. Instead of being proud of me for having the integrity and the guts to give them up, Judy's first thoughts were (naturally and rightfully): "How many did you really bring in here?" and "How serious could you be about quitting if you brought those in with you?" One hundred percent valid and appropriate questions as viewed from my present state of mind. But in my drug-bleary mind of yesteryear they seemed unfairly accusatory. How blind I had been.

The same evening that I had given Judy the four pills, I had also called my mother and told her that I had hidden a quarter of a gram of heroin and ten Lorcet 10s in her linen closet the day before I went into rehab. (I had hidden the drugs at her house in case I couldn't handle going straight. I felt deceitful, of course, but I had been scared to death of getting clean, and I had just been covering my bases. Also, I had hidden them at Mom's house because I feared Judy would ransack our house and might find them. I couldn't allow that to happen.)

My mom's immediate response was an incredulous, "You hid *heroin* in my house?"

I told her that I indeed had, and I told her the reason I had. But on that fourth day in rehab I told her I was done with drugs and asked her to flush everything down her toilet for me. My mother *claims* that she then asked, "How much could I get for it?" My mom has a great sense of humor (which is not something I usually let her know I know), and she may very well have said that, but I don't recall it.

Aside from the discovery of pneumonia, the doctors learned from my blood tests that my liver counts were all way off the scale. They were unacceptably elevated. The good news was, they told me that if I ceased my use of alcohol and narcotics there was a good chance that my readings would return to normal.

I remember getting some phone calls from friends in those first few days in the medical ward. I remember making a few as well. Gabe called from Alaska, and I talked to Drew Olsen and John Parker, among others. I also received many visits from Judy, my mom, and my brother Tim. My stepson Casey and his girlfriend at the time, Blazer, came to see me as well. I was very touched by their visit and happy to see them.

I was also blessed with several visits each from Tom Work, Mark Mitchell and Doug Knutson. Mark and Doug were co-workers, and both are also "friends of Bill W." Mark had fourteen years of sobriety at the time, and Doug had eighteen (both remain sober to this day). Mark became my Twelve Step sponsor—a person to talk with about recovery and about working the twelve steps. Doug became a close confidant as well. Along with my family and Tom, I owe these men a debt of gratitude I can never adequately repay. I often credit Mark with being highly instrumental in saving my life and for continuing my introduction into recovery after leaving rehab.

But the first person I owe my life to is, of course, my beautiful wife. Judy was the one who had discovered my heroin use in the first place and had had the courage to confront me about it. She put up with *so* much over the years. Toward the end of my active addiction it was almost unbearable for her. I remember in the last few weeks of my use I had passed out on the toilet on several occasions. Heavy opiate use will sometimes make it difficult to begin urinating, and this particular symptom had hit me full force. (My body was shutting down, trying to tell me the heroin was damaging my system.) It could take me as long as fifteen to twenty minutes to "get going" when I was in one of my heavier stupors—which was most of the time in those last few weeks. Because of the exorbitant amount of time involved, I would sit down when going to the bathroom. While waiting to "get started," I would often pass out. There were several instances when I wouldn't regain consciousness until a couple of hours or more later.

When I was confessing this to Judy several weeks after I had gotten clean, she looked at me as if I was incredibly daft and said, "I know—I *saw* you." How idiotic to think that I could pass out in the bathroom for hours at a time and not be noticed by my own wife. In retrospect, I recalled with horror how close to being in an opiate-induced coma (or to death) that I was. The depths of my stupors were revealed in those restroom visits. I would come to a couple of hours or so later, still sitting on the toilet, but all hunched over with my body having fallen against the wall of the bathroom. I was told by the hospital staff in rehab that one's breathing can become so shallow on opiates that eventually some people just stop breathing.

The magnitude of my intoxication those last couple of months was also revealed in my daily ritual while driving. I was so supremely wasted in those final weeks of addiction that it was everything I could do to drive to work and back without passing out. I employed all of the usual methods of trying to sustain consciousness—blaring music, putting down windows, even slapping myself—but I would invariably nod off and find myself leaving the road, being jarred back to consciousness by those little bumps on the highway shoulders. I would end up literally shouting in gibberish as fast as I could talk, for extended minutes at a time—totally nonsensical, strung-together, alien-sounding syllables—in a desperate attempt to keep from passing out. As insane as that was, I still didn't think I was all that loaded because I was experiencing no euphoria from my drug use. Even when I wasn't quite as wasted, I couldn't for the life of me keep my car from weaving all over the road. And because I didn't think I was all that high, I seriously thought my car was out of alignment. When I first drove it in sobriety I actually thought someone had had my car aligned while I was in rehab. I truly did.

Mark brought me some recovery literature my second week in the hospital. He was anything but preachy or bossy to me when it came to suggestions about recovery. He knew from experience that addicts and alcoholics don't like to be told what to do, so he shied away from any such sort of approach. (They say: "You can tell an addict, but you can't tell him much.") He would nudge me in the right direction and then patiently wait for me to follow his lead. He was also there on that eighth day in rehab when they told me about Luke dying from an overdose of the heroin I had purchased. I broke down and bawled like a baby that day. Or as I heard someone I respect very much say, who happens to be a policeman in recovery named Larry: "I'm no longer afraid to show my emotions. I don't cry like a baby anymore—today I cry like a man. I have learned that it's okay for a man to cry."

Mark has been there for me since day one of my recovery. He helped spur me to go to meetings, and he encouraged me when I was down (which was often in those first months). I will always credit Judy for literally saving my life and both Judy and Mark for making sure I *stayed* alive. Mark is well known and well-loved in our circles, and deservedly so. I know of no one who has helped others more than Mark has.

Doug Knutson was also extremely instrumental in helping to keep me sane, during early recovery in particular. This was no easy task, dealing with someone as insane as I was. I was truly touched by the visits he paid me in rehab and by his encouragement in the ensuing months (and years). I remember my first day back at work—I was completely falling apart. I was no more ready to face eight hours of a normal work day than I was to run the Boston Marathon. As I sat shaking at my computer, my mind racing a thousand miles per hour, Doug came up from behind me, gently put his hands on my shoulders and softly said, "Sometimes it's *one minute* at a time, bud." People often don't realize how much such a seemingly small gesture and a few kind words can do to help someone who is struggling.

I had no idea what they were going to do for me in rehab. No clue whatsoever. What they did for me, beyond the medical help, was introduce me to Twelve Step recovery programs. We had six or seven hour-long meetings every day, all dealing with recovery. I heard a lot of good things in those meetings. I don't remember a lot of specifics, but I recall isolated moments. I remember one young man about twenty years old slowly scanning the room one morning and saying, "Man, I look around, and I see all you people in your thirties and forties and fifties, and I think, *Maybe I haven't hit rock bottom yet.*"

A twenty-five-year-old woman (who had lived on the streets much of her adult life) chimed in, "Why does everyone feel like they have to hit rock bottom? Why can't you just settle for this is as low as I care to go?" She looked at the younger guy and said, "To me, rock bottom is death."

I've always remembered that. (And it was a prime example of how even people who don't necessarily have what we want can have something worthwhile to say. This is one of the reasons open-mindedness is identified and heralded as a main spiritual principle of recovery.)

Several years later I heard a different slant on "bottoms." Someone said: "They say we all have different bottoms. But I believe we all have the same bottom. We hit bottom when we put down the shovel and stop digging." It's true. No one else is digging that hole for us. It's *our* hole. We are the only ones that can throw down the shovel.

There was a speaker who had eighteen years clean and sober who came and talked to us one evening in rehab. I remember him saying, "It will take, on average, one to two years for most of you to get back to an even keel physically, two to three years to get back to a more normal level mentally, and four to five years to begin to achieve a decent emotional balance."

I blurted out, "That's a hell of a thing to tell someone with seven days clean."

He asked me, "How do you eat an elephant?"

I thought for a second and answered, "One bite at a time?"

He replied, "That's right. Try to eat the whole thing at once, it will kill you every time." I learned a lot of bumper sticker sayings during my stay in rehab, and hundreds more as I attended meetings out in the real world. These little sayings helped save my sanity on more than one occasion. When I first got clean, I could barely string two sensible sentences together, it seemed. My mind was severely clouded for quite some time. But I could remember one-liners. I wrote down my favorites and put them in my wallet so I could refer to them in times of need.

One of my favorites has always been, "How important is it really?" It reminds me of the book title, *Don't Sweat The Small Stuff—And it's All Small Stuff*. But in early sobriety the thing that helped me the most was the simplest thing imaginable. Three words, actually. When I was tempted to drink or to use (which was quite often in those first few months), I would tell myself, "It doesn't work." Just that simple: *It doesn't work*. I knew then (and I remain convinced today) that my way didn't work, and it would never work. I had researched the subject very thoroughly for three decades. I had become convinced to the core of my being of the futility of drug use. It became clear to me that drugs would never make me the person I wanted to be, nor take me where I wanted to go. I don't always necessarily know where it is I want to go, but I know for sure where I don't want to go: I don't ever want to go back to where I was. I need to be vigilant about remembering that there is only one thing that will take me back there, and that is to pick up a drink or a drug. As far as sayings go, my contribution with regard to relapse is: "For a brief relief, I double my grief."

When I talk with newcomers about recovery, I often cite the example of a famous celebrity who was about to enter rehab for addiction to painkillers. A reporter asked one of the physicians in charge of the expensive rehab center that the man was about to check into, what exactly would they do for him. The doctor replied: "Beyond medically supervise his detox? Twelve Step program." (He said "Twelve Step program" like it was a given.) "We have nothing better. I wish there was something that worked one hundred percent of the time, but there's not. Percentage-wise, Twelve Step programs are the most successful things available."

It's disconcerting to me that people have sometimes been fed false notions about Twelve Step programs. One of the most glaring untruths is that people in Twelve Step meetings just sit around and "bitch and moan and complain." Nothing could be further from the truth. In any segment of society there will be people who feel the need to complain on occasion. (Try to spend a couple of hours at work without hearing someone "bitch or moan or complain.") But the vast majority of the people are talking about solutions to their problems. I am continuously inspired by the courage, strength, and hope that others share in these settings. The rooms are filled with some of the most compassionate, caring and loving people in the world.

Perhaps the best thing about Twelve Step programs is that they are based on a "Higher Power of our own understanding," and not some God or religion that human beings contrived and added countless rules and regulations and qualifications to. (Unconditional love is unconditional love, for God's sake.) Twelve Step programs are spiritually based, not religiously based programs. As the saying goes: "Religion is for people who don't want to go to hell and spirituality is for people who have already been there and don't want to go back."

EARLY RECOVERY

I spent twelve days in rehab. My first day back in the "real world" I went directly to an outpatient meeting (as had been suggested to me), which turned out to be an extremely beneficial thing. I was so far removed from any sort of mental or emotional balance it was frightening. I needed to talk to people who were feeling like I was. There were eight or nine people gathered in a room for that first meeting. Most of them had fewer than two weeks clean. One guy had forty-five days, and I remember being intimidated by his time. I sat there thinking, *Why did they put this old-timer in here with us?* Perspective is indeed an amazing thing.

It was in this first meeting that I met Jake Thompson, who was twenty years my junior. Jake's main drug of choice at the time was meth, whereas mine had been opiates. In spite of our differences, I discovered early on that we were on very similar wavelengths. Jake's a good looking, blondish young man about six feet one, with a quiet demeanor and a ready smile. I had actually met him in a small orientation gathering before the meeting. We weren't in the room but about two minutes when I made a sarcastic remark about something, and I espied Jake's grin. I knew in that instant that we were kindred spirits. It's funny how connections between people can exist among seemingly totally disparate individuals. They say that the disease of addiction does not discriminate. It is equally spread among people regardless of age, sex, race, or religious, economic or social backgrounds. As my good friend, Tim Myers, says, "Addiction doesn't discriminate—but the good news is, neither does recovery. It is available for free to anyone who wants it."

Jake and I became close friends fairly quickly. After orientation we stood outside waiting to be called into the group meeting. I remember the two of us joking about the slogan made famous by Nancy Reagan: "Just Say No." We slapped our foreheads and said, "Why didn't we think of that?" Of course, as much as I've joked about her little slogan, the fact is that the first thing one has to do *is* to say "No." But, at the time, what was most important is that Jake and I needed to laugh. In fact, we needed to know that we still *could* laugh.

The meeting was led by a man named Ted Dorsey. He was to be our counselor for the three-month duration of our outpatient sessions. He turned out to be a great guy, a very authentic person with a genuine concern for people in pain. On that first night everyone in the room shared their story, one by one. I found it frightening to share for ten or fifteen minutes in a roomful of strangers, yet somehow I knew it was "do or die" time again. If I didn't face my fear then, would I ever be able to? Although I was terrified, by the time I got going I was fine. Sharing from the heart always removes the fear.

DAY 13

The morning after the outpatient meeting I reported back to work for the first time. But because I was so physically weak and mentally depleted, I had to leave at noon. I had never felt so out of place in all my life. The thought of having to face another day like that was more than I could bear. I decided to go to a doctor to see if he would prescribe something for the acute anxiety I was experiencing. I didn't have a regular physician that I had been seeing in recent years. I opted to go to a clinic in Gresham that I had visited on occasion when scamming for narcotics. Because my history with this clinic was not exactly cemented in integrity, I decided to bring along someone who by virtue of their mere appearance would exude more credibility than I was bringing to the table. I called my mother. She agreed to go with me, naturally.

When we got to the clinic, I signed in and saw that Dr. Johannsen was on duty. Waiting in a doctor's office at the age of forty-six with my mother at my side was humiliating, of course. But the first thing I said when Dr. Johannsen came into the room was that I had been less than honest with him in the past about my level of pain and my need for narcotic medication. I told him that because of my past behavior "I currently have no credibility." Then I pointed to my mother and introduced her, saying, "Today, she is my credibility."

I explained to the good doctor (and he is a very good doctor *and* human being) that I was now in recovery and that one of the things I had learned in my short stay in rehab referred to cleaning up our past and making amends when possible. I proceeded to make my amends to Dr. Johannsen right then. He was very understanding.

I then told the doctor that I was experiencing tremendous anxiety. I said it felt like there was a knot in my stomach the size of a soccer ball. I confided to him that if I didn't get something to help me with this anxiety, I was either going to get loaded or I was going to kill myself. (I was not being melodramatic. I was being completely honest, as opposed to my past visits with the doctor.)

I was a "basket case" (whatever the hell that means). Dr. Johannsen told me that he didn't want to get me started on anti-anxiety medication because the better-working ones were habit forming. Instead, he prescribed an anti-depressant for me that he said would also help to calm me down some. He also gave me something (I don't recall what it was) to help reduce the knotted feeling in my stomach. Dr. Johannsen was very supportive and very complimentary to me for having the courage to get clean and to come in and be honest with him. I thanked him for his compassion and apologized once more for my past transgressions. He told me not to worry about it. Then he looked at my mother and said, "I suspect a lot of people, but I never suspected your son."

The medicine took the edge off enough to keep me from whacking myself or getting loaded. I'm fairly certain, in retrospect, that much of the therapeutic benefit was of a placebo nature. In truth, I felt an immediate sense of relief the instant I swallowed that first pill. Just the idea, the hope, that I might soon be experiencing some relief was enough to relax me a great deal. Hey, whatever works. It was better than a gun in my mouth or a needle in my arm.

Over the next couple of years I saw Dr. Johannsen on five or six occasions. A few of those visits were regarding anti-depressants. (Although I never found one that did the trick for me without eventually experiencing intolerable side effects, I was at least willing to give them a try. I had reached a point where I was willing to follow whatever suggestions were presented to me, provided they appeared to be healthy ones.) Two of the visits were for standard physicals, including blood tests. It was from Dr. Johannsen that I found out my liver counts had returned to normal after about nine months of not drinking or using.

Dr. Johannsen and I developed a great relationship during these visits. The clinic was often extremely busy, and there would usually be just one doctor on duty. In spite of this, Dr. Johannsen would come in and converse with me for a good twenty minutes each time. He expressed tremendous interest in my recovery, and it touched me immensely. After my first couple of visits in the early months of my sobriety, Dr. Johannsen told me he was impressed with where I had come from and with the progress I had made. He told me that he was proud of me, as a father would his son. His compliments meant a great deal to me. At one point he told me he had a son who was a psychiatrist in the military and was stationed overseas. He was in charge of addiction related problems for military personnel all over Europe. At that point he asked me for permission to talk with his son about my case. I told him I had absolutely no problem with that. I told him that I was doing my best to never hide anything again. Hiding things had gotten me into a world of hurt in the past.

True to his word, on my next visit a couple of months later, Dr. Johannsen said he had discussed my case with his son. He had been glad to get some input from him, and I was glad to benefit from this "coincidental" resource as well. Dr. Johannsen is now retired, but I shall be forever grateful to him for the time he spent with me, for his endless words of encouragement, his concern for my well being and the genuine compassion he showed me from that first visit on Day 13 and throughout the next couple of years.

DAY 14

In the early evening of Day 14 I spilled some grape juice on the carpet in our living room. Although all human beings experience such lapses in dexterity from time to time, the fact was that my physical coordination had been noticeably hampered by my drug use. And it would continue to be messed up for a while, I learned in my outpatient classes. There is a term for the physical (and mental) impairment that is a direct result of chemical imbalances induced by drug abuse. That term is PAWS—Post Acute Withdrawal Syndrome. This physical impairment, coupled with my hyped-up behavior, was enough to plant doubt in Judy's mind about my sobriety. My brain chemistry was so out of balance that I, a recovering opiate junkie, had been acting like a fricking tweaker (meth addict) since I had gotten out of the hospital. I just couldn't settle down. Although the medicine Dr. Johannsen had prescribed for me had indeed taken some of the edge off, nothing was going to work magic overnight. I know today that most of the work has to come from within. As they say: "Recovery is an inside job." In addition to the time it takes to physically restore chemical imbalances, it takes a great deal of time to psychologically adjust to an entirely new way of living.

In any event, Judy accused me of being loaded after I spilled the grape juice. I was devastated by her accusation. At first I had been just plain angry. *How dare she accuse me of being loaded?* I had expressed my dismay to her, asking her how she could witness what I had gone through in the last couple of weeks and think that I would get loaded again, especially so soon. She told me that I just wasn't acting normal. Of course, neither of us really knew at that point what the hell normal *was* for me. I hadn't been completely clean and sober the entire time we had known each other.

I very quickly went from being angry to being horribly sad about what my addiction had done to the trust in our relationship. Nevertheless, I went to my outpatient group that night and began ranting about my wife accusing me of being loaded. Thank God for my fellow recovering addicts. They were as incredulous about my attitude as I had been about being accused of being loaded. In a nutshell they said, "How many years did you manipulate and deceive and lie to your wife about your drug and alcohol use? And you expect her to trust you after a couple of weeks?"

To which I had responded, "Well—yeah." I did have a half smile on my face when I said this, recognizing, with the help of my comrades, the absurdity of my expectations.

At any rate I told Ted, our counselor, that I desperately wanted to get a U.A. that evening. (I was legitimately clean, and I wanted Judy to know it. Yes, I had been angry about being accused, and yes I bitched about it when I got to my outpatient group, but underneath all the anger was a truly deep sadness over what my use had done to the trust in our relationship.) Our meetings took place on the grounds of a hospital, Mt. Hood Medical Center, and Ted told me where in the hospital I needed to go to get the urine analysis done.

The results of the U.A. were negative for drugs, of course. The funny thing was, Judy had ended up believing me within a few minutes of having accused me. She had seen the hurt in my eyes and had heard the genuine pain in my voice. Regardless, it was important to me to have proof on paper because, again, I had no credibility as yet.

DAY 20

On Day 20 I had an appointment with John Emerson, the counselor I had contacted a few days before getting clean. I had left for the appointment on time but in the haze of my early recovery I had forgotten the piece of paper bearing the address of the place. I recalled only that it was on Southeast Division Street, somewhere around 30th Avenue, I believed. But I couldn't find it for the life of me, and the closer it got to my two o'clock appointment time, the more frantic I became. I don't know why it had been so very critical to me to be on time. I think the main thing was I didn't want Mr. Emerson to think I was late because I had been out getting loaded. Also, it didn't help that I had an extremely short fuse in those early months of recovery. (I had never considered myself an angry person until I got clean. In those first few months, the slightest thing could set me off, it seemed. Coupled with my new-found temporary lack of physical coordination, my emotions could be easily triggered when things didn't go my way. Something as simple and seemingly mundane as dropping a tool in the garage or a fork in the kitchen might set me off.)

I couldn't call "information" on my cell phone because Judy had taken my cell phone from me (I will get to that in a moment). So I scoured the streets looking for a pay phone in order to look up the address in a phone book. As the minutes flew by, I was becoming more and more aggravated. Thanks in large part to the emotional maturity I was brimming with at the time, I began racing around corners in my little Nissan Sentra, purposely making the tires squeal. (I hadn't been able to get them to squeal in the normal fashion—as in "peeling out" from a stop. The Nissan didn't have near enough power for that. But it was evidently very important to me at that moment that I somehow make noise with my tires.) After speeding around one such corner, I continued my two-year-old tantrum by tossing one of my recovery books across the front of the car, slamming the innocent object up against the passenger door.

After more frantic searching and continuous swearing, I found a phone booth and hurriedly began combing through the yellow pages. However, this maneuver only served to add to my exasperation because I couldn't remember the name of the non-profit organization Mr. Emerson worked for. I ended up calling my sponsor, Mark, who did a good job of calming me down. I told him how upset I was. I told him I was losing it and that I didn't want to feel that way anymore. And I told him about throwing the book across the car.

Mark had patiently listened to me rant and then simply asked, "Was there anyone in the car when you threw the book?"

"No," I answered.

"Well, that's not so bad then," he replied. "You didn't hit anyone."

After Mark's calming influence I was able to somehow remember the name of the place and I finally got a hold of John Emerson. By this time it was too late to make it to the appointment. I related my frustration to Mr. Emerson, sounding like a madman, I'm sure. But he listened to my ravings as patiently as Mark had. When I was done venting he simply said, "Well, you learned something very important today, didn't you?"

I couldn't fathom what I had learned and told him so.

John answered in the most soothing tone imaginable, "You learned that the world did not end."

Oh, yeah. He was right. The world truly hadn't ended. It had been the perfect thing to say. Thanks to Mark and John, I survived Day 20 and went to bed that night, still clean and sober.

With regard to having my cell phone confiscated by my wife, the situation was as follows: After I had arrived home from the hospital I asked Judy if she had seen my cell phone. She took a deep breath and bravely told me that she had taken it. (I say "bravely," because in my addiction she had become accustomed to my getting very self-righteous and/or defensive whenever I was questioned about anything.) I told her that I needed that cell phone to call people. (Recovery programs stress the importance of maintaining contact with fellow recovering addicts.) Judy simply told me that we had a home phone I could use.

It turned out that my wife was willing to give me the benefit of the doubt, but that she was deathly afraid of my dealer calling me on my cell phone. I tried to convince her that he had never called me before (he hadn't needed to—I had called him religiously) and that she had nothing to worry about. But she held fast and I decided I owed it to her to heed her concerns.

After my experience trying to locate John Emerson and a phone booth, however, I broached the subject again. Aside from that frustrating event, I was now driving forty miles to work each way. (Our company had moved to Woodland, Washington by this time, and I was commuting from our home in Gresham, Oregon.) It was a prime opportunity to stay connected with people in recovery. Judy decided I was sincere about this conviction and agreed to give me back my phone. I tried to console her by telling her that there was no way Alejandro (my last dealer) was going to call me after almost a month of not hearing from me.

Within an hour of getting my phone back, Alejandro called. I was truly shocked. I recognized his voice immediately, of course. There was no mistaking that thick accent. I instantly informed him that I was "done." I told him that I had been through rehab and that I was quitting dope for good. The man who previously had had no trouble interpreting what I said when I was paying him a hundred dollars a day, had suddenly become unfamiliar with the English language. He acted as if he didn't understand me.

I repeated to Alejandro that I was quitting drugs. "No mas," I said. "That shit killed my friend and I'm done with it." Then I told him never to call me again. I had refrained from swearing at him and directly blaming him for Luke's death, thanks again to the insight of my outpatient group. When I had first told my peers about my wife taking my cell phone and of her concerns about my dealer calling me, they had agreed with her. They, too, believed he would call me. *Was I the only blind person on this planet?* I remember one guy from my group had said: "You were handing the man a hundred dollars cash every day. He's not going to suddenly forget that income. Dealers dream about finding 'reliable, no-hassle customers' like you."

I had responded by telling my group that I still didn't think he would call, but that if he did, I was going to cuss him out for killing my friend, Luke. Again, the group had come through for me. They asked me what the hell I was thinking. They reminded me that I really didn't know this guy from Adam. He might not take my calling him a murderer lying down. They told me I had no idea what he was capable of. The man was dealing heroin, for God's sake, not selling lemonade on the street corner. I rebutted by saying he didn't know where I lived. They reminded me that he had seen my car almost every day for months. He could very easily have written my license down and could trace my address if he wanted to.

So, thanks to my friendly local group of recovering addicts, I didn't start ripping into Alejandro about killing Luke. I chose my words carefully and then hung up the phone. I then immediately called my cell phone carrier and requested a new number. The lady told me it would cost me thirty dollars to change numbers. I told her that sounded like a lot for just a new phone number (not remembering at the moment that I had ended up paying a *hundred* dollars for Alejandro's phone number). She told me that if it was an emergency situation she could change it for free. I jumped all over that. I told her that yes, indeed, it was an emergency situation.

"It's a matter of life and death," I told her. "Mine."

The lady was cool. Without asking any questions she changed the number for free.

DAY 21

Day 21 was the day that I met Meg in her faded blue Chevy Caprice to listen to her account of Luke's death. A very sad, but also very poignant, experience.

DAY 22

On this day a *very* close family member ended up in the intensive-care ward at Mt. Hood Medical Center. I shall call this person "Ken" out of respect for his anonymity. Suffice it to say he had three grand mal seizures that day, brought on by the use of methamphetamines. He was in a meth-induced psychosis when I received a frantic call from Judy. Judy rarely panics, so when I heard her losing it I knew something had to be terribly wrong. I was on my way home from work, still a few miles away. I became frantic to get home. I raced through the crowded streets of Gresham in rush hour traffic, at times hitting more than seventy miles an hour.

I arrived home and burst into the house to find five paramedics and firemen working on Ken. Judy was sitting on the floor of the hallway with her knees up to her chest and her hands over her mouth. I had never seen her look so shocked.

Judy and I spent the night in the hospital wondering whether or not Ken was going to live. It was an extremely traumatic night for the two of us. At twenty-two days clean and sober, I was in no state to be handling this kind of emergency. My mom and my brother Tim came to the hospital and proved, once again, to be invaluable support. With their help, Judy and I both got through it, as did Ken. Today, thankfully, Ken is off the meth and doing great.

DAY 56

I continued to go to one or two meetings a day. It was suggested to me that I go to ninety meetings in ninety days and, as I said, I had made a commitment to follow healthy suggestions. I remember specific days that were troublesome in those first ninety days of sobriety, and Day 56 was among them. From the onset of my recovery it had been difficult handling a normal workday without getting overstressed. I found myself taking deep breaths all day long in an effort to calm down. (One of the things I read in those early weeks of recovery was that the normal breathing of most people is too shallow—that we should "breathe into our bellies" as a way of relaxing.)

On Day 56 I was feeling particularly stressed. I just couldn't relax—at all. I tried deep breathing over and over again that day. I tried praying. I tried going for a short walk. But on this day, nothing was working. For some reason, I was losing it—and losing it big time.

I called Mark out in the shop and told him I wasn't doing well. He told me to try to relax, that "This too shall pass." But, again, nothing seemed to be working that day. Mark related to me that although he was my sponsor, that didn't mean he was always going to know the right thing to say. He told me to hang in there, that things would get better. But I was wigging. In my mind it seemed as if no consoling words from others *or* actions on my part could possibly be enough to snap me out of whatever the hell I was in, and I certainly didn't feel like "things would get better."

I told Mark I was going outside for another walk. When I came back a few minutes later I was feeling slightly better, but it wasn't long before the anxiety was back full force. I hated the instability of early recovery. I felt so damn raw. I recognize now, of course, that almost everyone feels that way when they first get sober. We had blocked out our emotions during most of our active using days. We hadn't had to deal with things head on, clean and sober, for a long time. When we first get clean we have to learn how to do that. It's like learning to walk all over again. On that 56th day, in my severely distressed, raw state of emotion, I wanted out badly. I simply didn't want to do this life thing anymore. There was just too much pain involved.

At that moment I happened to glance up at the bulletin board that hung above my computer desk. There, fastened with a push pin, was a newly written sign, and I recognized the handwriting. It was Mark's. Apparently he had come to the office to see how I was doing. In my absence he had written a note and pinned it on the wall.

In big letters, it read: **"YOU CAN START YOUR DAY OVER AT ANY TIME."** Below that it read: **And remember, a great man once told me, 'It's only steel.'"**

I could start my day over at any time. Wow! Whether or not I had heard that particular saying before, I don't recall. What I do know is that it was exactly what I needed to hear at that moment. It seemed like such a revelation. No matter what had happened two hours ago, or ten minutes ago, or even five seconds ago—I could start anew in this very instant. It was quite a novel concept to me. *Every moment is new. No one has ever experienced this moment before.* No matter what has happened in the past, I have the option to view this new moment from a fresh and more positive perspective. And I *always* have that choice. This was good news indeed.

The "great man" who had told him "It's only steel"? Well, that had been me. I had told Mark that very thing a long time prior to Day 56, on a day when *he* was suffering from the stress of the job. "What goes around comes around" applies to good things, too, I suppose. Mark had proved himself wrong. He had known exactly what to say.

DAY 89

I continued to attend a meeting or two a day, doing the "ninety in ninety" that had been suggested to me (my meeting streak had started on my seventh day in rehab, after I had been transferred back up from the medical ward). However, on Day 82 of my meeting binge I had almost broken this streak. I had been back to work full time for about six weeks at this point, and I was exhausted. I was still experiencing weakness from the pneumonia. I was also continuing to suffer the effects of detoxing and of chemical imbalances. I was physically, mentally, and emotionally drained. When I had gotten home from work that day I plopped down in a recliner and said to my wife, "You know, eighty-one days is close enough."

Without looking up from the book she was reading, Judy responded with the brief and simple remark, "Can't cut it, huh?"

There was an endless combination of words that my wife could have uttered at that moment, but those were the ones that did the trick. No addict worth his salt likes to be told that they can't do something any more than he or she likes to be told *what to do.*

"I can cut it," I told her. And I got up off my butt and made it to a meeting. I kept my streak alive with the help of my remarkable wife, Judy.

STONES

About six months into my recovery I found out I had kidney stones. I had been experiencing pain in my lower back that didn't feel much like muscle strain or anything else I had ever felt. I had several fairly severe attacks in this region, including one that took place in front of Judy just after we had gotten into the car one evening. I hadn't even put the key in the ignition when I was suddenly struck with a shooting stab of pain in my lower back. Out of reflex I pulled the lever that tilted the seat back. In a prone position, I began writhing in pain for several minutes. The writhing was accompanied by constant moaning. The thing about kidney stones is that they only hurt when they try to move inside your body. When they stop moving, they stop hurting. So when it was over I put my seat back in its normal position and went on with my life. As I started the car, I looked over at Judy and said, "That kind of hurt."

Judy's eyes were practically popping out of her head. "*Kind* of hurt?" she responded, flabbergasted. "You were writhing in agony for three or four minutes. That's not normal."

I thought about it and decided she was right. (Once again, I'm just not all that bright. Without others to guide me, I'm really kind of floundering at sea much of the time.) I went to the doctor shortly after that. He told me it sounded like kidney stones. The first thing they did was take a urine sample. Then this medical specialist, who I had never been to before, called me into his office. We didn't go into a regular, patient waiting room—we went into his office. I sat down in a chair across from his desk, and the very first words out of this doctor's mouth were: "There are three types of cancer we could be dealing with."

I immediately looked over my shoulder to see who it was he might be talking to. (Knowing full well that there was a wall inches behind my head, and there was nothing or no one else, but he just couldn't have been speaking to me—we had been talking kidney stones, I thought.)

284

The doctor proceeded to rule out prostate cancer, thinking I was still too young for that. Then he mentioned bladder and kidney cancer. I sat there speechless while he went through his ten-minute dissertation on the various types of cancer, how they usually showed up, and how they were treated. I waited until he was finished with his cancer lesson and then confusedly inquired, "What happened to the kidney-stone theory?"

"Oh—it could still be that," he replied, acting as if his cancer spiel had just been routine.

Who was this guy?

It turned out to be kidney stones. A few days later I went to a hospital where they injected me with some sort of dye in order to view my stones. The results showed that there was one stone that was too big to pass. They also said that it was located where it wasn't going to move much further without help, so they scheduled me for surgery. The doctor explained to me that they would insert a tube up through my penis and then feed a camera into the tube so they could see what they were doing. Then they would shoot a laser through this tube and bust up the stone. Finally, they would insert a tool through the implanted tube and use it to grab the chunks of broken up kidney stone.

I had listened with astonishment to the various gear they were planning on bombarding my member with. When he was done, I said, "Doc, it's really not all that big." I paused to let that sink in. "We can't just be shoving tubes and cameras and tools up there, en masse. Besides, that's going to hurt—*a lot*—don't you think?"

The doctor explained to me about microscopic sized instruments and that I would be completely under anesthetic. In the end I decided to let the specialists do their thing on my thing. It appeared obvious to me that I couldn't perform the operation on myself. Everything went as planned—the surgery was successful. I was still going to have to pass pieces of stone, they told me, but they would be comparatively small. The biggest problem now was that I was going to have to pee through a urethral tube that had just had cameras and tools and things shoved up and down its throat. As such, it was now just an open, raw, bleeding wound. An open, raw bleeding wound that I had to pass *acidic* urine through. They, of course, wouldn't let me leave the hospital until I urinated. So, when I was able to, I did. The pain was beyond excruciating. I had never experienced physical pain of that magnitude. The "moving kidney stones" had been a cake walk compared to this.

The kicker was I had no painkillers given to me other than ibuprofen. My choice. They had offered me narcotic pain medication several times. Hell, they had practically tried to ram them down my throat. The day before the surgery the doctor had told me I would be getting pain medicine, and I had told him I didn't want any. I had let him know right from the get-go that I was an addict. (To this day, that is the first thing I tell any doctor that I haven't seen before—and that's only to protect me from me. I get any of the guesswork out of the way, and any potential temptation to take painkillers without anyone being aware of my history.) Even so, right before surgery, the doctor asked me what I wanted for pain medication. I told him again that I didn't want any. I told him that if the pain got too much for me I would call him. In spite of my very clear feelings on this subject, when I was still unconscious and in the recovery room, the doctor went to my wife and mother (who had both come to the hospital) and asked them what I might want for pain medication. Thankfully, they both told him the same thing—that I didn't want any. (For years, I scratched and clawed and pleaded with anyone and everyone to get my hands on narcotic painkillers. Now that I was trying to stay away from them, offers were flying at me from every direction, it seemed.)

Anyway, I poured my goddamn acidic urine through this open, raw, bleeding wound of a urethral tube without pain medication. And it hurt like holy hell. I couldn't accomplish the act of urination for the next two and a half days without literally screaming in agony while doing so. About halfway through the second day I called my friend Tom and told him I couldn't take the pain anymore. I was going to have to call the doctor for medicine. Tom told me to hang in there, that the worst part was almost over. He had been through the same surgery a year or so prior, which was why I had called him. I knew he would give me honest input, based upon actual experience. Of course Tom had been given narcotic painkillers after his surgery, but even with the pills he said it had still hurt like hell, and he could tell me at what point the pain had begun to subside for him. He told me to just make it through that second day if I could, and it would start to get easier. Tom knew how badly I wanted to avoid taking narcotics if I could. So I focused on the original pact I had made with myself before the surgery. I had told myself that only if I passed out from the pain would I ask for narcotic pain medicine. The beauty of this pact was, of course, that if I passed out, I wouldn't be needing any painkillers because I'd be unconscious. In other words, I wasn't going to take narcotic pain medication no matter what.

When I was sharing this experience a week later with a fellow recovering addict, he looked at me and said, "You need to have more faith in your recovery."

I looked at him with astonishment and said, "Man, you're one of the main reasons I didn't accept pain medication from the doctor." This particular addict had recently had eleven years of what appeared to me to be very good recovery and had relapsed because of taking painkillers for kidney stones. Did he not see the parallel there?

Anyway, I made it through the ordeal, and it taught me that we can take a lot more pain than we think we can. About a year later I had a lady tell me that she would rather go through the pain of childbirth ten more times (she had three children) than go through kidney stones again. (And she had just been talking about the pain of *having* the stones—she had not had the surgery to have them removed.)

About six months later a customer from work, an owner and operator of a welding and fabrication shop, called and told me he was going to have the exact same operation in a couple of days. Remembering my surgery, he was calling to get my input on the matter. I told him what I knew and what he could expect as far as pain. The following Monday (four days after his surgery) he called me. Without saying hello, he said, "I just wanted to tell you that if you went through that without pain medication, you are one tough son of a bitch."

"Not that tough," I told him. "Just scared."

There *are* healthy and responsible ways that a recovering addict can take narcotic painkillers if one has legitimate pain and truly needs them, but at six months clean, and with my past relationship with pain pills, I just didn't feel comfortable doing so. I'm grateful that thus far I haven't had to take anything other than aspirin or ibuprofen at any time in my recovery.

OVEREXPOSED

There was a moment, I recall, at around sixteen months sober, sitting with my wife in our kitchen, that I found to be inexplicably bizarre. It occurred on a day that rivaled a Day 13, Day 20 or Day 56 for insanity and intolerability. As I sat down at the kitchen table I began continually raking my hands through my hair in frantic fashion, complaining one more time to my wife about how I couldn't handle this "sober" thing. *Life was just too damn hard for this head of mine*, I told her for the umpteenth time.

It was a hot summer day, and I had my shirt off. While I continued ranting, Judy walked around behind me, and every once in a while she would lightly touch my bare back. I could feel her breath on my skin and I got the sense that she was inspecting me closely. At the end of my four- or five-minute diatribe on the horridness of the human condition (and specifically the horridness of *this* human's condition), Judy walked back around in front of me. After waiting a few seconds to make sure I was done venting, she looked at me and said, "Well, you don't have melanoma."

Well, thank God for that! I thought to myself. *Where the hell had that come from?* was my next thought. I felt completely disconnected at that moment. I looked at my lovely wife and said, "Of the 437,000 insane thoughts that have been racing through my addled brain today, whether or not I had melanoma had definitely not been one of them." I paused, then added, "Until now."

Judy began to laugh. She recognized that, like two ships, we had just passed in the night without seeing each other. If I hadn't said it before, I shall make clear one point. I am blessed with having a wife (and a mother) who are without a doubt the two best listeners I have ever known. They are truly amazing. Good listeners are relatively rare in this world, and I am graced with having two of them in my life. I guess it probably seems even more amazing to me because I have always rather sucked at it—listening, that is. (I've made a concerted

288

effort in recent years to become a better listener and am making slow progress. I'm sorry—were you saying something?)

But after having had to listen to me rant and rave on a multitude of subjects over the years, and especially having had to listen to the insanity of my ramblings in early recovery, Judy was certainly more than entitled to have an occasional lapse of the listening mode. Completely out of character for her, she had barely heard a word I said. That aside, she had medically cleared me of melanoma, so things could have been worse. Never mind that I had been so out of sorts that I was once again questioning the very worthiness of life itself—now that I knew I was melanoma-free, what could I possible have to fret about?

We had both chuckled over that one. The irony is that about four years later I actually did come up with melanoma. My wife's probing me that day had not just been an idle moment of boredom. She knew I had taken in a lot of sun in my life and was genuinely worried that I might contract melanoma someday. (Her timing was a little off from my perspective, but she had done it out of concern for my well being.) Judy had a couple of relatives who had died from this very deadly form of skin cancer, so consequently her sensitivity to the disease had been naturally heightened.

After having been to the doctor in September of 2004 for a physical *and* to have a mole on my back checked out (that Judy didn't like the looks of), I got a call at work from the doctor I had seen. His exact words were: "Well, you tested positive for melanoma, the deadliest and most aggressive form of skin cancer."

After my head went *Whoa!* I settled back in my office chair and said, "What do we do?"

The doctor told me that we needed to remove the mole right away. I scheduled an appointment for surgery for the next afternoon, hung up the phone, and buried my head in my hands on my desk. It's quite a shock to actually hear the dreaded "C" word applied to you, especially when used in conjunction with such encouraging terms as "deadliest" and "most aggressive."

I have been blessed in the work world to have been surrounded by great people all of my life. They have always been there for me. Sue and Karen were the first to comfort me, followed by Lisa and Diane. I'll be forever grateful for the support all of my co-workers have given me over the years, in this situation and in many others. I have been truly fortunate in this regard.

The first couple of hours after hearing this bit of news I was more or less in a state of shock. But after a while I simply accepted what the doctor had told me. There was really nothing I could do about it, I knew. The doctor had told me they would cut out the cancerous mole and then a biopsy would be performed on the surrounding tissue to see if the cancer had spread at all. I would end up having to wait five or six days to get the final verdict. Although it wasn't the most thrilling way to spend the better part of a week, I really didn't sit around and think about it too much. "What will be, will be," I told myself. I was grateful for having learned new ways of dealing with things.

The news was good. The cancer had not spread. However, having the words "most aggressive" and "deadly" still fresh in my memory, I asked the doctor what would have happened if I hadn't come in for another year or so. He told me that I might not have been around—melanoma can spread that quickly if not caught in time. So, once again I owed my wife Judy my life. I certainly wouldn't have noticed that mole on my back. (I *hadn't* noticed that mole on my back.) Yet, something about the shape or color of the mole had concerned Judy, and she pestered me for two months to go to the doctor before I finally did. And I'm very glad I finally "listened" to her.

MIRACLE/MYSTERY

Mitch had ended up getting clean and sober a couple of months before I did. He had gone down to Eugene to detox, and for some reason it finally had a lasting effect. I remember him calling me a few times to see how I was doing. He'd gotten clean shortly after I had started using heroin. I told him I wanted to stop but didn't know how. He kept repeating to me that I couldn't do it on my own, that I needed help. He was very compassionate and supportive.

Ironically, we both ended up getting clean in the same calendar year. Judy and I ran into Mitch at a recovery convention in Tacoma, Washington, several months after I had gotten clean. He had almost a year clean and sober by this time. A true miracle, considering the man had rarely gone more than a few days without a drink or a drug (and all of those occasions were in a detox facility of some kind).

I remember I spotted him that day at the convention. There was a crowd of people off to one side of us, and suddenly I said to Judy, "There's Mitch!" She wanted to try to spot him by herself before I showed her where he was. She had seen him a couple of times back in our using days. Judy scanned the crowd and finally gave up. So I pointed him out to her and she exclaimed incredulously, "*That's* Mitch?" She was truly shocked. She had never seen him sober and cleaned up. "Wow! He's kind of cute!" I remember her saying.

Mitch and I talked for almost an hour that afternoon at the convention. He was full of recovery—that's all we spoke about. It was just such an amazing transition, I could hardly believe it. But there he was, clean and sober, looking good, and spewing recovery talk from the heart. Judy had been apprehensive at first, but after about thirty minutes of listening to Mitch and me, she could tell he was serious about his sobriety. She hadn't said two words up until that point. Suddenly she looked at him and asked, "What was different this time, Mitch?"

Mitch pondered it for a few seconds and then said, "I don't know for sure.

I had heard all of that stuff a hundred times in detox units and it never stuck. I guess maybe this time I finally listened with my heart instead of my head."

Sadly, at twenty months clean and sober, Mitch relapsed. He had given in to his chronic back pain one day and had gotten some narcotic painkillers. It was like letting a monster out of a cage. I remember him calling me from Eugene asking if he could come detox at our house. I reluctantly said to him, "You know I can't let you do that, Mitch." I told him that Judy was happy with me now, that she had grown to trust me, and that I just couldn't put the onus of having someone detoxing at our house on her. (I knew how messed up Mitch could get, and the truth of the matter was that I couldn't handle it, either.) I feel guilty about that to this day, but the reality is that Mitch and I wouldn't have mixed well in that scenario. I wasn't exactly a rock of stability in my early recovery. And I knew that with Mitch having relapsed he would probably be quite tempted to use again, especially if he was staying with one of his old drug-running buddies. I also knew how persuasive Mitch could be. And that frightened me. I couldn't risk my sobriety at that point—not even for an old friend. I also knew there were places he could go in Eugene to detox. He had been to a ton of meetings in those twenty months. Surely there was someone down there (with a little less personal history) who could more realistically help him and direct him. I had done the safe thing by turning him down, yet it still troubled me to tell him no.

And it bothers me to this day, years later, because whether Mitch is dead or alive, I simply do not know. I know nothing of his current whereabouts, I am sad to say. I have not heard from him in years, not since that day he called to ask about detoxing at our house. But I think of him often and hope with all my heart that he is okay.

I had first begun talking about writing my memoirs back when I was hanging with Luke and Mitch. I remember Mitch asking me if he would be in my book, to which I had replied, "Of course you will, man." He seemed extremely pleased to hear that.

We had quite a run out there. God bless you and keep you, Mitch, wherever you may be.

BIRDS OVER WATER

A crucial step in my recovery has been reaching out to the still-suffering addict. One of the most rewarding things I do in this regard is visit hospitals and prisons. The first time I went to a treatment facility to speak to addicts was a very special night for me. As I have explained in detail, I had been plagued for years with a fear of speaking in public. When I had slightly less than one year clean and sober, a lady asked me if I would like to share my "experience, strength, and hope" at a rehab ward in a hospital. Actually, she hadn't really put it in the form of a question. She stated that Mark had said I would be interested in doing this (good ol' Mark—always looking out for me). Although the mere thought of speaking to a group of people immediately threw me into a state of panic and ensuing dread, I accepted her invitation. As much as the thought of it scared the hell out of me, my desire to face and overcome my fears (this one in particular) won out.

I was told to contact a "Lawana M." at a Sunday morning meeting in East Gresham. The following Sunday I went to this meeting and found Lawana. I introduced myself and asked her about this speaking-engagement thing. She told me it would be at Portland Adventist on March 28, a week and a half away. I related to her that I was quite petrified, and that I didn't know if I could go through with it or not. I wanted to, I told her, but I was worried. She told me that I would be just fine.

But in my apprehensive state I looked at Lawana and asked, "What if I freeze?"

Now, she could have said any number of things in response. She could have given me a mountain of advice (she had been talking in prisons and hospitals about recovery from addiction for years). She could have laid a bunch of psychological mumbo-jumbo or recovery talk on me. In fact, I'm quite convinced I could have spent ten years on a couch with the best shrink in the land and not gotten what I was about to get from Lawana. Two words. Two very simple words that had an immediate and profound impact on me:

She simply looked me in the eye and said, "So what?"

So what? Yeah—so what? I thought immediately about what those words meant to me. I said to Lawana, "Yeah, you're right! *So what?* No one is going to get loaded if I freeze. No one is going to die. The world will not end." Another profound revelation from a very simple sentence, given to me at precisely the moment it was needed.

So I gathered my courage and went to Portland Adventist on March 28, 2000, one year *to the day* that I had gotten clean. That in itself was a "God shot" to me—one year to the day that I had gotten clean and at the very hospital where I had gotten clean.

I was nervous as hell that night, of course, before I started. Lawana's "So what?" words hadn't eliminated my fear, but they had taken enough of the power out of it to get me to walk through those doors in the first place. Once I started speaking, though, it was like magic. The fear left almost instantly. The dozen or so addicts that were there in rehab that evening cried with me and laughed with me. I will never forget that night. And I will never forget Lawana for helping to supply me with the courage to go through with it.

I went back to Portland Adventist a couple of times with Lawana and her husband Dennis, both of whom have over twenty years clean and sober and continue to go to hospitals and prisons several times a month to this day. They are a remarkable couple who have continually reached out to help the still suffering addict/alcoholic. I owe these two people a great deal and will always be grateful to them.

Dennis and Lawana soon asked me if I wanted to take a meeting into Oregon State Penitentiary with them. I agreed. That was another gratifying, albeit initially intimidating, experience. I eventually got clearance to go to a number of different lock-down facilities, mostly in the Portland area. These commitments instilled a purpose in my life that had been lacking since my college days—back when I was searching for a meaningful career. I found that I didn't need to have a job that was saving the world. I could begin to find a sense of fulfillment through volunteer work.

Eventually I was asked if I would like to go to Portland Adventist once a month on a different night from when Dennis and Lawana were going. I agreed, and have been going there ever since. I choose a different person in recovery to take with me every month, and it has been one of the most rewarding experiences of my life. That monthly commitment has been highly instrumental in aiding with my continued recovery. It has kept me clean and sober on several occasions. It is always a great experience and I have had some truly special moments on some of those nights.

On one of my visits to Portland Adventist I met a man by the name of Vincent, who was a patient in rehab there. I was standing up by the nurse's station shortly before heading down the hall where the meeting was to take place. I saw this person sort of milling about, not really doing anything—just kind of standing near me. I said hello to him, and he gave me an unsure smile back. Then an amazing thing happened. Within less than two minutes we were deeply engaged in a conversation about spirituality on a level that I had only really reached with a couple of other people in recovery. You just didn't find a lot of people that believed in a spirituality outside of mainstream religious conventionality, even among addicts who had been anything but conventional in their lifestyles. Although recovery programs emphasize open-mindedness and finding "a Higher Power of your own understanding," it seems a large percentage of addicts end up pursuing mainstream religious avenues. And that's great—whatever works. Most addicts do, however, change from the concept of a punishing God, that many of us had been raised with, to a God of unconditional love—and that to me is a critical (and progressive) shift. But I had explored spiritual thought that strayed from conventional Western religious thought. I found a real connection in Eastern thought—but not with any one religion. My influence came from a variety of sources—both Eastern and Western. As someone once said: "There are many archers, but there is only one target." The truth is the truth, regardless of what name you put on it.

In any event, Vincent and I hit it off immediately. After the meeting we talked further and I gave him my phone number. I said earlier that addicts rarely call when you give them your phone number. Vincent was one who did call. From that night in Portland Adventist when I first met him a seed had been planted that would develop into a great relationship for the next couple of years.

Throughout the period of time that I was conversing with Vincent, I was continuing to have my ups and downs. Vincent, on the other hand, once he had the first few weeks of recovery under his belt (he had been five years clean and sober before he relapsed), seemed to be fine. He was always so upbeat and positive. I thoroughly enjoyed each of our conversations. And as weighty as some of these conversations became, there was always humor interspersed among the seriousness. Vincent could come up with some very spiritually-minded, esoteric types of statements, but he could also be very down to earth and quite humorous, as well.

There was one particular day I was giving Vincent my new theory on being tired. I told Vincent that when I'm tired now, I merely close my eyes and tell myself that *I am not my body, nor am I the entity that feels tired.* I told Vincent that I would focus on the fact that *my True Nature has boundless energy and that I was only experiencing fatigue through the relative illusion of the body.*

Vincent listened to me politely and then simply stated, "When I'm tired, I just take a nap." Great response. (I take naps now, too.)

At almost three years clean I went through a very rocky period. I was once again battling a severe depression and was feeling suicidal. I was struggling to make it through each moment and truly didn't know how much longer I could take the psychic pain I was experiencing. For a few weeks' time it was everything I could do just to get up and go to work. On one cold winter day in early March, I was having a particularly difficult time. I forced myself to get ready for work, but on the drive there I was considering calling in sick from my cell phone and then heading back home. At one point I began to beg God to give me a sign of some kind, something, *anything*, that I could glom onto in my hour of need.

As I was crossing the Columbia River on the 205 Interstate Bridge, I happened to notice a seagull floating peacefully in the sky over the water. The thought suddenly struck me as to what tremendous freedom birds represent. They cannot fall from the sky and therefore have no fear of heights, as many people do. Nor can they drown—they float on water effortlessly—so they have no fear of water, as many people do. They are totally free up there. I continued drifting off into thought about this visual representation of freedom. I decided then and there, in that moment, that I would make "Birds over water" my new mantra of peace. When things were not going well, I decided, I would visualize this image and by so doing, hope to bring some peace into my heart.

Within moments, however, my mind drifted back to its recent mode of insanity, and I quickly became distraught again. No amount of positive thinking or images of birds over water could allay my angst. I spent the next fifteen minutes of my drive completely mired in anxiety and woe. Tears were streaming down my face as I battled my inner demons one more time.

Less than five minutes from the Woodland Industrial District where I worked, is another bridge, this one spanning the beautiful Lewis River. I had been crossing this bridge daily for almost three years and I had rarely seen a single seagull anywhere near it. But as I came upon the bridge on this particular day, a truly miraculous sight literally overwhelmed me. Not one, not two, not five or ten or twenty—but literally *hundreds* of seagulls were floating above the Lewis River that morning. On the north side of the bridge the highway continues to follow the path of the river for another half a mile or so. And all along that stretch of the river, wherever one looked that morning, hundreds of seagulls flew and hovered about thirty feet or so above the water. A virtual wall of birds covering the sky above the river. *Birds over water.* My God—I couldn't believe it.

I continued to cry, but they were now tears of joy and gratitude. I was not so self-absorbed to believe that this "miracle" had been created simply to soothe my tortured soul—and yet, I had no other explanation for it. It was truly an overwhelming spiritual experience for me. Whether or not this scene had been created for my benefit was not significant. The fact was that twenty minutes prior I had been begging God for a sign of some kind and five minutes after that I had suddenly and inexplicably decided that "birds over water" would become my mantra of peace—and, lo and behold, a mere fifteen minutes later there they were, hundreds upon hundreds of "birds over water," for as far as the eye could see.

When I got to work I mentioned the birds and was informed that it was smelting season and that the seagulls showed up like that every year for a two- to three-day period. Well, okay—that was the logical, physical explanation. I had evidently not seen them, or not noticed them on prior years. And yet, what could explain the fact that on this specific morning I had begged God for some sort of sign and then moments later had established a mantra of "birds over water" and moments after that seen this mantra in action?

When I had told Vincent about this event a few days later, he had said, with the utmost sincerity, "You manifested those birds."

Well, I certainly didn't know about that, but it sure beat the hell out of "When I'm tired, I just take a nap." I do know that for me, it was one of the most profound experiences of my life. I had subsequently made it through another bout of suffering without doing anything rash, and experienced some growth along with it.

Somewhere along the way Vincent and I lost touch. I'm not sure what happened, really. At one point I left a few messages and didn't hear back from him. But he was there for me during a time of both struggle and growth and he added immensely to both the joy and the beauty of my journey. Here's thinking of you, Vincent.

DEPRESSION PARTIES

A couple of months before my "Birds Over Water" experience, I had once again sought help for my depression. Mark had seen a flyer about a man named Douglas Bloch who was giving a talk on depression and anxiety at Portland Adventist Medical Center (my alma mater). I decided to check it out. There was a phone number listed in the flyer Mark had seen. I called it, and Douglas returned my call. He was a counselor in the field of depression and anxiety who was starting up group meetings. He said his approach was one that combined psychological tools with spiritual ones. He was a published author of about a dozen books, including *When Going Through Hell, Don't Stop.* I joined a group of his that was going to be meeting on Monday nights.

The group met weekly for a period of six months at the home of Douglas and Joan (his lovely wife) Bloch. They were similar to Twelve Step meetings except that in these "depression meetings" we had more time to share, and we also got direct feedback, both from Douglas and Joan and from one another. One of the things Douglas stressed was having each of us write a vision statement—an affirming summation of what we envisioned for ourselves. This helped a great deal in reinforcing the positive thinking I was attempting to develop.

We also had occasional social get-togethers, taking turns holding them at each others' homes. People at work would ask me what I was doing on certain weekends and if we happened to be having one of these gatherings I would tell them that I was going to a "depression party." The response was predictable: "A depression party? What the hell do you do at one of those?"

"Oh, we just sit around with our heads hanging down, wondering aloud why we bother to live," I would answer, messing with them a bit. In reality, we laughed and joked at these gatherings probably more than at most parties I had been to in my day. However, if someone was hurting during one of these festivities we would know about it and console them as much as we could. For the most part, though, the best method of consoling was to help them join in the fun and the laughter, helping them to get out of themselves.

Laura, Cathy, Kathy, Linda, Pat, Sharon, Dick, Jane, Jim, and I were original members of that depression group. Diane and Frank came along a little later, and there were quite a few of us that met monthly for a couple of years even after the group had stopped meeting with Douglas and Joan. These people were all very influential in helping me through a tough period in my life. I was the only addict in the group, but we all shared a common bond nonetheless. I was probably the closest to Laura (whose husband happened to be "a friend of Bill W"). We all helped each other through the months (and years) and though most of us have lost contact, a few of us still email each other once in a while, and I shall never forget any of them.

I have continued to stay in occasional contact with Douglas over the years as well. He and I have a common interest not only in the fields of depression and anxiety, but with regards to spirituality as well. We are of fairly similar minds as to our concept of a Higher Power, much like my friends Tim and Vincent. The two of us even took a trip together to attend an interactive retreat in Seattle one weekend.

Douglas, who has given frequent talks at various venues for years, asked me once if I would go with him to Coffee Creek Correctional Facility to help him give a presentation. He said he would talk about recovery from depression for about forty-five minutes, and he wanted me to give a talk on recovery from addiction for a similar length of time. He had become more aware in recent years of the connection between depression and drug abuse, and an extremely high percentage of prison inmates have addiction problems. Of those, a significant percentage also suffer from depression and anxiety.

Of course, my initial reaction was one of fear. Though I had been speaking at prisons and hospitals for a couple of years by this point, those talks were for fifteen or twenty minutes, and the average "audience" was ten to thirty people. But I knew it was a positive and healthy thing for me to do, and I had trained myself to say "yes" to such offers without thinking about them first. So, I agreed to go with Douglas.

Coffee Creek is a women's prison located in Wilsonville, Oregon, just a few miles south of Portland. I had been there a number of times with Dennis and Lawana to bring a meeting to the women in medium security there. (The three of us still make it down there a couple of times a month each, and the ladies who attend the meetings are an endless source of inspiration to us.)

Douglas and I arrived at Coffee Creek on the evening scheduled for our presentation. We were to be speaking in the minimum-security section of the prison that evening. As we approached the room where the presentation was to be held, I caught a glimpse of the women through the glass in one of the doors. I instantly panicked. It turned out there were sixty-one women in there, and the sight of that many people scared the hell out of me. I immediately said (out loud), "I can't do this!" My comment was to no one in particular—it just sort of spontaneously erupted from my mouth. Neither Douglas nor the guard nor counselor that were accompanying us acted as if they had heard me, and something kept me moving forward.

When we got into the room a moment later, a couple of the inmates smiled at me. They had recognized me from the meetings in medium security. This relaxed me a bit, and I sat down in a chair up front while Douglas led the introduction for the evening. He had me speak first, and the strangest thing happened. The instant I started speaking the fear was gone. I mean *gone*. To hell with the fear—suddenly I wasn't even slightly nervous. My Higher Power was at work once again.

It's funny—sometimes at a regular meeting where I know everyone, I can still become momentarily gripped by the fear of speaking. I usually just shrug it off, mentally noting it as merely past conditioning. Then I go on speaking and the fear generally subsides as I talk. But for some reason, whenever I go to speak at a prison or a hospital or rehab center, there is no longer any fear. It never comes up—ever. I sometimes may become slightly anxious before I start, but that's it—truly a miracle in my book.

I often share with patients in rehab facilities, particularly at Portland Adventist, that you could have put a gun to my head before I got clean and sober and told me to come in here and talk to you and I would have said, "Go ahead. Pull the trigger—please!" Because not only would I have been too paralyzed by the fear to go through with it, I didn't want to live anymore at that point anyway—at least not the way I had been living.

About nine o'clock on our evening at Coffee Creek, after the question-and-answer period following our presentations, Douglas caught me completely off guard. He suddenly mentioned to these sixty-one women that "Gary is turning fifty years old in about three hours, and I was wondering if we could all sing 'Happy Birthday' to him." Seconds later I was being serenaded by Douglas, a few prison officials and sixty-one female prisoners.

Not "bad people," just "sick people" trying to get better, the same as me.

I wish people that stereotyped addicts and convicts could attend some of the meetings I have been to in these places. I'm not saying they're all angels—they most certainly are not. But the ones that attend meetings are generally sincere about changing their lives (only about one percent of the prison populations show up for Twelve Step meetings, and the ones that do are usually pretty serious about it). Their faith, their acceptance, and their words are truly inspiring.

The patients in rehab facilities and the inmates in prisons have taught me a great deal about judging books by their covers. Mainly, not to do that. I heard someone once say, "People who judge, don't matter. And people who matter, don't judge." As I said much earlier, I am not particularly biblically minded, but there are a couple of sayings from the Bible that cover it best: "Judge not lest ye too be judged." And "Let he who among us is without sin cast the first stone." Many of the people I know and love today are people who would be prematurely judged in a negative light by large segments of society. Some of my best friends today are convicted felons, for example. However, they have served the time behind bars that society dictated should be their just punishment. They have gotten clean and sober and have made their amends to the best of their ability. They have turned their lives around, and I am proud to call them my friends.

WEDDING DAYS

As my niece Jennifer was growing up, she always told me that I would walk her down the aisle one day. (As I mentioned, her biological father had killed himself while on drugs when she was very young.) That day finally came when she was twenty-five years old. She called me and said, "Uncle Gary. It's time!" I was excited and honored. That was in the fall of 2000, and I was thankful that I was able to walk her down the aisle after I had gotten clean and sober. It was much more special to me that way.

She made a beautiful bride. Jennifer was six feet tall in her bare feet by the time she reached adulthood, and with me at five foot nine we had to practice the aisle walk to get our strides in sync. I'm a fast walker, and Jen (with her long legs) and I have always been miles ahead of her mother, Pennie, and my wife, Judy, whenever we have gone someplace together. Though we normally walk about the same speed, it's entirely different when you're doing an arm in arm, slow, aisle walk. Practice as we might have, we never did get it right, and she ended up giggling most of the way down the aisle, which got me to laughing as well. It was much better that way, anyway. It was true Jennifer form.

The wedding took place on a yacht out in Newport Bay, California. I was honored to have the first dance with Jennifer at the reception following the ceremony. Her maid of honor, Michelle, and I danced to the song, "C'est La Vie," which had been played in the movie *Pulp Fiction*. We may have looked nothing like John Travolta and Uma Thurman (well, Michelle looked just fine, but I'm certainly no Travolta), but we had a blast regardless. I do believe that my wife and I were the only two on the boat who weren't drinking. It was the first time in my life that I had danced sober (at least in front of other people), and I was pleased to find out that I had no trouble with it at all. I think I cared less about what people thought when I was sober then I did back when I was drinking. Anyway, everyone seemed to have a great time.

Okay, so Jennifer got divorced eleven months later. Hey, it happens. Besides, I figured it would allow me another chance to walk her down the aisle again someday.

And sure enough, it did. A few years later Jennifer's boyfriend of three years, Robert, called to ask for my blessing and for "my daughter's" hand in marriage. I was deeply touched. I gave Robert an enthusiastic, "Yes, of course!" He's a great guy, and I was very happy for them.

A few weeks after Robert called, Jennifer phoned and said, "After you walk me down the aisle, Uncle Gary, why don't you just keep going and marry us?"

I responded, "Well, for one thing, Jen, I'm not a minister."

But my "little girl" wanted someone close to her to officiate the ceremony, to make it more personal, and she also wanted some humor added to the occasion. I couldn't disappoint my "daughter," so I got on the Internet and a short time later I was an ordained minister of The Universal Life Church. When I told my dear Catholic mother about this, she thought I was being sacrilegious. But my friend and Twelve Step sponsor Mark thought it was pretty cool and asked me if the process cost money. I replied, "Well, they ask for a donation, but I figured that as long as I was being sacrilegious I might as well be cheap, too." (I have since donated some money—I didn't want to incur any negative spiritual karma.) But seriously, as I said at the wedding, Jen's and Roberts' hearts were in the right place, as was mine. Nothing else should matter in the eyes of anyone's God. This is, of course, only my (now sacred) opinion.

MUSING ON MEDS AND MOMENTS

The roller-coaster rider of recovery is not for the faint of heart. It takes perseverance, determination, and a lot of help to stay clean and sober after a lengthy bout with active addiction. When the road has gotten too slick, I have used every means at my disposal to stay on the path. Once in a while, I have skidded completely off the road, and it has required a variety of resources to help drag my sorry carcass back up on the highway.

My straying from the path led me to some severe bouts with depression and anxiety in those first few years of recovery. And when the tools I had learned from Twelve Step programs and other resources didn't seem to be enough to lift me from the fog, I sought help in the form of counseling and sometimes, medication (sorry, Mr. Cruise). Although I believe that most of our therapy must come from within, in the form of a complete change of perspectives and attitudes, we often need help to do this—to combat the negativity that permeated our lives for so many years.

I love the way Thoreau described the magic of perspective:

> I know of no more encouraging fact than the unquestionable ability of man to elevate his life by conscious endeavor. It is something to be able to paint a particular picture or to carve a statue, and so to make a few objects beautiful. But it is far more glorious to be able to carve and paint the very atmosphere through which we look. To affect the quality of the day, that is the highest of arts.

As I stated previously, the narcotics I took in the past initially did more to alleviate my anxious and depressed states than anything the psychiatric community had ever done for me. Of course, as I have also stated, this alleviation was of a false nature, and though the pills and the alcohol brought me temporary relief in the early years, they eventually led me to an even deeper level of despair.

Though I had tried anti-depressants sporadically over the years, I had never found one that did the trick. Of course, I was still using and drinking during many of those trial periods, which pretty much eliminated any therapeutic potential these psych meds had. I also now know that anti-depressants are not in any way magic pills. That is, you don't just start swallowing these things and expect to be cured. Any medicinal therapy must be conjoined with a shift in one's attitudes and thinking processes. This shift can be accomplished through a variety of methods, but ultimately boils down to the responsibility of the individual. I can read and/or hear all sorts of wonderful things from a variety of sources—but unless I pick up the tools that are presented to me and start applying them in my life, my healing and growth will be limited, at best.

I need to change the way I think, the way I view life. I was the one that developed certain negative attitudes in life—I have to be the one to "un-develop" them. I was the one that learned to react to certain situations in certain, now predictable ways—I have to be the one to unlearn these reactions, and to ultimately learn new ones. A psychologist I visited in my early months of recovery told me something I've never forgotten. He said, and I'm paraphrasing: "We teach ourselves to react to certain situations in certain ways, and our brains are very good at remembering where they've been taught to go." He told me that I had taught myself negative ways to react for a number of years and that now I was trying to build a new path. He said that it was only natural that my mind would revert to the older, well-worn path quite often while I was constructing this newer, more positive path. But "with time, dedication and persistence, my mind would eventually follow the positive path more often." He was right, of course. We *can* learn to think and to react differently.

Also, if I want to have some serenity and joy in my life, I can no longer blame my past for anything. Sure, one's past may directly or indirectly be responsible for how one learned to react to certain situations in life. One's past experiences may also be indirectly responsible for the current emotional states one finds oneself in. But where does it end? It's possible that a person may have had the most messed-up childhood imaginable, but at some point one has to stop playing the victim. I heard a speaker once say, "Victims don't stay sober." I believe he is right. Nor do "victims" gain any sort of true or lasting serenity in their lives.

The Dalai Lama has a great quote regarding letting go of the past or letting go of resentments. The Chinese government overran the Tibetan people and their country decades ago, forcing the Dalai Lama to flee his homeland. They virtually enslaved the people of Tibet and destroyed over six hundred of their beautiful, priceless monasteries. In an interview years ago, the Dalai Lama was asked what he would wish for the Chinese government and the people responsible for ravaging his country. He calmly replied, "I wish them nothing but peace."

The interviewer was a little taken aback and retorted, "After all they've done to you and your people, how can you say that?"

The Dalai Lama answered, "They have taken everything else from me—should I let them have my mind as well?"

Another favorite parable of mine regarding resentments is the following:

Two monks in the sixteenth century decided to go on a year's trek. As part of their discipline, they agreed not to have any contact with women during this time. Shortly into their journey they came upon a river that needed to be crossed. On the riverbank sat a woman, obviously unable to cross the river on her own. The older of the two monks proceeded to put the woman on his back and take her across the river. He then set her down and continued on his way. The younger monk couldn't believe what he had seen. He was upset with the older monk for having gone against their agreement, and so early on in their trip. The more he thought about it the more he fumed. After a few hours he could stand it no longer. Seething with anger, he finally yelled out, "Why did you carry that woman?"

The older monk looked serenely at the young monk and replied, "I set her down ten miles ago. Why are *you* still carrying her?"

Stories like that are powerful examples, pointers to a more peaceful and a saner way to view life. We do not let people walk on us, but when something is done, it is done. Stewing about the past or fretting about the future serves absolutely no purpose.

I personally have very little to blame outside of my own choices in life for how things have transpired in my life. Genetics may very well have played a part in some of my anxiety, depression and addiction—but I believe that those things only rose to the surface based on actions I engaged in. I was not a particularly anxious person before I took drugs, for example. Nor had I suffered from depression in childhood. But regardless of the reasons for my life being the way it is, at some point in time I must put the responsibility of changing it upon myself, if I indeed want change.

As my friend Tim Myers said to me once, in regards to a fellow recovering addict's continued insistence on their past being a source of pain for them: "Yes, but what has that got to do with now?" So very, very simple. Such a beautifully simple notion, to be able to view the present without the tainted mirror of the past or, indeed, without the foggy perspective of the future clouding our vision, yet so difficult for most of us to put into practice. As Emerson said, "What lies behind us and what lies before us are tiny matters compared to what lies within us."

It boils down, I have come to believe, to staying in the moment, to recognizing, ultimately, that there is no other moment. I used to hate it in my early recovery when people would tell me to stay in the moment. I would sometimes rebut with, "Evidently you're unaware of the type of moments I'm having." Or I would say, "What if the moment sucks? Why would I want to stay in it?" At first I didn't understand the notion. The simple explanation is, of course, that we are staying in the moment simply because we have no other choice. This doesn't mean that if we are in a bad space that we perpetuate the negativity of the moment. It doesn't mean that we apathetically settle for, "This is as good as it's going to get," either. It is simply pointing out to us that if we accept things as they are in the moment, rather than perpetuating them through one form of negativity or another, then that moment has the potential to be transformed. Indeed, it cannot help but be transformed, for we change how we feel by changing how we view the present moment. It's inevitable. In this way, the power of the pain from our past is converted into our strength for today.

But, again, the key is to first accept things as they are in the moment. A friend of mine, Eileen Norris, once sent me a text message citing an old Zen saying: "If we understand—things are as they are. If we don't understand—things are as they are." Nothing we can do can change what already is.

Ralph Waldo Emerson put it like this:

These roses beneath my window make no reference to former roses or to better ones. They are for what they are. They exist with God today. There is no time for them. There is simply the rose. It is perfect in every moment of its existence. But man does not live in the present. He postpones or remembers. With reverted eye he laments the past, or heedless of the riches that surround him, he stands on tiptoe to foresee the future. He cannot be happy and strong until he too stands with nature, above time.

And stringing together a few quotes from Eckhart Tolle:

"Do you treat this moment as if it were an obstacle to overcome? Do you feel you have a future moment to get to that is more important? There has never been a moment in your life that was not 'now', nor will there ever be. The 'Now' is as it is because it cannot be otherwise. When you say 'yes' to what is, you become aligned with the power and intelligence of Life itself. Only then can you become an agent for positive change in this world."

I recall reading a quote from a woman in her eighties. She had been asked about her life, and she responded with, "Oh, I've had my moments. And if I had to do it all over again, I'd have more of them. Just one moment after another, instead of living so many moments ahead of each day."

Today I am content to experience the moments of my life without all the wildness and craziness of my yesteryears. When I was about a week clean, still in the hospital, I had begun making a list of ways that I could replace my high—little adrenalin games I could engage in to stave off the boredom I felt I was soon going to be facing. But in a moment of clarity I suddenly recognized that I couldn't bungee jump 24/7. I realized fairly early on that if I could find some peace within, then anything I did would be enjoyable, regardless of the amount of adrenalin it activated. True peace knows no boredom. There are activities that can enhance our physical experience on earth, and people can also assuredly add to our enjoyment in this realm, but no event or person can ever begin to provide us with the lasting peace we seek. That peace comes from a deeper place. This higher power can be accessed from within ourselves. I like a quote by Agnes Repplier: "It is not easy to find happiness in ourselves, and it is not possible to find it elsewhere."

I believe that certain people (and books, etc.) are put in our lives to aid us along our respective paths. I believe that a higher power speaks to us through other people at times, and that if we keep an open mind (and an open heart) we will hear what we need to hear when we need to hear it.

My friend Tim Myers, for example, has been an extremely positive influence on my life since I've been in recovery. I feel that our meeting was no accident. The circumstances by which we met seemed ordinary enough at the time, but in retrospect they were quite remarkable. (I won't go into details, just trust me on this one.) Tim and I share similar views with regard to a higher power. We have had countless hours of discourse regarding spiritual matters. We have read some of the same literature and have been to forums put on by different spiritual leaders during the years I have been in recovery. We traveled to Canada together on one occasion and spent a few days in Vancouver, British Columbia at a mini-retreat of sorts. We also play a lot of golf together—along with our good friend, Charlie McClain, and others—we do like to have fun on occasion.

I tell people who are new in recovery not to be discouraged. As I have stated, my first few years of recovery were anything but stable, and "fun" was a very fleeting notion in those days. But with perseverance and earnestness—and sobriety—life can truly become worth living. I have continued to experience bumps in the road, but am more fully aware that hard times are a part of life. These hard times can be eased by shifting our perspective, by avoiding getting wrapped up in the negativity that can sometimes present itself in our lives.

THE THIRD PLANE

Another invaluable tool that I have received in recovery is meditation. When I finally met with the counselor John Emerson (after missing my first appointment with him), one of his suggestions was to begin meditating. I balked at first, citing lack of time as my excuse. I told John I had taken a course in Transcendental Meditation a quarter of a century prior, and they had suggested meditating twice a day for periods of twenty minutes each. I said it would be difficult to find that kind of time. John rebutted with, "Do you have two minutes a day?"

I told him, "Well, yeah—sure."

"That's a start," he said.

John recommended a book that contained some very helpful hints on meditation, and I was grateful for his input. There are a number of approaches to meditation, and there exists a variety of tips on how best to reach a relaxed state of mind. Whenever we close our eyes and try to relax, most of us are met by a bombardment of thoughts. Rather than trying not to think, the phrase I found most helpful as to what to do with our thoughts is: "Don't fight them and don't invite them."

Imagery is often helpful. A key suggestion for me was to imagine that our True Natures are like the deep calm waters of a great lake or an ocean, and that our thoughts are merely ripples on the surface. One night in my early recovery when my mind was going a hundred miles a minute (some refer to this as "race brain"), and I was becoming extremely anxious and agitated, I used this imagery to help calm me down. It worked.

About a year and a half into my recovery from drugs and alcohol, I had an experience in meditation that seemed at the time (and still does in recollection) to be far more real than any of the other moments of my life (with the exception of the experience I had when my dad lay dying on the operating table, which seemed equally "more real"). I had been meditating for longer periods of time

311

in the preceding months, often sitting for an hour or more in repose. (Today, although I don't meditate as often or as long as I used to, it remains a valuable tool that's readily available to me.) On one particular session I had a moment of such intense depth that its profundity remains with me to this day (and sharing it may irrevocably cement me in Lala land in the minds of many). As I sat cross-legged on the couch in our basement, I was suddenly overcome by a realization of startling clarity—the realization seeming to be "clarity" itself. In that instant, it was as if there were no longer any questions about anything, and that I ("I" no longer being "me," but simply the life force that was animating me) somehow knew that everything was all right (identical to the feeling that I had while my dad lay dying years before). This realization was accompanied by a sense of incredible peace and profound joy. Then I was suddenly catapulted from this dimension of "knowing" into an even greater dimension of "not knowing." It was as if this clarity of knowing was contained within an infinitesimally vaster field of unknowing. And it was while immersed in this state of not knowing that an even deeper sense of contentment and utter joy existed. For it became immediately apparent to me in this instant that only in "not knowing" can there be a full sense of "wonder." It is while engaged in wonder, *without having to know the answers,* that we can feel truly alive and purposeful, and therefore truly whole.

Not long after this experience (maybe I had just needed a nap), my good friend Missy Rees called and asked if I would like to go with her to a training session on meditation being held at the Gresham Library on the upcoming Saturday. Missy has been a very close friend of mine since my early recovery, and I love her dearly. She is twenty-five years younger than I am, but again, I have found that age is not a barrier when it comes to friendships unless one makes it so. Missy has helped me a lot over the years, particular in my early recovery whenever I battled with a bout of depression. She relates to this form of suffering and on a couple of these occasions showered me with gifts to help boost my spirits. As I sit here typing I can see a little treasure chest she bought for me a number of years ago when I was in a very low place. She filled this small box with all sorts of thoughtful little trinkets, including a candle, a heart-shaped stone with "Willingness" engraved on it, a card with a spiritual saying, etc. And she always spoils me with something thoughtful on my sobriety birthdays. I have tried to respond in kind.

Although I felt I had already received plenty of instruction regarding meditation, how could I say "no" to my dear friend Missy? I asked her how she had heard about the seminar and what seemed special about it. Missy told me she had spotted a flyer with a guy's picture on it who "looked like he would know how to meditate." I asked her why she had thought that and she told me, "He has a long white beard and he's wearing a turban." Well, that certainly iced it for me. Everyone knows that bearded, turban dudes are the best at meditation.

So, off we went to the Gresham Library one Saturday morning for our instruction on meditation. The "bearded turban dude" didn't make it. Evidently, he was the guru worshipped from afar. He may even have been dead—I don't really recall. A man in his forties and a lady in her, like, eighties, came to instruct us. It proved to be a rather bizarre experience.

Missy and I (and the overwhelming crowd of four others that showed up for this gig) were given several mantras to memorize. We repeated them aloud over and over again in unison. Nothing in English, I assure you, and if I were to repeat any of these secret mantras to you I would be breaking a sacred trust and they would become completely ineffectual for me (that is, if I were actually using them), *and* I might possibly lose my mind (again), or perhaps have a voodoo doll in my likeness receive 1970's-voltage-level shock treatments or something. I don't really remember what they told us the exact retribution for such a breach would be. I only recall that it wasn't pretty. Although I gave up saying these five mantras within a few days of having received them, I still remember one of them. So does Missy. Of course, this secret is remaining with us to the grave. Although neither of us is particularly worried about losing our minds (been there, done that), we *are* a little concerned about the whole potential voodoo thing.

Immediately after being brainwashed with the mantras, the six of us were asked to close our eyes and plug our ears with our thumbs. We obediently complied. It was suggested to us that we try to imagine a holy figure, such as the turban dude. *This is where they whack us over the heads and drag us to their compound and make sex slaves of us,* I began thinking.

After sitting there dutifully with our eyes closed and our ears plugged for a few minutes, we could hear the man and lady going around whispering things to their new-found cult members. I couldn't quite make out what they were saying, but soon the lady was whispering in *my* ear.

"What do you hear?" The lady was suddenly asking me. She sounded excitedly expectant, as if I should be hearing something, what with having uttered our mantras and trying to envision the turban dude and all.

I didn't want to disappoint the little old lady—after all, she seemed quite nice and appeared to be relatively harmless. But I didn't want to lie to her, either. So, I simply told her the truth: "I don't know. Just a kind of 'ringing' in my ears, I guess."

This delighted her no end. With unbridled exuberance she exclaimed, "Good! That's the third plane!"

Well, I was pumped. I hadn't even heard the first two planes, but somehow I had been blessed with experiencing the third one.

"You just try to stay there!" the elderly lady encouraged me, as if I had broken through to some high spiritual level not usually found by their novice cultists.

In spite of the fact that I found the whole scene to be extremely ludicrous, I've got to admit there was a part of me that felt a bit proud for having found "the third plane." And here I had thought it was just a ringing noise. To this day, Missy is ticked off about not having experienced the third plane, or the first or second one, for that matter.

Sure, we joke about our experience occasionally, but neither one of us is coughing up the mantra.

ON NEGATIVE THINKING

My head has taken me to some crazy places over the years. The good news is, that once I stopped adding to the problem by feeding my mind with drugs and alcohol, I gave myself a chance to correct some of that madness. With the help of my Higher Power and a support group that includes family and friends from a wide variety of sources, I have been able to make great strides in finding peace in this life. The negativity that, in one form or another, plagued me for years, both before and after I got clean and sober, has gradually dissipated. It is now (on most days) but a shadow of its former Herculean self. For that, I am truly grateful.

When it comes to negativity, I have learned that if I simply let my negative thoughts and feelings be, without labeling them or judging them *and* without fighting them, they move on much more rapidly. When I find myself mired in an emotionally unpleasant state, I have learned that if I could simply put an end to it by consciously wishing it, I would have already done so. But it seems the more I resist them, the more I give them life. I can continue to try to do battle with them, but I know from experience that this is a painful and fruitless endeavor. So, rather than consciously resisting them (which always involves tension and is never liberating or comfortable) I can begin to carve a more peaceful, freer state of being, simply by not feeding my negativity. I've made many a negative mood much worse by catastrophizing my thoughts or by becoming immersed in self-pity. There is no magical solution, that I am aware of, for ridding oneself of unwanted thoughts or emotions. It took time to develop negative thinking, and it takes time to develop a more positive frame of mind. By recognizing and allowing that which already is, simply "to be as it is," I automatically herald in a new perspective, a gateway to peace. One of the more beneficial approaches to dealing with negativity is simply to detach oneself from unwanted thoughts or feelings. In the Buddha's philosophy, "attachment" was to be avoided in all matters, pleasant as well as unpleasant.

315

There is little serenity to be found in "clinging" or "attachment" of any kind. The Buddha exclaimed: "It doesn't matter what we are grasping. When we grasp, we are losing our freedom." He said that the liberated person has a mind that "no longer seeks resting places."

Redirecting my thinking can be helpful, or doing something physical to distract myself from unwanted thoughts and emotions. It's not about suppressing these things. We are not denying their existence. On some level, we have already noted their existence by letting them to come to the surface. Now we simply accept them and allow them to move on. We can aid in this transition by developing a disinterest in them, similar to the detachment the Buddha talked about.

This is not to imply apathy. We can learn to view our suffering from an impersonal perspective, coming to know that we are not merely our thoughts, nor are we simply the mind that contains these thoughts, nor are we the suffering that can evolve from these thoughts. Who and what we truly are lies beyond all of this. Our True Nature is much deeper than these things, yet also contains these things. Eastern philosophies often use the term "witness" or "observer" to indicate this True Nature, this "impersonal watcher." In a way we are simply learning how not to be ruled by the mind. The mind can be a great tool, but it makes a terrible master.

I have read many helpful books regarding these matters and have heard many influential ideas expressed by people from all walks of life. When I've read or heard something that resonates with truth (somewhere within me), I have been very earnest (not always successful, but at least earnest) in applying what I have learned, or sensed, to my life. By coming to an understanding of some very powerful tools such as "surrender" and "acceptance" (terms which seem to be at the core of every major spiritual modality), and then applying these things in everyday life, there can come a much greater awareness, a deeper presence, and a more fulfilling sense of peace.

Seemingly simple sayings can be powerful pointers to the truth and can often aid in freeing oneself from a suffering state of mind. One such favorite of mine is: "Worry does not empty tomorrow of its troubles—it empties today of its strength."

A friend of mine, Roxy Hobbs, put it another way. She called it "suffering twice needlessly." We worry about something that's coming up and when this "something" arrives, it is rarely as bad as we imagined and often entirely different than we imagined. Even if it does occur exactly as we envisioned, we have now "suffered twice needlessly," for our worry changed nothing. But as is more often the case, when the "something" is not as bad as we had imagined, then we need not have suffered at all.

I heard another recovering addict say: "Ninety-eight percent of my life can be going along just great, and what do you think I focus on? That's right—the two percent that isn't going great. Maybe that's a human trait. But I think it occurs mostly out of habit, from past conditioning that 'tells me' to view life from this negative perspective."

An Indian philosopher and spiritual teacher spent fifty years of his life traveling and spreading his wisdom. Toward the end of his days, as he was speaking to a large throng of people, he asked them, "Do you want to know my secret?" The people anxiously leaned forward, listening attentively. He simply said: "I don't mind what happens."

There's a lot of power in that statement, and I've found that this wisdom can be applied in a variety of forms. I can say to myself, "I don't mind what happens, *including* the emotions that I experience." I have tried this with "fear," which usually comes in waves or pangs, saying, "I don't mind my fear." It's amazing what happens if we truly incorporate this sentiment into our mind set. It can have miraculous results.

With persistence we can recondition ourselves to look at life from a more positive perspective. We may have a beautiful yard, for example, full of gorgeous trees and plants and grass, yet instead of appreciating them, our past conditioning may compel us to focus on the weeds in our garden of Eden. The good news is that we can retrain ourselves to begin focusing on the flowers in life rather than the weeds.

HIGHER POWER

Recovery has allowed me to develop a concept of a Higher Power of *my own* understanding, as opposed to someone else's. I love what one of the earlier teachers of Buddhism said: "Do not believe what others tell you—not even the Buddha. See for yourself what brings contentment, clarity, and peace. *That* is the path for you to follow."

I can never adequately express my concept of a Higher Power in words. (As Taoists say: "The Tao that can be expressed in words is not the Tao.") I can, however, try to express what it means to me to believe in a Higher Power (or God, if you prefer). I have heard it said, "I would rather believe and be wrong, than not believe." And surely, there would seem to be more comfort in believing than in the alternative, but I prefer a quote by Thomas Jefferson: "Question with boldness even the existence of God; for if there be one, he must more approve of the homage of reason than that of blindfolded fear."

This I have done—in both sober and not so sober states of mind. At various points along this odd journey called life, I would find myself teetering in the back yard, a glass of Potter's rum in one palm and nothing but a handful of tortured questions in the other. There I would sway, shouting up at the heavens an assortment of drunken rhetorical inquiries and pleading demands:

Why do you allow such suffering in this world, God?
If you exist, show me a sign!
Why am I out here talking to myself?

and other such irrational babblings. Most of my life, I have believed in a Higher Power of some kind, yet this belief has obviously wavered from time to time. In such moments, I have often questioned the meaning of life. To me, personally, the notion of existence on this planet without the presence of some sort of Creative Intelligence, seems purposeless. When mired in such states of doubt, I have been known to express some rather bizarre sentiments.

I remember at about two years clean and sober, I was having a trying day at work. And my mind began "doing its thing." The whole idea of working in the world of steel began to seem completely ludicrous to me (I had encountered such feelings before, but at that moment, I was *really* getting into this feeling.) I had often experienced stress at work, and dealt with it in different ways (with varying degrees of success and failure). But on this day "the idea of dealing with stress," in itself, seemed ludicrous. *Nothing* seemed to make sense.

At that moment, Leslie (who I had worked with for almost nine years) happened into my cubicle. Leslie had always been one of my favorite co-workers—bar none. We had become quite close over the years. She had started working in steel when she was just eighteen years old. Anyway, she had come to ask me a simple, work-related question, but my head was mired in the midst of this insane questioning about a seemingly insane world when she began speaking.

Before the poor, sweet girl could get three words out, I suddenly hurled my pen against the wall and then reaching down, pulled an adjustment lever beneath my seat, flinging myself dramatically back in my chair. With my arms spread wide, I looked at a now perplexed young Leslie and shouted, *"What are we doing here?"*

Leslie sheepishly replied, "I was just going to ask you—

"No—I mean, *here*—" gesturing to some imaginary point in the heavens. "What are we doing *here*—on this planet? In this universe?"

Poor Leslie, of course, couldn't answer. (Who could?)

I began to chuckle (the chuckle of a madman). "I'm sorry, Leslie. I'm just crazy right now." (Obviously.) We ended up having quite a laugh at my temporary insanity and somehow it made us both feel better that day.

So have gone the ramblings of my mind, off and on, for years.

Here are my reflections in a nutshell:

Either there is a God (or Higher Power) or there isn't. (I prefer the terms "Higher Power" or "Consciousness" over "God," in that the word "God" can often conjure up pre-conceived notions, many of which seem severely lacking in open-mindedness.) More and more, science itself is turning to a higher power, or consciousness, to explain some of the inexplicable matters *of* science. They are discovering what almost has to be interpreted as conscious connections between separated units of seemingly unintelligent matter, which defy any reasonable physical explanation.

As my simplistic "86% theory" suggests: if there *is* a Higher Power then It must be everywhere and within all things at all times (It would not be in just 86% of the universe, nor would this Higher Power be present only 86% of the time). And if there *is* an intelligent Higher Power underlying the universe, then it would seem logical that there must be some sort of purpose to all of this.

If I believe that these things are true, and I have come to believe that they are (for a variety of reasons, both logical and experiential), then the next step in logic has to be that "nothing is wrong." If I accept that everything happens for a reason, or ultimately serves a purpose, then nothing, absolutely nothing, can be wrong. Everything is as it should be. There is great peace in this acceptance.

This doesn't mean that when something tragic happens in my life or in someone else's, that I walk around preaching "Nothing is wrong." I will feel sadness at the loss of a loved one, for example, but on some deeper level I can come to know that "things will truly be all right." As Eckhart Tolle so eloquently puts it: "Even within the seemingly most unacceptable and painful situation is concealed a deeper good, and within every disaster is contained the seed of grace." And it doesn't mean that I don't try to make things better when I'm able, or strive to achieve things. It simply means that I accept what comes as it comes, to the best of my ability, knowing that ultimately it serves a higher purpose.

This attitude brings me peace. I can recognize and affirm that thoughts and emotions have only the power that I lend them. In fact, no person, place, thing, or situation has power over me, because my power comes from within—this Higher Power is available to me at all times—and I can surrender to that Power any time I so choose.

I have come to believe that our True Natures are one with this Higher Power, the Source of all things. I have also come to believe that the ground of this connectedness, and therefore of our True Nature, is one of unconditional love and unfathomable peace (a belief founded on brief, but powerful experiences and reinforced by the related experiences of countless others over the millennia).

For reasons that remain a mystery to me (and at least six or seven others), this True Nature, at least as it manifests itself in this material universe, has somehow been covered up.

It is my belief that our ultimate purpose here is to uncover this True Nature.

For most of us, it appears that we must apply effort to accomplish this. But perhaps it is better accomplished by giving up effort (the effort to control outcomes), and by surrendering ultimate control of life to this Higher Power. I have learned in recovery that it is in the expectations of outcomes that lack of serenity is bred. We continue to take the next appropriate step in life, we "do the footwork" as it has been phrased to me, but we leave the outcome up to the Universe, which is a much more sane way to live.

The irony of it appears to be that when we begin to discover this secret, we see that effortlessness can become one of the byproducts of our efforts. I believe that if we can learn to fall in love with the mystery of life, rather than trying to control it, we will find that there is great power and peace in this discovery.

But then again, I'm relatively insane.

I wish you all peace.

EPILOGUE

In October of 2005, a couple of weeks after I initially finished writing this book, my youngest stepson Casey, my "little buddy" and Judy's baby, died of a heroin overdose in the basement of our home. He was thirty-two years old. Finding him like that was the most devastating moment of my life. Frantically running upstairs to tell Judy that we had lost a second son was the most excruciating.

Losing one child is an utter travesty. Losing a second is an abomination. Sometimes my heart aches so much for Judy's pain, let alone mine, that I think it will actually burst into little pieces.

It started two years prior for us with Casey. I had initially inserted into these pages a piece of Casey's story under the assumed name "Corey," but had decided to omit it. Casey was a private person, and I had wanted to respect his anonymity. Sadly, it may have been this private nature, an unconscious resistance to become more vulnerable, that contributed in some way to his tragic end. And it wasn't that he didn't attempt to open up more—because he most certainly did. It's just a very difficult thing for many of us to know how to do in any consistent way. It was the drugs, of course, that killed him. He wanted so badly to live without them. And he tried. God knows, he tried. He tried so hard.

Back in August of 2003, my wife had called me at work one morning and told me that Casey was at our home, and that he was addicted to heroin and he wanted help. We were both shocked at this revelation. Although we had known that Casey probably smoked too much pot, we had no clue that he was into anything heavier than that. He was thirty years old when he came to us for help. He had been on his own since he was eighteen and had always supported himself, always worked. He always gave the impression that he was pretty on top of things. He genuinely seemed to enjoy life. But there was hidden within Casey a pain we were unaware of, an anxiety he couldn't cope with.

He revealed to us over the next couple of years that the only way he felt he could handle this angst was with the use of drugs. The ironic fact that his drug use over the years served to exacerbate this discomfort seems beyond question to me. I had experienced the exact same thing in my life.

I harbor guilt—a guilt that, for the most part, I can let go, but at times it haunts me. I ask myself if Casey would have even tried heroin if he hadn't seen me "successfully" come out the other side of a heroin addiction. I know that when Judy first told him I was in rehab kicking heroin years ago, he had broken down and wept. He had looked at her through the tears in his eyes and said, "Nobody ever makes it back from that." And then he saw me come back from that. There are several key things in life that can haunt me if I let them, Michael and Casey's deaths first and foremost among them. But I have to continue to believe that everything in this world comes to serve a higher purpose. I have to believe that.

I had rushed home from work that day in August of 2003 to find Casey lying on the bed in the spare bedroom. When he first saw me he looked up through his tears and cried out, "Can you help me?"

I told him that if he was a hundred percent honest and a hundred percent willing, he could be helped. But that if he wasn't, there wasn't a soul on this planet that could help him.

We checked Casey into rehab, and when he got out I started taking him to meetings. He tried in the best way he knew how to stay clean and to find some serenity in his life—to get back the serenity and happiness he remembered having as a child.

In the ensuing weeks, we learned that Casey had had occasional suicidal thoughts since high school, something he had never shared with anyone. Over the next couple of years, as we tried to help him recover from his addiction and find some peace within himself, he attempted suicide twice.

Casey and I had begun attending meetings together those first few months. But at some point during this time he relapsed without our knowing. A few weeks later he had ended up in a motel room on 82nd Street trying to take his own life with an overdose of heroin. He had left a suicide note. This was no cry for help or for attention—it was a very real attempt to end his life. When the maids came to clean his motel room on a Friday morning, Casey lay unconscious on his bed, hidden from view behind closed curtains and a locked door. After several minutes of pounding on the door the maids summoned the manager, who retrieved the special tool needed to open the bolted door. (A few days later I went to the motel to personally thank the maids for their persistence. I brought them cards and a couple of small gifts as tokens of our appreciation. They said finding someone like that had always been their biggest fear.)

The ambulance had rushed Casey to Portland Adventist Medical Center, where he spent two and a half days in intensive care. He was unconscious for two of those days. The manager of the motel said that the paramedics had told him it was a good thing check-out time had been eleven o'clock and not noon— that's how close to death he had been.

I remember getting the call from the intensive-care unit. One more fucked-up phone call in our lives, in a pair of lives filled with too many fucked-up phone calls. Casey had not been home for four nights. We had started to worry after a couple of days of not hearing from him. He had a girlfriend, we knew, although he didn't talk about her much. It wasn't unusual for him to be gone for a couple of nights, and he didn't always call us to let us know where he was. He was thirty years old, after all. We didn't want him to feel like he was being parented at that age, and he was very sensitive to that scenario. The fact that he was back living at home with his parents embarrassed him. I tried to tell him that it was no big deal. People develop setbacks in their lives, and they often need help to make it through them. It was certainly nothing to be ashamed of.

The hospital was initially unable to contact anyone regarding Casey because he had minimal ID on him, and no phone numbers. His last name did not match my last name, so there was no way to connect him to us. He must have blurted out our name or phone number when he had briefly regained consciousness on that third day in ICU. (We never knew for sure how they got our number, and we were too disturbed to delve into it when we arrived at the hospital.)

After intensive care, Casey was transferred to the psych ward on the first floor of the hospital, where he spent five days. On his second day in the ward I had one of my scheduled monthly visits to the chemical-dependency unit on the fourth floor. That night I took two of my friends from recovery with me, Joe and Dennis. We each shared for about ten or fifteen minutes. It was a very emotional night. I told the patients that my youngest stepson was down in the psych ward on this same night after having tried to kill himself in his addiction. After the meeting, Joe and Dennis wanted to go downstairs and visit with

Casey. The compassion these two men showed my son was truly heartwarming. I saw love in action that night.

Casey made it a few months before he relapsed again. He had gone to meetings for a while, but then had stopped going. He had stopped seeing his mental-health counselor and doctor as well. I told him at that point that he couldn't live with us anymore, that it wasn't working (we were trying the "tough love" thing, since nothing else had worked). A couple of weeks later, he attempted suicide again. He ended up at OHSU hospital, where he spent a few days in one of the medical units before being transferred to their psych ward for a month. We got a call from his girlfriend telling us where he was.

When he got out of the ward a few weeks later we allowed him to live with us again. We had only forced him out in the first place, of course, because we felt it was the best thing for him at that point. Everyone we had talked with had agreed that he wouldn't hit his bottom as long as he had us as a cushion to break his fall. It seemed sensible to us. Well, so much for theories. I have found that there is no black and white, no definitive right or wrong, when it comes to decisions regarding helping someone who is struggling to stay clean. (We tried everything from tough love to total co-dependency to everything in between, and we still lost two out of three sons.) You can only follow your instincts and hope for the best.

Casey managed to stay clean for a few months, but relapsed again in the summer of 2005. And once more, we didn't know he had relapsed—or at least, weren't *sure* whether he was using again or not. I had suspected on a number of occasions that he was using at different times over those last two years, but I simply never wanted to believe it. I would usually end up telling myself that I was wrong.

He used most of that summer without our knowing. One minute I would be saying to myself, *He's using—I know he's using—why am I denying it?* Then, a few hours later I would find myself saying, *Maybe I'm wrong.* I just didn't want to face it.

It was my friend, Walt S. who finally confronted Casey. Walt had gotten to know Casey through recovery, through meetings. In October of 2005 Walt was painting the outside of our house and when I came home from work one day he informed me that Casey was strung out on heroin.

I remember saying to Walt, "You think he is?"

To which Walt had responded, "No. I *know* he is." Walt had been through it enough himself and knew the signs. He also wasn't as emotionally involved as Judy and I and therefore not as prone to denial as we were. He told me that he was going to go in and talk to Casey when he was done cleaning up. I said, "Please do." It was obvious to me that I no longer knew how to help him.

Walt confronted Casey. Casey came clean. I ended up taking him to Hooper Detox a couple of days later. Hooper is *not* the Hyatt Regency. It's "the last house on the block" for many addicts and alcoholics in Portland. But it's a good place that provides a much-needed service. In addition to helping people detox, they attempt to help people find outside counseling, housing, etc. You can hardly ever get into Hooper on the first day you go there. It usually takes several days of going there at seven in the morning before a bed becomes available. Our good friend Millie, who had talked with Casey about recovery on several occasions (wonderfully inspiring talks that Casey truly appreciated), came down with us. He got in on his third attempt.

Casey spent eight or nine days at Hooper. The goal was to find him long-term residential treatment once he got out, since staying with us had proven not to be the answer. But it takes time to get into such programs, and Casey came back from Hooper to live with us until he could get into a place. He stayed in the bedroom downstairs where he had spent most of the previous two years. Every day upon his return from Hooper, Judy and I would talk to him about how he was doing, much as we had done for the last two years. Casey had also seen counselors, been in outpatient programs, and been to meetings off and on during this time. And he had been taking anti-anxiety and anti-depressant medications as prescribed and was on them again.

That last week of his life Casey told me he was having cravings to use like he had never had before. I would call him from work during the day to check on him. He would tell me that he was struggling. He was continuing to experience suicidal thoughts and overwhelming urges to use. I told him to hang in there, that those cravings to use would ease with time and that his suicidal thoughts would become less intense as well. I talked to him about acceptance and surrender and love and hope and perseverance and perspective, about staying in the moment, about meditation and the Serenity Prayer and anything else I could possibly think of to help him get through his turmoil.

But my words couldn't save him. My friend Kim H. (whose son had also struggled with addiction) said to me one day, "Gary, if there were magic words, we would have said them long ago."

On the Friday before Casey died, less than thirty-six hours before he passed on, I called him at home from work. I asked him how he was doing. He mentioned again his strong urge to use. He told me on that day that he *knew* he was going to die from "this."

I said, "You mean addiction?"

He said, "Yes."

I responded, "Yes, you're probably right. If you continue to use, it will probably kill you."

That evening Casey got a call from Walt. He had asked Walt to sponsor him just a week before. He was trying his best to make things work. Casey went downstairs and talked to Walt for quite a while. When he came back up I was sitting at my desk in the den typing on my computer. I asked him how it had gone with Walt.

Casey said, "Good. He helped me a lot." And then he suddenly leaned over and threw his arms around my shoulders and began to sob. He cried like I had never seen him cry before, like he was releasing years of pent-up suffering, or trying to. He cried like a person caught between hope and despair, a cry I had become all too familiar with in my own life. He was clinging to a hope that perhaps he *could* conquer his demons, and attempting to resist the despair that he might never be able to.

The next day Casey went with me to the store for something. On the way, the song "Losing My Religion," by REM, came on. We both remarked how we liked the song. It was the last song I remember hearing with Casey, of the thousands of songs we had listened to together over the years. That became the first song we played at his funeral, and it brings me to tears as I type this several months later. There is a line in this song that has haunted me since his death. It goes: "Oh, no—I said too much—I haven't said enough." I know in retrospect that I, that we, gave Casey everything we had and then some. It simply wasn't enough. I only know that Casey wanted to live, that he wanted desperately to be free of his pain. And now he is.

I believe in my heart that Casey served a great purpose on this Earth. His story, for one thing, has helped a lot of people. His pain has allowed others to reach out—and they, in turn, were helped by doing so. No one can measure that. No one can diminish its greatness. And while Casey was here, for *most* of the days of his life, he brought joy to others. He brought them love and laughter and compassion. He gave of himself to many, and this is how he will be remembered by those of us who were lucky enough to have known him.

On that last Saturday evening we held a small family party for my brother Tim (Casey's favorite uncle). Tim's fiftieth birthday was coming up on Monday, the 24th of October, 2005. Tim's two daughters went with me to buy decorations for the party. Later, Tim came over with his two boys, and Mom joined us, too. Judy and Casey made dinner. My mom and Tim remarked how good Casey looked, how well he seemed to be doing. I wasn't so sure. I remember looking at him at one point in the evening and thinking, *My God—he's loaded again.* And yet, once more, I just didn't want to believe it.

My brother's car was crowded that night. I don't remember why. I offered to take Samantha and Chrissy home. My brother lives only five minutes away. After I put on my coat, Casey said goodnight to everyone. My niece, Chrissy, for whatever reason, snapped a picture of Casey hugging me. It's the last picture I have of him with me. It was the last picture ever taken of him. My back is to the camera. Casey's arms are around me, and his eyes are closed. It's as if he is not just saying goodnight, but good-bye. I love that picture. There is a tenderness and a compassion on Casey's face that speaks volumes to me, even though his eyes are closed. Casey had a lot of love in his heart. He loved his family a great deal. I know he wanted to stay with us.

That next morning Casey never got up. We waited and waited for him to come upstairs. It wasn't unusual for him to sleep in until late in the morning, sometimes even until noon. He wasn't working. He had been going to college off and on the last couple of years, but wasn't currently. He had wanted to get into the health profession, he had wanted to help people. But he hadn't been to school in quite a few months. His sleeping in had a lot to do with depression, I'm sure. It's so sad. He was always such a happy kid.

Shortly after noon, Judy and I each took a nap, she on the couch, me on a recliner in the same room. We woke up at about the same time. I asked Judy if Casey had come upstairs yet. She said no, a worried look covering her face. I remember saying, "Shit."

I went downstairs and called out Casey's name as I approached the closed door of his bedroom. Instinctively I knew something was terribly wrong. I opened the door and saw him. It is a sight that will haunt my memory forever. He died on his knees, at the foot of the bed. His left arm and his head were resting on the bed, his right arm down at his side, his right hand on the floor. Near his hand I saw the spoon with the brown stain of heroin and I knew it was over. I cried out, "Oh my God! Casey!" I bent over quickly and touched his neck. He was cold and stiff—ice cold, and stiff. He had been gone for hours.

Hysterical, I raced upstairs to Judy, taking two or three steps at a time. As I ran down the hall to the living room where she was, I could see her sitting up on the couch, a look of unspeakable horror frozen on her face.

"No! No! No!" she kept shrieking.

I was repeating, "He's gone! He's gone! He's gone!"

Judy's hands, up by her face, shook violently from side to side, as if trying to shake off the truth. "No! No! No!"

This could not be happening—not again. Oh, my God, not again.

I clutched her as hard as I could, rocking her back and forth, whispering forcefully in her ear over and over and over again, "I'm going to make this okay! I'm going to make this okay! I'm going to make this okay!" I remember it like it was yesterday. The agony and the horror of that moment will never leave us.

At some point I said to Judy, "I have to call 911." I didn't want to let go of her, but someone had to be called. I grabbed the phone. "Please help us!" I remember saying. I was so hysterical, I was almost unintelligible. "Please hurry!" I needed, we needed, someone—anyone—someone to come tell us it wasn't true, someone to lie to us, someone to make it all go away.

But no one could do that for us.

I called Walt next. He lived fairly close. I knew we needed someone to help carry this burden. He came quickly. Then I called my mom. She called my brother Tim. I would have called a hundred people I think—part of me wanted to fill the house with people, fill the house with living, breathing human beings who could by their simple act of "being" negate the presence of death.

But no one could do that for us.

Mark was the last person I called at the time. He came rushing in the door, crying. He has sons who have experienced addiction problems. He hugged me like he had never hugged me before, clutching me, comforting me as best he could.

Mom, and then Tim and his girlfriend Laura arrived a bit later, as did our friend Millie. Everyone did their best to comfort us, and in some measure it worked, because we are still alive. I wasn't sure it would be possible to live through the death of a second child, but somehow we did—somehow we have. We have lived through the death of Michael, through paramedics and emergency rooms and calls from intensive cares and psych wards and rehabs, and now this. The thought of having to face this had entered our minds, of course. But the thought and the reality don't intersect. Nothing can prepare the mind and the heart for something that tragic. Nothing.

The following evening my friends Gabriele and Lonnie came by with a beautiful plant and some chocolate and bread and cheese. They were followed by friends Michelle and Brian, who brought us the most awesome flowers. Phone call after phone call, card after card, bouquet after bouquet came in those first few days following Casey's death—countless expressions of love and compassion and support. Those gestures somehow kept us from sinking into an even deeper despair.

Neither the medical examiner nor the police saw any evidence of suicide and ruled it an accidental overdose. We agree. However, as Casey's good friend Niki said to me a few days later, "Every time we use, it's like a suicide attempt." And she's right. We never know what's going to happen. Whether it's a drink or a drug, we don't know if this could be the time we get into a car and kill ourselves, or worse yet, someone else. We don't know if this fix might be our last. We don't know when our heart might finally say, *Enough. That's enough. I've had enough.* We just don't know.

The day after the coroner took Casey away, Judy and I were forced to begin discussing arrangements. Casey's dad, Al, and his stepmother, Betty, and brother, Darin, were driving up from Los Angeles. They wouldn't be here in time to help with the initial arrangements. Judy's sister Pennie and our niece Jennifer were flying up from California in a couple of days. Judy and I, still in terrible shock, had begun talking about when to have the funeral and such. We decided fairly quickly that the services would be on Friday and would be held at the chapel in the funeral home where Casey was. We started talking about where to have the reception afterwards, and it was beginning to get complicated and somehow that just didn't seem right. Judy mentioned food following the services, and I wasn't ready to handle thinking about that.

I said to her, "I haven't thought that far ahead." I was beginning to feel overwhelmed. Our pain was still far too deep for us to have to worry about these things. It just wasn't right. And then I said, "We know enough people that certainly *someone*, someone like Doresa, will help with that." I have absolutely no idea why Doresa's name came into my head. No idea at all. Doresa Dressler is a lady in recovery who has over twenty years clean and sober and I knew her from meetings. But it wasn't like we were particularly close or anything at the time. We had talked on the phone only once since I'd known her. But *fewer than five seconds* after my comment to Judy, the phone rang and it was Doresa.

Doresa told me she just wanted to call and offer to "take care of all the arrangements for the food following the services." She said she had already contacted all of her "girls" (other women in recovery), and it was all set. All I had to do was say yes.

Tears began streaming down my face, as they are now. As they do whenever I think deeply about the significance, the coincidence, of that moment. I looked at Judy and said through my tears, "It's Doresa. She wants to take care of all the food following the services." I could barely speak.

Judy just looked at me and said, "Oh, my God." She was as awestruck at the coincidence of the moment as I was.

My faith was bolstered in that instant, as it is every time I think deeply about the "coincidence" of that moment. In fact, during a time when my faith could easily have faltered, it was instead strengthened. Strengthened by the overwhelming love, compassion, and support we received in countless ways following Casey's death.

When we were debating over where to have the reception following the services, thinking our house too small for the number of people that would probably be coming, our good friend Teri Hoffman called and offered to secure the Masonic Lodge down the street from the funeral home. She and Doresa, and Mark and Kathy, and Wendy Ortiz, and Jeanne Langdon, and many others took care of everything that week. Blazer, an ex-girlfriend of Casey's, and our niece Jennifer, each made awesome collages of Casey for the services. All we had to worry about was the service itself.

In the first few months following Casey's death my faith wavered at times, and on occasion, still does. There have been moments since his death when I have felt completely disconnected with life, sometimes feeling *What is the point?* But my faith has been quickly resurrected by talking with people and by recalling various acts of compassion.

So many people have meant so much to us during our times of grief. I would love to thank them all individually, but that would be impossible. Close to two hundred people came to Casey's service. We were once again overwhelmed with love and support from family and friends. Many of Casey's friends from over the years were there, some of whom we hadn't seen in many years, some whom we had never known. At least half of the people there were from recovery—most of whom had known Casey at least casually if not more deeply.

I wrote and gave the eulogy for Casey's service. We wanted his memorial to have a personal touch. I was unsure, however, whether I would have the strength and courage to deliver the eulogy in front of a large group of people—to make it through without falling apart. When I mentioned my insecurities to Mark, he said, "Of course you will. You will be surrounded by family and friends who love you and Casey." His words gave me strength.

The packed chapel showed how many lives Casey had obviously touched. There is a verse that Judy and I chose to put on the cover of the funeral booklet. I close this book with it and with some final thoughts on Casey as taken from his eulogy:

> You can shed tears that they're gone,
> Or you can smile because they've lived.
> You can close your eyes and pray they'll come back,
> Or you can open your eyes and see all they've left you.

Casey has left us his wonderful spirit and many good memories. We all loved him so much. I have only mentioned Casey's battle with addiction today in the hopes that his death won't be in vain. I know in my heart that his message will be carried to others for years, the message that drugs kill, that they rob us of who we are and adversely affect many lives. I know Casey would want his story to be heard, if it could possibly help someone else.

Throughout most of his time on this earth, Casey had a tremendous exuberance and love for life. He had a warm, kind and giving spirit. He was such a happy kid. He was the most inquisitive child I have ever known. He was constantly asking questions, always curious about the things of this world. I loved that little guy. Although drugs gradually diminished some of his zest for life, underneath it all, we could still see the real Casey. If only *he* could have. If only he could have fully taken in the love that was offered him. If only he could have taken the love that is present in this room today and bottled it and drunk it and taken it into his heart, he may have been freed from his pain.

We will always remember the true Casey, the Casey who had a quality about him that immediately drew people to him. The Casey that somehow could quickly find a place in other people's hearts. The magical Casey that loved to laugh, that had such a winning and vibrant smile, that had such a warm and loving heart, right up until the very end. These are the memories we will carry with us. These are the memories that will lift our spirits in times of sadness. It is said that "God gave us memories so that we might have roses in December."

Casey was my little buddy. I loved him so much. We all love you so much. God bless you and keep you, Casey. May you rest in peace."

AFTERTHOUGHT

I cannot predict who will stay clean and sober and who won't. Nor do I have the power to get anyone clean and sober or to keep them clean and sober. That particular piece of truth has been slapped upside my head pretty hard. Nor do I fully understand why some people get to keep the gift of sobriety and others don't. But it has been my experience that we can increase our odds of remaining sober by staying connected with people in recovery, by cleaning up the wreckage of our past and by helping others.

The disease of addiction is a deadly serious affair. It robs us of who we are, it destroys lives, it shatters families, it demoralizes, it emaciates, it kills.

But while there is life, there is hope. I pray that all suffering addicts, indeed, that all suffering beings of *any* affliction, are able to at least experience some hope. With hope, and with life, anything is possible.

ACKNOWLEDGMENTS

I could take up a dozen or more pages if I were to thank everyone whom I felt compelled to thank here. I suppose "acknowledgments" by definition are mostly for those who have helped in some way in the production of the book in hand. However, in a memoir of this nature, there are countless hundreds who have inspired and touched my life and therefore placed their imprint on my writings here. I shall do my best to more concisely enumerate those who were most directly involved, but I reserve this addict's right to obsessively digress on occasion (and to unintentionally omit people who truly mean a lot to me).

First and foremost my dear wife, Judy. Without her encouragement and faith in my abilities (or her perceived notion of my abilities) I don't know how long I could have, or would have, persevered in this endeavor. My sons Michael, Darin, and Casey, only Darin of which still survives this world. The pages of this book have become mostly for them. My parents, Amby and Margaret—the best possible guides ever, without question. My brothers Joe and Tim—who shared my upbringing in all its glories and disappointments. My beautiful niece, Jennifer, who became the daughter I never had, and my nephews and nieces Josh, Jeremy, Samantha, and Chrissy—all special to me beyond words. My dear sister-in-law Pennie, Jen's mother. My Aunts and Uncles: Mary and Gordon (RIP) Morgan, Luigi, and Marilyn Serio. My cousins Louie, Tony, and Vinnie Serio—(yes, my cousin Vinnie), and their spouses Janelle, Jennifer, and Judy. My cousin Bill Morgan and his wife Lavonne, cousin Mike Morgan and his wife Nancy Babka. Nancy is one of three lawyers in the family (all female), and she helped me in my search for an attorney to consult with on specific legal matters regarding the publication of this book. And cousins Dan, Pat, and Colleen Morgan. My godparents Virginia and Dom Miranda (may they RIP) and the rest of the Miranda clan, especially my cousin Gary and his wife Patty. Gary is an extremely talented writer whose input regarding my book encouraged and helped me as much or more than anyone.

I'd also like to thank attorneys Trish Flanagan and Ken Kissir for their invaluable help and advice. And a special thanks to Rob Hanewall for the cover of this book.

My friend and "editor," Shelley Bennett, who helped me untangle numerous convoluted sentences in the first one hundred pages. My second batch of friendly editors: Michele Cameron, Gabriele Hardin, Teri Hayes—ladies without editorial credentials, perhaps, but also perhaps without professionally-biased perspectives. My fifth friendly editor, Teresa Fuhrer, who was as encouraging and helpful as the previous four women (I sense a pattern here). And my first professional (and first male) editor, Doug Marx, whose advice I sometimes listened to and sometimes didn't. (Anything you found lacking in this book is on me, no one else.)

My Twelve Step sponsor and close friend, Mark Mitchell and his fiancée Kathy and her daughter Lauren. The line from the AA Book *We Are Not Saints* was written before Mark was born. Well, okay, he's not a saint—but he's pretty damn awesome. And some of my closest friends, in *no* particular order, both from recovery and from a more normal life, including work (except customers—I'm not going down *that* road): Oh God, I'm sure to leave someone out—if I do it's because I hate you and you are not worthy of drawing breath: Paul Prutch, Tom (who spoon-fed me in rehab) and Katie Work, Doug Knutson (my *other* recovery guide, God help us all), Mike and Edie Porter, Debra, Mike and Joe Cleary, Mrs. Cleary, Sister Marion Loyola (Mary Hill, RIP), the Woods, the Roths, the Gendrons, the Neibergalls, the Lydons, the McMahons, Debbie Manion Green, Dave Kessler, Gil Urata, Dave O'Brien, Tom Mitchell, Chris Hertel, Mike Lynch, Shawn Ball, Dave Beck, Kim Milligan, Mike Eaton, Dan Feltz, Joe and Jeanne (RIP) Feltz—thanks again, Joe, for saving my life (I was drowning at Cove Palisades in the 1970s—well, not the whole decade), Dan and Laurie Depaola, Peggy Depaola, Jim Feltz, Scott Kessler, Mike Ball, John Parker, John Emerson, Dr. Gordon Canzler, Dr. Luther Johannsen, Dr. Craig Montgomery, Douglas and Joan Bloch, Laura Zalent, Jane Spence, Patricia, Sharon, Dick, Cathy, Kathy, Linda, Jim, Tim and Terry Myers, Charlie McClain, Millie Dukes, Jake Thompson, Missy Rees, Ben Randolph, Shelley ('Da Pimptress) Slayton Hicks, Frank Hicks, O.E. Cieloha, Carissa Parker, "Curly Fry" Dave Cahill, Kelly Lett, Sue Holmes, Jim and his daughters ("Don't leave me hangin', dawg") Brandy and Jamie, Glenda "my Chi girl" Gould, Walt Seamons, Dana Seamons, Kim Holden, Kyla

Cadieux, Jackie Suzi, Dennis Bennett, Dennis Cox, Joe "Double-booking" Ballard, Kevin Gaunce, Teri Hoffman, Annalee Purdy, Sally Pritchard, Dennis and Lawana Matthews, Doresa Dressler, Larry Young, Roger Bearman, Roger and Stormy, Tom and Ruth, Ed Hayes, Karen and Paulie, Ron and J.J., Debbie Olson, Julie Mitchell, Eileen Norris, Juliet Buckley, Roxy and Jeff Hobbs, Phillip Blomberg, Rick, Rob and Joyce, Donald S., Steve Galloway, Sandie Wilkens, Lisa Overton, Lonnie Helzer, Maggie Presting, Marcie Winters, Donna Crane, Bruce Gibson, Lenny Z., Roy Hamilton, Lonnie B., Robert and Brandon Bonner, Greg and Terry Zook, Sue H., Dan O., Casey Zimmerlee Palmer and Matt Palmer, Matt Cassidy, Commodore Matt Decker, Jeff and Teri McCarty, Treva, Jeff Stiles, Jeanne Langdon, Wendy Ortiz, Cindi (Miss Oregon) Dove, Tony, Doug and Amy Tadina, Chardonn, Gary H., Sheryl Martin, Nick Durham, Rachelle Batalgi, Becky Counts, Janene Ray, Terry Johnson, Joe Popp, Ruth, J.J. Nystrom, Blazer, Niki Eatman, Friggin' Jim Hunt (RIP), Misty, Earl Hightower, Bill W., Dr. Bob.

Lisa Miller (my "work wife"), Leslie Dawson Forgey (my "work daughter," my LF and BFAW), Sue Melton, Karen Bauer, Diane Contreras, Jim Burks, Lloyd Kegney, Leslie Koontz, Margaret Townsend, Kevin Cox, Eric Summers, Cheryl Peterson, Laura Lee, Don Wolfe, Brad Sether, Mike Williamson, Bill Raybell, Lori Fontyn, John Norman, Ken Matzek, Mike Hill, Katie Lucia (who still needs to be on American Idol), Tim Manwell, Barry Carmichael, Sam "Kahn!" and Debbie "Watchalay" Chinakos, Zephram Cochran, Emily Yeager, Misti Matta, Corrine ("No, *I* 'da Ho") Crawford, Julie Murdoch, Roger Hearson, Doug Banks, Ben Traub, Casey Bennett, Rick Lakefish, Craig LaCross, Alan Sheasgreen, Brian Kirby, Natalie, John, Holly, Gary and Karen Bryon, Jeff Ohlson, Mark and Maggie Holbrook, Pat Armstrong, Mike Shefchek, Doug Pagel, Al Humbard, Dick Gourde, Leo Wayne Moore, Chris Munson, Fred Harris, Mark Peebles, Mike Swartout, Art and Sharon Charboneau, Oren Donnell, Ted Hilbert, Steve Williams, Don Brown, Gary Steiert, Gary Wilkes, Larry Grierson, Doug Goldstein, Roy Renk, Steve Pendergrass, Nedjatolla Vahid Tari (my Irish friend).

Also, the women at Coffee Creek Correctional Facility (too many to list, and anonymity precludes it anyway, but some of the ladies there are the most inspirational people imaginable, bar none), the men at Columbia River Correctional Institute (ditto), The Justice Center, Multnomah County Correctional Facility and Oregon State Penitentiary (only two, but very memorable visits to the latter); as well as the steady stream of addicts and alcoholics who took up residence and attended with me monthly recovery meetings at Portland Adventist Chemical Dependency Unit for the eight years I went there until the unit was physically transferred to another facility. There are too many among these facilities who have meant so very much to me that I dare not start a list of names, Buffy (yes, I actually know a woman named Buffy—and she is neither a vampire slayer nor a ditzy blond—well, she's certainly no vampire slayer.)

I could go on enumerating the countless people, words and deeds that have meant so much to me in my life, but it would take more time, space, and brain cells than I have left. (Also, I am still evidently such an obsessive whack job that I wanted to put asterisks on some of the above names from the preceding paragraphs, but talk about a haven for hurt feelings.) There are *so many* people whose words and actions have touched my life in such significant ways, it would be impossible to do them all justice. I have met scores of good people both in my recovery from drugs and alcohol and from earlier times, each of whom has blessed my life in some way. I have mentioned a number of them throughout this writing, and quite a few more in this section, but if I were to attempt to compile a more comprehensive list, I would undoubtedly leave a crucial someone out by accident (and most certainly already have). At the risk of further oversights, suffice it to say that "you all know who you are," and I thank each and every one of you from the bottom of my heart. I remain eternally grateful for your words of wisdom and encouragement, your acts of kindness and love, your hugs, your smiles, as well as your countless prayers. *You are* how life and recovery work.

I wish each of you, and all who tread the path (which is every human being), eternal peace, love and joy.